GET REAL!

THE UNTOLD STORY:
SEXY, SCARY, SCANDALOUS
WORLD OF REALITY TV!

ISBN: 1-59777-584-3

Library of Congress Cataloging-In-Publication Data Available

Book Design by Sonia Fiore
Cover Illustration by Rob Fiore

Printed in the United States of America

Phoenix Books, Inc.
9465 Wilshire Boulevard, Suite 315
Beverly Hills, CA 90212

10 9 8 7 6 5 4 3 2 1

GET
REAL!

THE UNTOLD STORY:
SEXY, SCARY, SCANDALOUS
WORLD OF REALITY TV!

BY
MIKE WALKER

PHOENIX
BOOKS

 **Dedication**

To Jennifer Aniston, who observed:

"We have an obsession with Reality TV!...

Humiliation. Degradation. What's going on?...

I have no interest in that 'Idol' shit!"

BEHOLD THE ESSENCE OF REALITY....

HERE'S AN "AMERICAN IDOL" MAKEUP SECRET:
PRODUCERS CONFISCATE ALL EYELINER AND MASCARA FROM
FEMALE GUESTS—AND NOT BECAUSE RYAN SEACREST MIGHT
NEED MORE. THEY DON'T WANT THE GALS WEARING THE
WATERPROOF KIND—AND THEY INSIST MAKEUP ARTISTS USE STUFF
THAT RUNS LIKE WATER, BECAUSE IT MAKES THEM
LOOK EXTRA-WEEPY WHEN THEY LOSE!

—from Mike Walker's Gossip column, *National Enquirer*

FADE IN....

Here's how this book began. As the gossip columnist for a national newspaper, I cover that state of mind called Hollywood, which—just an eye-blink ago—meant the glittering world of showbiz: movie stars, actors, singers, rapper, dancers, TV/radio hosts, and those dead-eyed studio executive dicks known as "Suits"...the ruthless, faceless organ-grinders who make the monkeys dance.

But with the dawning of the New Millennium, America's fickle TV fans— yes, I mean *you!*—triggered a dramatic and unexpected shift in viewing tastes that generated gigantic ratings for so-called "Reality TV" shows; gritty, unscripted extravaganzas like "Survivor," "Fear Factor," "Temptation Island," "The Amazing Race," etc., starring so-called "real people" embroiled in sexy, scary, even dangerous situations.

But this unscripted reality trend really exploded when celebrities suddenly discovered that exposing their private lives generated career-hyping fan exposure—a slam-dunk tradeoff! Suddenly, Hollywood A-listers, B-listers, has-beens and wannabes hopped aboard the Get Real Express: Ozzie Osbourne...Paris Hilton...Britney Spears...Anna Nicole Smith...Danny Bonaduce...Whitney Houston...and brash-Brit unknown Simon Cowell, fronting his reality-meets-karaoke breakthrough, "American Idol."

Andy Warhol's "15 minutes of fame" theory was suddenly coming true—albeit in 60-minute segments.

The new reality genre tippy-toed into the Hollywood dream stream quietly at first, then gathered steam as trend-junkies began buzzing about a 1989 Fox series called "Cops"—a show so scarily "real" it could arrest your heartbeat.

"Cops!"

The riveting Fox series featured jittery, cinema-verité police video of wild, heart-thumping car chases and crashes; thugs fleeing police pursuit through sleazy trailer parks; belligerent booze-fighters violently resisting arrest; and drunken redneck wife beaters...many of whom were actually wearing wife-beaters.

"Cops!"

It played like a crackhead's nightmare. And, man…was it addictive. Fox-TV had nailed it! A new era had dawned, and I knew it when I idly asked my then pre-teen daughter—a feminine little thing whose main interests were pink clothing, dollies and baking cookies—"Honey, what's your favorite TV show?"

Princess answered promptly, "'Cops,' Dad!... DUH!"

By 2001, Reality TV had captured the national imagination, steam-rollered the programming landscape and flattened the Hollywood playing field. The industry's movers and shakers—those crafty studio Suits—loved reality shows because they were easy to produce and CHEAP, eliminating the need to pay big buck$$ to the snotty, high-priced weasels known as "scriptwriters." By 2005, even TV's finest scripted shows like "Friends" and "Everyone Loves Raymond" were passé! Suddenly, it seemed, everyone in America was either (1) a rabid fan of Reality TV, (2) auditioning to be a participant or contestant on an upcoming show, or (3) trying to create the next reality blockbuster like "Joe Millionaire" or "Queer Eye for the Straight Guy."

The reality of just how sizzling hot Reality TV had become really hit home when two major studios, MGM and Fox, suddenly proposed—out of the blue!—reality shows starring ME, your humble author! More about that later…but while chatting with my big-shot New York literary agent about these approaches, and the sudden dominance of Reality TV, he said, "Mike, that sounds like your next book. You're a take-no-prisoners gossip columnist and showbiz expert. Why not write your snarky take on how the Reality TV phenomenon changed the face of show business?"

(NOTE TO WANNABE AUTHORS: Here's a hard-nosed, in-the-trenches tip from a No. 1 *New York Times* best-selling author—namely me.)

TIP: Whenever you get a legitimate bite on a book idea—i.e., someone might actually cough up real money—never hesitate.

On the very day of our discussion, I sat down at the keyboard and wrote Agent Dan a pitch letter that outlined why the whole world's waiting for the ultimate book on Reality TV—written by me, of course. The rest, as you will see, is history.

Dan Strone
Trident Media Group
New York, N.Y.

Dear Dan,

"Get REAL!"

    Words to live by—and the title of my new book.

    To say that America's having a love affair with Reality TV would be pussy-footing. In fact, we're locked in a sweaty, lustful embrace with a low-rent genre that didn't even exist a decade ago. Why? What fueled Reality TV's rocket-like ride to ratings glory?

    Money and sex drive all human endeavors, and showbiz more than most—so when Hollywood moguls discovered the irresistible business model of Reality TV, it worked like Viagra. Suddenly, the Suits were bellowing:

    "Stars?... Who the hell needs *stars?*... Who needs to pay insane salaries to Julia Roberts, Angelina Jolie, or Jennifer Aniston? Get me has-beens who'll work cheap...get me Anna Nicole Smith, Whitney Houston, Danny Bonaduce! Better yet, get me complete unknowns who'll work for next to nothing! Everyone wants their 15 minutes of fame...so we'll turn nobodies into household names for a dime on the dollar, then dump them!... Hey, is this a great business, or what?"

    Thrilled at screwing the on-screen talent out of money, it took the Suit a couple of extra heartbeats to appreciate an even more rewarding and exciting aspect of

Reality TV. "Hey, wait...this Reality TV crap writes itself because it's 'real,' right? So why pay scriptwriters those ridiculous union salaries?... What? You're asking me how can we get away with that? Because America's hot for this stuff! Look at the ratings! Rather than watch pretty actors performing fictional scripts, people are getting off watching people *just like them* undergoing physical and mental torture...and experiencing illicit sex. People watching this stuff *identify* with 'real people.' And they absolutely ADORE the spectacle of has-been stars humiliating themselves like trained monkeys for a chance to revive their faded careers. God, *is this a great business, or what?"*

But enough of economics, let's get right to the nitty-gritty: SEX!

Is Ryan gay? Is Simon? Did Paula jump the bones of that cute "American Idol" contestant? Did Paris and Nicole rodeo-ride those young bulls in Arkansas while enjoying "The Simple Life"? Who killed Anna Nicole Smith's son? Was Anna Nicole murdered? Is Howard K. Stern Larry Birkhead's secret gay lover? And *which* is the bitch? (Enquiring minds want to know!) Are Howard and Danny colluding to steal the fortune baby Dannielynn stands to inherit from the estate of Anna Nicole's dead sugar daddy? Talk about "reality" exploitation. Even as this book goes to press, Larry's negotiating for a "Bringing Up Baby" Reality TV show.

No wonder Reality TV is here to stay. You couldn't write this stuff and sell it as fiction because no one would believe it—but now you must believe it, because it's...real! Right?

Make no mistake about the longevity of this genre: it's queer, it's here...and it's unionizing.

Flashback: Twenty years ago, the movie "The Running Man" seemed like a science-fiction pipe dream, with its storyline of convict Arnold Schwarzenegger gambling his life against the prize of freedom—or the booby prize of instant death. Millions watched as government agents gave the budding "Terminator" a running start—then launched a manhunt with intent to execute him on a national TV show hosted by real-life "Family Feud" star Richard Dawson.

Today's reality? Even as I write this, the Writers Guild is out on strike, refusing to write movie or TV scripts until the studios give them a bigger piece of the profits pie. But would the studios have been bold enough to face the horror of shutting down shows if they didn't know that they can always produce reality shows to fill TV schedules? Think I'm kidding? The writers went on strike in late 2007—and the networks quickly ordered a whopping 50% more reality programming for 2008. (And here's an ironic twist that just occurred to me—it was the writer's strike in 1988 that spawned the first reality TV shows, like "Cops" and "America's Most Wanted." So in a strange way, the writers spurred the creation of the monster that just might come back and eat them alive in the new strike. Studios and networks are jeering, "We've got reality—who needs you guys?") The Writers Guild of America went on strike to seek relief from "exploitation." But pity the writers of reality shows, because they do not rely on the Writers Guild, or any other union, so studios are free to exploit them in the most sadistic ways—and frequently do. That's why the front page of a recent *New York Times* arts section featured this watershed headline:

"Union Plans to File Suit for Reality TV Workers!"

The *Times* story exposed a dirty little secret—the brutal reality of how Hollywood's exploiting this new genre, forcing producers to work 18-hour days in unstable jobs that offer no healthcare or pension benefits. Nearly 1,000 writers, editors and producers, have signed with the Writers Guild of America to force networks and studios to negotiate a union contract. That's no surprise to students of the fast-growing Reality TV phenomenon, which has now spread worldwide. After all, if viewers want to watch real people react to "real" situations—e.g., live mice released in a ladies' locker room—who needs writers? This stuff writes itself, right?

Consider, if you will, the wildly popular show with this snappy title:

"Terrorism In The Grip Of Justice."

It aired nightly in war-torn Iraq, with virtually every TV set tuned to a gritty, violence-tinged government roundup of terrorists, who were herded into a barbed-wire compound lit by floodlights, then ruthlessly interrogated for your viewing pleasure by the Scorpions, Iraq's elite police force.

So far, no executions, but...stay tuned!

Can the "Running Man" be far behind?

Nobody's actually been killed on a Reality TV show yet, but....

Consider: In 2003, the Sci-Fi Channel reached for the outer limits of "real" TV. An angry female contestant on Sci-Fi's "Scare Tactics" show, hosted by notorious "Beverly Hills 90210" Mean Grrl Shannon Doherty, filed a lawsuit claiming she'd suffered emotional and physical trauma when producers abducted her—then forced her to witness a staged murder by an unearthly "alien" she believed was real. This bizarre lawsuit was just one of a growing number of complaints filed against networks and TV producers. As a result, insurance premiums are rising fast—but don't assume that the added cost will kill the allure of getting rich quick off cheap-o reality shows. The Suits will compensate for added premiums by shaving the paychecks of frantically eager-to-work non-union writers fighting to get a foot inside Hollywood's door. And talk about wacky lawsuits! Even squeaky-clean Pax Network was sued by a fitness trainer, who claimed he was injured when producers tricked him into lying down on a moving conveyor belt at an Arizona airport and...*OOWWW!*...his leg jammed in the mechanism and he was badly injured.

Flashback: Who hasn't heard the phrase, "Smile... you're on Candid Camera!" Reel back a few decades to The Beginning, when the only "reality" on the television landscape—other than actual news and documentaries—was the relentlessly Milquetoast, hidden-camera spoof show, "Candid Camera." Back in that kinder, gentler America, we gasped when news shows unveiled video clips from truly savage Japanese reality shows that featured, for example, real people buried neck-deep in sand and covered in honey—screaming in agony as killer ants attacked and snacked! Such sadism would never play in America, sniffed the TV Suits. They even pooh-poohed MTV Generation offerings like "The Real World" and "Road Rules," dismissing them as puerile flash-in-the-pans (Or is it flashes-in-the-pan?). But then...a new day dawned. Trend-sniffing Suits woke up and smelled the reality coffee when murder suspect O.J. Simpson led the Los Angeles police—and all of America—on the infamous "Bronco Chase." This bizarre, slow-speed chase of a star/murder suspect became one of the highest-rated TV events in history. Suddenly, showbiz sat up and dropped its coke spoons! Stars, agents, managers, networks and producers joined in a creative orgy—and birthed the ground-breaking, trashy tell-all genre known as "celeb-Reality TV"...and they did it with the full cooperation of stars who were only too eager to expose their dirty linen: Bat-biting rocker Ozzie and his coo-coo clan, The Osbournes...Anna Nicole Smith, who just missed dying on camera...DebuDitz Paris Hilton and her out-of-control stage mom, Kathy..."Partridge Family" moppet-turned-'roid-rager Danny Bonaduce, who told VH1 his onscreen suicide would make great TV...Bayou Bimbette Britney Spears, who couldn't stop giggling about how she loved fucking her gold-digging him-bo Kevin Federline, y'all.... Let's not forget Donald Trump...and Martha Stewart...Farrah Fawcett...Rockers Tommy Lee and Gene "KISS" Simmons...Whitney Houston and Bad, Bad Bobby Brown...and even O.J. Simpson mounted a TV reality show—a killer idea that died quicker than you can say "Bruno Magli shoes." You've gotta hand it to the Hollywood Suits—they're quick studies! Once they realized that voyeurism triggers a short-circuit between crotch and cerebral cortex, they eagerly began to stretch the

*envelope, green-lighting truly unspeakable horror shows...
like "Being Bobby Brown," starring the R&B jailbird and
his then-wife Whitney Houston. Horrified* New York Post
*TV critic Linda Stasi reviewed the result of their
"reality" pairing and headlined:*

"Stop Bobby! The Price of Fame Just Got Too High!"

Ms. Stasi, bravely fighting waves of nausea,
described this key scene:

"The reunited couple and entourage go to a restaurant,
which opens up specifically for them. While they are
eating, Whitney brings up that always-popular dinner
conversation: the importance of pulling bugs out of your
rectum. Then Bobby tells one of his dinner guests, *'Don't
smother my food with your boogies!'* If this doesn't cause
high-speed remote-controlled disconnect, then wait until
next week to hear Bobby discuss how he pulled something
other than a bug out of his wife's rectum. Yes. And then
he demonstrates which fingers he used.

"To this brilliant conversation, Whitney enthusiastically responds: 'That's love! That's love! That's
black love!'"

Ironically, just below Linda's story, the *Post* ran
a piece with this revelatory headline:

"We're Watching More TV Than Ever."

It cited a study showing that in 2005 the average
person watched 30.7 hours of television each week—up from
27.9 in 2001.

Give the people what they want?

Or is it...a sucker's born every minute?

I report, you decide.

Question: Would you have guessed, just five years ago, that the Suits would be slavering to present prurient jaw-droppers like the Sundance Channel's "Trans-Generations"—a reality show that observes college-age kids changing sex? Parents of the scholars were totally riveted, as you might imagine, wondering if their kids were contemplating a gender/genitalia switch. Just imagine the letters home: "Dear Mom, Guess what? I'm now a DUDE!.... Love, Samantha.... P.S. You always used to call me 'Sam,' so no big deal, right?"

Think that's a shocker? Did you ever watch "The Vomit Game" Howard Stern used to play on his E! TV show? Who could forget the episode where a guy hurls on a gorgeous girl's feet—and a Stern employee licks them clean! No wonder Pope John denounced Reality TV!

Let's hope the Pope won't be shocked by the racy celeb anecdotes from my *National Enquirer* column that pepper this book. Here's an exclusive that titillated my readers when America went stark-raving nuts over the first season of Fox TV's "The Simple Life," starring Paris Hilton and Nicole Richie:

> Hot on the high heels of Mary-Kate Olsen's anorexia bombshell comes my shocking gag-me-with-a-spoon scoop: During the Arkansas sojourn of "The Simple Life," svelte-figured Paris Hilton regularly sneaked away from the cameras to hog hearty on greasy fried foods and pizza...then dashed to the bathroom for lengthy barf-a-thons, reveal owners of two local eateries! "That girl could really pack away the

food," marveled the proprietor of a joint Paris patronized. "Not just healthy foods—real greasy fried stuff. Then she'd rush into the bathroom and keep it locked for about 20 minutes, each and every time. When she was done, I knew I had to go in and clean up. She wouldn't leave it messy, but the smell was distinct. I knew that someone had been throwing up in there. It happened every time she came in, like clockwork!" The sexy million-heiress had a monster appetite that astounded the locals, confided another restaurateur. "Paris came into our place just about every day. When the cameras were off, she'd shovel the food into her face—mostly cheese pizza.

"And we knew to give that girl her space when she wanted bathroom time!"...BURP! (Oops... pardon me!)

That breathless anecdote illustrates interesting points about the appeal of Reality TV. For example:

1. Why are even the most vomitous reality episodes hypnotically fascinating? Why don't we avert our eyes as the horror unfolds?

2. Is Reality TV really reality? Everything is not really as it seems, it seems, and even though we all suspect that all reality isn't really—like, real—we just don't care!

3. Celebs behave badly, and always have—but what fun catching them red-handed on camera. YUMMY!

4. NEWS FLASH: Confirming our darkest suspicions, celebs really are whores. WHEE!

5. So-called real people are "attention whores" who fight to get on reality shows, then allow slicky-boy Suits and producers to abuse them, lie to them, embarrass

them, work their butts off for free—and even con them out of money!

6.Reality TV producers are often manipulative tyrants, but Hollywood studio Suits abuse, cheat and terrorize them—which is why these abusers-turned-abusee's are suddenly screaming, "UNION-IZE!"

And here's the best part: Reality TV stars often become so famous that even movie stars kiss their butts! This item from my column illustrates the point perfectly:

> After hearing JUSTIN TIMBERLAKE's snotty sneer that "American Idol" winner TAYLOR HICKS "can't carry a tune in a bucket," this mind-boggler's truly hilarious: "Pirates of the Caribbean" mega-star JOHNNY DEPP, dining at swanky Ivy in BevHills, leaped from his seat and rushed over to introduce himself when "Superman" stud BRANDON ROUTH walked in—and started raving about how he's a huge fan! Totally stunned, young Brandon stammered, "I can't believe you want to meet me...I'm a huge fan of yours!" Just then, as Depp and Routh stood trading praise, in walked—you guessed it!—Taylor Hicks. Instantly, the two movie idols rushed to the "Idol" idol, gushing like star-struck kids...raving that they're HUGE fans!! Dumbstruck, from-the-sticks Hicks barely managed to squeak a strangled, "Thanks..."—then grabbed a notepad from the hostess and begged for their autographs. Buccaneer Depp and Super-Dude Routh happily obliged, but Hicks really got his kicks when they begged him for his signature ("X"?). Hey, TimberSnake...not counting CAMERON DIAZ, how many Hollywood superstars suck up to you like that?

Coming up are tips on how YOU can pitch your own Reality TV project and get in on the fun. Trust me, if you have a halfway decent idea, networks will drag you in off the streets...which is exactly what happened to me when I half-jokingly told a Hollywood pal about my way-out, too-wacky-for-prime-time idea for a reality show. That person called another person—and next thing I knew, I was sitting in meetings with Fox TV development execs, one of whom admitted:

"Mike, your show about female virgins is as close to an absolutely original idea as anyone ever gets in this Reality TV business—which means I've only seen it once before."

You'll read the treatment I wrote for Fox. It will give Reality TV wannabes an idea of how to present a pitch. And even though my show is still unsold, it's all a matter of timing in Hollywood. I truly believe virgins are ripe for the plucking, so to speak. In fact, one network recently put out a casting call for "male virgins" for "a new reality series."

So...are you ready to rumble, Dan? America needs to get real. Alert Publisher's Row, and let's holler, *"ACTION!"*

Really, Yours Sincerely....
    Mike

(AUTHOR'S NOTE: Agent Dan sold my book, dear Reader—get ready to *"Get Real!"*)

* * *

Chapter *One*

PEEK-A-BOO + SCHADENFREUDE = WHO NEEDS SHAKESPEARE?...
THE FIRST RULE OF REALITY: PARIS RULES!... WHEN WONG IS RIGHT.

Let me begin by welcoming the newcomers, if there are any, to Reality TV—the Super Bowl of Voyeurism! In just a few short years, Reality has exploded. It's a major phenomenon. Even the so-called "experts" have quit predicting the death of the trend. And here's the dirty little secret that drives the juggernaut—summed up in a wink-wink-nudge-nudge tagline I wrote for the syndicated tabloid television show I created, "National Enquirer TV":

You *know* you want to watch!

Admit it. You *can't* tear your eyes away from the train wreck of Reality TV. You tried it, you liked it—and now it feeds your new-found craving for *real* kicks, not that pale, make-believe stuff on scripted TV.

When was your first time? You probably don't remember. Your Reality TV addiction probably happened gradually—just crept up and caught you by surprise. Before you knew it, you were hooked—mesmerized, perhaps—by the titillating thrill of witnessing real danger as real-life "Cops" tackled some meth-crazed, wife-beating redneck in a trailer park. Or was it when you vicariously endured physical and mental stress on "Fear Factor"—and discovered the sheer fun of being frightened while sitting safely on your sofa?

Did jolts of sexual electricity tingle your nerve-ends as you ogled half-naked "Temptation Island" hotties & hunks seducing committed couples into committing adultery? And were you aware, as you giggled helplessly at the drug-addled antics of "The Osbournes," that you'd let these Brit loonies worm their way into your heart until they became your adopted, dysfunctional family?

Admit it: you shivered watching the scary "Anna Nicole Smith Show"—cringing as the blowsy, aging ex-stripper shoved mammoth breasts into young son Daniel's face and cooed, "Do you love Mommy?" And do you remember how you gagged—horrified that a mother would commit such a filthy act in front of her own child—when she laid face-down on the bed in the master bedroom of a house she was inspecting and humped it vigorously, purring, "I'm so *horny*!"?

When the Anna Nicole train wreck hit TV, Internet bloggers shrieked that someone should call child services to rescue Daniel from the sordid reality of his mommy's show. Legally, of course, that was a long shot because Daniel was already approaching 18. And even though his drug-addled mother was hardly a perfect role model, there's no question they had a close relationship. And Daniel apparently wanted to join her on the show, most of the time, anyway. Nevertheless, the boy's father, Billy Smith, told a reporter, "It just doesn't feel right (to put Daniel on TV). I don't see how it can be a positive thing for him."

In hindsight, a tragic understatement!

Daniel joined Mom and her creepy lover/lawyer Howard K. Stern in the Bahamas just after the birth of his baby sister, Dannielynn—then died suddenly of a drug overdose in suspicious circumstances!

In death, reality icon Daniel made headlines like a major Hollywood star. Ten thousand stories hammered out the news of his passing, proving that Reality TV had captured the national imagination so completely that millions of people ended up truly caring about this young man. And when Sleazy Mommy, in the perfect career move, suddenly kicked the bucket under mysterious circumstances, she whipped up a Perfect Storm of tabloid hysteria. The Playboy pinup/Marilyn Monroe wannabe, long consigned to the has-been trash heap, was suddenly resurrected as a glittering, deathless Monroe-esque icon through the magic of Reality TV.

You know you wanna watch!

Here's the reality, Reality Fan: *You're hooked.* Like millions of TV viewers, you've come to the conclusion that sitcoms, soaps, dramas and documentaries are insipid substitutes for the lubricious embrace of silly/sexy/scary Reality TV.

Oh, sure…you still turn scripted shows on.

But they don't turn *you* on!

Why? Here's Reality star Paris "The Simple Life" Hilton explaining it all in her famously pithy prose:

"Like…*DUH!*… It's so hot!"

Right on, Paris! Reality TV's appeal is irresistible because it's visceral—an edgy thrill that starts percolating deep in our innards. And that's *so* understandable, right? Because for a human being, there's nothing—with the possible exception of watching Brad do Angelina—that matches the thrill of spying on real people reacting to unreal, unrehearsed confrontations; ordinary folks like thee and me suffering mental and/or physical and/or sexual torture. It's so deliciously "peek-a-boo-I-see-you-but-you-can't-see-me." It's enjoyment derived from the troubles of others, or what the Germans call *"schadenfreude"*—which roughly translates as: "It's not enough that I am happy…what's important is that you are miserable!"

Reality TV perfectly defines the old joke about the difference between tragedy and comedy. To wit:

When *I* slip on a banana peel and bust my ass, that's tragedy. But when you slip on a banana peel and bust your ass…that's COMEDY!

Think about it. Thanks to Reality TV, we no longer need a Shakespeare or a Seinfeld to artificially, albeit artfully, re-create The Human Comedy. Today, we can watch the real thing…starring "real" human beings. With Reality TV, the small screen is no longer a mere projection device—it's a blast-in-the-ass magic window, allowing the viewer to experience the same forbidden, naughty thrills that motivate the Peeping Tom. It triggers an addictive rush that literally re-wires your brain. It morphs you—in one headlong, heady whoosh—from Passive Viewer to Peek Freak.

So hop aboard our unstoppable train. Time to get in on the fun, if you're still missing it! Join us as we fling open the Portals of Prurience and expose the Brave New World of Reality TV. But, please…as you innocently skip through our magical gateway, seeking thrills and adventure à la Dorothy on the road to Oz, contemplate one final, probing question—and answer honestly:

Ever feel just a teeny bit…ashamed?

Oh, forget I asked!

And, anyway, you're not *alone.* Far from it! For you—and for mega-millions of otherwise normal folks on our planet—mesmerizing psycho-drama that masquerades as good, clean TV fun has burgeoned from a home-grown sub-genre into a mind-blowing pop-culture phenomenon.

Why?

Because in our human universe, nothing beats guilty pleasure!

Take pornography. It's fun precisely because it's forbidden! And the same for voyeurism, that powerful human passion so roundly condemned by polite society. So…when the Wizards of Hollywood cleverly combined these naughty pursuits, the fun factor ratcheted straight off the charts!

After all, what scripted drama can compare to the vicarious thrill of spying on total strangers—people you know to be "real" and not actors—sweating in the real-life throes of sexual abandon or abject humiliation?

Critics sneer that Reality TV is sadistic, sordid, sex-drenched and stupid. Perhaps. But even during its most disgusting and depraved moments—e.g., when the jailbird/thug star of "Being Bobby Brown" explained to viewers how he dug a "doody bubble" out of wife Whitney Houston's booty—Reality TV is, to put it in rock-and-roll terms, "simply irresistible!"

But enough of sex, drugs, & rock and roll (…for now, anyway. We'll dwell on it endlessly in due course, of course!). Let us consider this serious question: What, if any, are the redeeming qualities of Reality TV—a home-grown American genre born out of the 1940s radio show, "Candid Microphone" and its long-running TV spinoff, "Candid Camera"? Is it *always* tawdry, tacky, execrable, exploitive…secretly scripted and staged by evil producer/trolls who manipulate all-too-willing human puppets?

And…is it ever really…*real?*

Again, let's ask one of the genre's major stars, Ms. Paris Hilton!…

Paris?

"Like, *Duh!* Don't you ever watch 'The Simple Life?'…Like, HELLO-*O-OO!*"
Thanks, babe. Well said.

Now, before you curl your lip in a superior sneer, dear Reader, never forget that Paris Hilton rated a major "That's *hot*!" with her Reality TV trifle, "The Simple Life." (And *do* stay tuned for exclusive backstage dirt that will be dished in upcoming chapters. Remember, you're in the hands of an expert here!) So, never dismiss Ms. Heir-Head as just another air-head. This Hollywood hottie's an icon who knows her business—and here's the message she's sending you: Never believe there's nothing *not real* about Reality TV.

Say *what?*

Oh, come on, people…Get *REAL!* And get ready to stand up and cheer!

Climb aboard our magic carpet for a swift ride to the first stop on our phantasmagorical tour—the frontlines of America's war against terror. We've got a copy of the *New York Times* on board, and here's a startling headline:

"In War's Chaos, Iraq Finds Inspiration for Reality TV!"

In a truly amazing *New York Times* story by Edward Wong, a Baghdad woman named Amal Ramzi Ismail stares at the wreckage of her home, destroyed when soldiers blew up a munitions dump nearby—then shrieks in excitement as an Iraqi TV crew pulls up in a van. They're from a home-grown show called "Materials and Labor," a program inspired by "This Old House" and "Extreme Makeover: Home Edition"…with a touch of "Apocalypse Now."

Unlimbering cameras, the crew begins filming laborers hired by the Iraqi TV network to rebuild Ms. Ismail's house!

"I get chills thinking about this," she says. "Words can't express how grateful I am."

Writes Wong: "Reality TV could turn out to be the most durable Western import in Iraq. It has taken root with considerably greater ease than American-style democracy. Since Spring 2004…a constellation of reality shows has burst onto TV screens across Iraq."

WOW!

America's gift to the war-torn and weary is…Reality TV! Hey, Britney, don't it just make ya proud, y'all?

Believe it or not, there are *other* Iraqi Reality TV shows—like the smash-hit called, "Congratulations!" It helps deserving young couples get married. In yet another popular program, TV crews roam the country passing out $1,000 prizes. And topping TV charts from Baghdad to Mosul is an extravaganza known, in loose translation, as:

"I Wanna Be Iraq Star!"

It's an amateur singing contest that bears such a stunning resemblance to "American Idol" that if Iraq was not at war, Simon Cowell would *sue*. But hands down, the Iraqi Reality TV show that really tugs the heart-strings is "Materials and Labor,"—which is hardly a snappy title. But Fox TV learned that a title can be too snappy, à la their creepily suggestive and quickly-canceled "Who's Your Daddy?" show. (If they'd called it "Abandoned Daughters Find Their Fathers," women might still be weeping over it every week!)

Incredibly, "Materials and Labor"—a home makeover show staged in the middle of a war zone—has financed the repair of six homes destroyed in explosions and air-strikes since its inception.

How's that for getting "real."

So be proud, America!

Smile, everybody…*You're on Candid Camera!*

Our invention, Reality TV, is a prime-time export. It's as American as apple pie, a genre created in our own image—brash, corny, flashy, smart, sentimental, sympathetic and strong. Now the whole world wants to join in the fun. Real People want to get sexy, get rich and famous, and help their neighbors even as they help themselves. And even though these *goldang furriners* have ripped off our Reality and made it their own, look on the bright side, folks. It's a stunning salute to America's legendary "can-do" spirit—and a major sign that we just might be winning their hearts and minds!

Reality TV: Born in the U.S.A.!

Because Americans are the *real*-est damn people on earth!

Yeee-HAH!

* * *

Chapter *Two*

WHO'S YOUR DADDY?... SHOCKING THE UNSHOCKABLE!...
THE FASTEST CANCELLATION IN TV HISTORY....
YES, IT'S A TRANSSEXUAL, BUT WE'RE BRITISH!

My day job as columnist for the *National Enquirer* is tough! Week in and week out, I'm charged with the gargantuan task of shocking unshockable America. To say I'm equal to the task would be false modesty, and dubbing myself, say, "the Da Vinci of Scandal," might be taking it a bit too far. But Howard Stern—describing my virtuosity at breaking behind-the-screen bombshells—once told his millions of listeners:

"Mike Walker is the Hemingway of gossip."

Here's a headline-making example of my handiwork that you just might remember—news that broke live on national television when Judge Ito dramatically stopped the O.J. Simpson murder trial and announced that he was stopping the trial because he urgently needed to read my just-published new book, "Nicole Brown Simpson: Private Diary of a Life Interrupted."

His action stunned the courtroom and the nation—and helped drive my book to the #1 spot on the *New York Times* bestseller list! (Thank you, Your Honor-san.)

A somewhat less earth-shaking scoop of mine—but people always seem to remember it—was my then-riveting revelation that soulmates Angelina Jolie and Billy Bob Thornton were walking around sporting vials of each other's blood on gold neck chains. Nobody believed it at first—until the press finally confirmed the story three *weeks* after I broke it!

But enough of idle boasts…the point is that my job, ferreting for gossip gold, suddenly got much more exciting when Paris Hilton, Britney Spears, Lindsay Lohan and Nicole Richie began shedding their inhibitions—not to mention their unmentionables—and started smashing up cars, doing drugs, cuddling lesbians, collapsing in rehab and ending up in jail. This new era of celebrity shame kicked off in 2005, fondly recalled by showbiz journalists as a banner year for shocking headlines trumpeting kinky sex and/or murder involving names like Michael Jackson, Robert Blake and Phil Spector.

Celebrity scandals that encompassed pedophilia and even murder once again raised a question that—in a lifetime of reporting on high crimes and misdemeanors by the rich and famous—had often been put to me by TV, radio and print interviewers:

"Mike, is there any crime that showbiz fans absolutely *won't* forgive?"

My answer always was, "Stars can bounce back from *any* crime if they do the right kind of spin-doctoring—and that includes drug abuse, shoplifting, assault, hit-and-run, rape, kidnapping and murder."

But since 2005, I've changed my tune just a bit. Early that year, two bizarre brouhahas triggered a violent shift in Hollywood's tectonic plates that shook Planet Showbiz to its core—and it forced me to modify my stock answer that stars almost always get away with murder. First, the world was shocked when Peter Pan-esque freak Michael Jackson was arrested, handcuffed and put on trial for child molestation! It was unprecedented and unsettling.

Suddenly, there was a new career-killer in town—sexual weirdness with kids.

It was, in Paris Hilton-speak, *so* totally toxic, image-wise! Showbiz, like any human enterprise, isn't just about hearts and minds. In the end, it always comes down to the numbers. When El Wacko released a CD following his courtroom ordeal, it sold a pathetic 8,000 copies in its first week. "That is, like, *so* not hot!"

"There you have it: the stardom-killer," I triumphantly told talk-show interviewers, like Ahab spotting the whale. "Now we've identified the one unspeakable crime fans won't forgive; a taboo that disgusts them so much they'll turn their backs on a showbiz idol forever. I'm talking about…."

Child molestation!

Amazingly, hot on the heels of that discovery, America's hard-to-shock TV audience identified yet *another* career-killing taboo—one coughed up out of the slimy, sadistic, sex-drenched world of Reality TV! Here was a crime so vile, in the eyes of viewers, that the mere *hint* of it enraged millions of fans…so much so that they literally killed a major TV series after just *one* episode.

Memo to Reality TV Moguls: You Suits have been put on notice—the viewing public has delineated a no-fly-zone in BadTaste-istan. Be warned and beware, moguls! TV viewers will open fire with lethal e-mail bullets if you dare to violate this just-delineated boundary. Refrain, therefore, from even a hint of TV Land's new taboo! Folks, I'm talking about:

Incest!

America has drawn a line in the sand for depraved producers. So with that in mind, let's take a tour of this new Forbidden TV Territory and present, for your salacious delectation, the author's nominee for the following category:

"Most Cringe-Inducing Scene in a Reality TV Show Produced by a Major Hollywood Studio."

(AUTHOR'S NOTE: When you purchased this book, you were enrolled automatically in my newly formed "Reality TV Academy of Arts & Sciences." Therefore, you are officially authorized to nominate your own choice for Reality's TV's most *"Eeeeeewwww!"* moment. But here's mine, dear Reader, and I'm sticking to it:)

*

Imagine, if you will, a beautiful and voluptuous blonde woman, dressed in a daringly low-cut black evening gown, whisked in the dead of night—like Tom Cruise in "Eyes Wide Shut"—to a magnificent mansion. There, she is presented to eight distinguished-looking older men…and told that one of them is the father who abandoned her at birth.

As the evening progresses, the men court the young woman. There is much coy laughter. A languid, flirtatious mood gradually pervades the drawing room. The men engage the young woman in conversation; vie for her attentions. She rewards them with demure smiles.

Then…a bizarre ritual begins. As she sits facing them, the men step forward, one by one, to dance for this ravishing beauty in solo competition. She watches intently as they strike

macho poses and flaunt their rhythmic prowess with dips, glides…subtle hip thrusts.
Finally, the moment of decision arrives. The young woman smiles enigmatically, then chooses
her man….

Whoa!

For one surreal moment, as you watch this show, the seductive mood lulls you into forgetting that this young beauty is not the prize in an illicit contest for sexual favors. And you remember how you suppressed a guilty urge to snigger the first time you heard the show's title, with its outrageous double entendre. And as the announcer cheerily bellows the show's name at the commercial break, you're struck by the utter absurdity of it.

You ask yourself, "What the *hell* was Hollywood thinking?"

Announcer: Now it's time for "Who's…Your…Daddy?"

(Applause.)

In late summer of 2005, over drinks at the Beverly Hills Four Seasons, I interviewed one of the creative minds behind the show that shocked America—and arrived DOA following a firestorm of outraged viewer e-mails.

"What *were* you thinking?" I asked this smart, experienced producer. "Surely, a roomful of Hollywood big-shots weren't oblivious to the sexual connotations of the phrase, 'Who's Your Daddy?' What possessed you guys to go with it?"

Before I reveal his answer, let's explore the meaning behind my aforementioned mantra that describes the Peeping Tom compulsion which drives Reality TV:

You **Know** You Want to Watch!

The phrase winks at our tacit hypocrisy about voyeurism. We can't tear our eyes away from scenes of hot sex and bloody violence because prurient curiosity is a natural human impulse. But so is guilt. That's the price we pay for our forbidden thrills, exacted by that strange human mechanism known as our "conscience." But even though we know we'll hate ourselves in the morning, human curiosity can't be quelled. It's why we run *toward* car crashes, not away from them!

Sex?

You *know* you want to watch sex! The Internet's raging growth was fueled by our multi-billion dollar porn industry.

Violence?

If the law allowed televised executions, we'd flock to stadiums, in numbers that would have shocked Caesar himself, to watch criminals flung to lions (or we'd catch live-action coverage on Fox News Channel).

But at the end of the day, as we like to say in Hollywood, our voyeurism has self-imposed limits. We are not savages, after all. That's why there's a visceral recoil from the two major taboos that have been imposed by every tribe of man down through the ages. Incredibly, however, in 2005 A.D., arrogant and/or ignorant Hollywood-ites ignored our tribal taboos at their peril, and were quickly punished for forgetting that child molestation and incest are still forbidden—even for superstars and Reality TV producers!

Ergo, the Court of Public Opinion swiftly declared Michael Jackson—and "Who's Your Daddy?"—guilty of "taboo chutzpah!"

"Who's Your Daddy?" paid the ultimate penalty! To say it died is an understatement. This turkey was ax-murdered! Nielson Media Research dubbed "Daddy" a ratings dud after it pulled just 6.3 million viewers, compared to 14.8 million for the Sugar Bowl and 11.3 million for shows on CBS and NBC.

And lest you think I'm over-emphasizing the viewing public's reaction to the incest issue—sniffing out kinky where none exists—hark to these harsh words from *LA Times* critic Paul Brownfield, who chided the show for "incestuous, orgiastic undertones."

Wrote Brownfield: "'Who's Your Daddy?' was selling a heartwarming reunion; it somehow didn't understand how gross it was. The woman, named T.J., was told that she would win $100,000 if she could guess which guy was her dad (she did).

"Curiously, the show took place at night...as T.J. mingled with the men at a cocktail party and later watched four of them disco dance. For much of the 90 minutes, she wore various plunging necklines as soft-core porn music played in the background, and steadily I grew confused—was she being sold into sexual slavery, or reuniting with her birth father?"

In his hilarious, dead-on critique, Brownfield describes the potential "daddy's" of lovely T.J. as "...mid-level professional types who looked like they'd probably hit on her if this were a Friday night at Bennigan's."

Hey-*ooooo!*

To be fair, the idea behind the show, a birth-family reunion, is emotionally powerful. Treated with a modicum of dignity—an admittedly alien concept in most Reality TV—it easily could have been a tear-jerker hit. Sadly, however, tacky titillation won the day. Yet it wasn't its crassness that killed it.

After all, wrote critic Sally Kalson in the *Pittsburgh Post-Gazette,* nobody got overly offended by the tackiness of such Reality hits as "The Bachelor," "Temptation Island" and "Who Wants to Marry a Millionaire."

Said Kalson: "Rick Rockwell plucked Darva Conger out of the harem and married her on a Las Vegas stage; scantily-clad singles on a tropical island tried to seduce committed couples into cheating on each other; and a backhoe operator posed as a rich playboy to woo a partner under false pretenses."

(And there was a British show that had guys competing to be the first to have full intercourse with a beautiful woman—who turned out to be a full-on transsexual. Lawsuits bloody well *flew* on that one.)

Aaahh, tacky, schmacky!

All too often, that is the defiant, derisive and dismissive response from our TinselTown Suits, Reality fans. Viewers, as any studio organ-grinder will tell you, LOVE tacky! *But not this time, moguls.* The exception proved the rule. What strangled this puppy was its skin-crawly, incestuous undertone.

"The most bizarre part of the entire tear-soaked schlock-fest was its implicit sexuality," marveled critic Kalson. "T.J., the searching daughter, was all grown up in the fullest sense of the phrase…she had long, blonde hair, amazingly plump lips and a suspiciously curvy frame, showed off throughout in low-cut, skin-tight outfits that revealed plenty of leg.

"The men, meanwhile, looked to be in their late 40s and early 50s. As T.J. chatted them up at a get-acquainted cocktail party, the flirtatiousness got a little creepy. Then it got more so. After learning that her father had been a disco dancer as a young man, she watched as the contestants took turns performing dance steps for her—some with a fair amount of hip action.

"At this point, 'Who's Your Sugar Daddy?' seemed a more appropriate title. Leave it to Fox to give the Electra complex a bad name."

Now…let's flash back to my interview with one of the show's creators. My burning question, you'll recall, was, "What the hell were you thinking? You must have known 'Who's Your Daddy?' is a phrase that evokes sexual connotations?"

He shrugged. "Sure, we thought of that. We kicked around a lot of title ideas, like 'Reunion.' But after discussion, we decided it was a clever title that described the show in a phrase that everyone's heard, but which has various definitions. We believed the show's theme spoke for itself, and no one would take a sexual meaning where none was intended."

Well, as Church Lady might say…"Isn't that *precious!*"

The winds of hell swirled up swiftly after Fox TV Network announced an air date. Adoption groups around the nation rallied members, who drowned the studio in a deluge estimated at 100,000 angry e-mails—literally clogging computers for days on end!

Fox—the mighty giant of Reality TV, and producers of many good, clean shows—might have withstood the onslaught from adoption advocates, whose main complaint was that birth parent reunion was far too emotional a topic for TV exploitation. And when the so-called "incest" angle began to leak out, it provided chewy fodder for all the "issue pimps"—snarky journalists, radio/TV talk show hosts and late-night comedians.

Fox really smelled the brimstone when "Saturday Night Live" took a savage shot that made America gasp…and giggle! On its "SNL News Update" segment, anchor-babe Tina Fey intoned with a devilish twinkle in her eye:

"Fox has announced a new TV show based on reuniting a daughter with the father who abandoned her at birth, and it's called 'Who's Your Daddy?'"

Instantly, the audience snickered lewdly. Tina raised an eyebrow, nodded and said, "Uh, huh!" As the laughter subsided, she explained:

"The show works like this: a young woman who was abandoned at birth by the father she never knew wins $100,000 by picking him out of a crowd of older men."

Staring deadpan at the camera, Tina zinged:

"And then…*she marries him!*"

The punchline totally killed the audience—and studio executives wished they were dead.

"Oh my God, this has turned into a nightmare," a hardened Hollywood veteran at Fox told me. "I've never seen such hate mail. Our computers are literally clogged. Sometimes bad publicity makes people tune in to see what it's all about—but this feels different. I think we're dead."

And they were. To their credit, Fox yanked the show after just one airing. Five other episodes are in the can, but you'll never see them until some genius realizes there's cult/camp gold in a DVD titled: "Who's Your Daddy?—The Lost Episodes!"

The embarrassing "Daddy" debacle could have been headed off by the then brand-new head of Fox TV Studios, former ABC-TV exec Angela Shapiro, who had stepped into her job just as "Who's Your Daddy?" went into production. While the show wasn't developed under her watch, Shapiro viewed the footage that had been shot, and reportedly found it distasteful for all the obvious reasons.

Curiously, instead of demanding changes, in the words of one Fox insider, "Angela went back to supervising the lengthy and expensive decoration of her new offices. For whatever reason, she just didn't seem to give a damn about a show she hadn't been involved in."

So "Who's Your Daddy?" set a new world record in a genre that's famed for hatching tasteless turkeys—and the record still stands:

"Fastest Cancellation in Reality TV History!"

(Applause.)

*   *   *

Chapter *Three*

REALITY TV'S FIRST DEATH.... 9/11 PROVES THERE'S NO ESCAPING REALITY.... MULTIPLYING LIKE BUNNY RABBITS.

How did reality programming "hijack" TV?

How about sex, scandal, dirty tricks and backstage celebrity secrets? You KNOW that's where we're heading, but first, let's dig deep into the dirt that surrounds Reality TV's roots!

In the Beginning…(drum roll)…there was "Candid Camera." The granddaddy of all Reality TV shows began life as the brainstorm of a bright young U.S. soldier named Allen Funt, who originally conceived and produced a radio show that featured the amusing gripes of his fellow GIs during World War 2. It aired on Armed Forces Radio and was called "Candid Microphone." The show clicked big-time with the troops.

After the war, in 1947, Funt sold "Candid Microphone" to network radio. The show, modified for a civilian audience, clicked again. Then Funt debuted "Candid Camera" on network television in 1948—and a phenomenon was born. The show ended up becoming the longest-running smash in history, but at the time, no one had any reason to believe that this funny little reality baby would grow into The Beast That Ate TV.

Viewed today, "Candid Camera" looks tame, even quaint. Funt—ironically, a man whose name literally evokes and embodies the word "fun"—was a genius at dreaming up pranks to pull on unsuspecting ordinary people, then letting the cameras catch the candid reality as they reacted in sometimes unexpected ways. So "Candid Camera" owned the fledgling reality genre—along with a few other unscripted shows pioneered by American TV, like "Truth or Consequences" and, later, "That's Incredible," "This Is Your Life," "Queen for a Day" and "The Price Is Right." These formats eventually were exported from the U.S. to countries all around the world. They were cheap to produce using native talent, and very popular.

In 1964, Great Britain's BBC aired another quaint forerunner of today's high-voltage Reality TV shows, a series called "Seven Up." The show, which still exists, was created around an intriguing premise: it followed the lives of a dozen seven-year-olds from all walks of life in documentaries that aired every seven years. The idea was to record how they reacted to changes in their lives as the years went by. Seven years after the first series, when the youngsters were 14 years old, a new series—titled "Seven Plus Seven"—was filmed and aired. The next installment, when they turned 21, was called "Twenty-One Up"…and so on.

The show wasn't "real" Reality TV because there was no plot—and there was none of the cynical manipulation for thrills and laughs so common today. It was simply a series of interviews, but it did introduce what was then a breakthrough idea: plucking ordinary people out of their ordinary lives, and transforming them into television celebrities.

The first "real" Reality TV show was "American Family," a truly weird, unsettling, but totally fascinating documentary series that debuted on PBS in 1973. Members of the Loud family were filmed day and night by a team of television producers who shot more than 300 hours of footage, then edited it down to the 12 hours that aired on PBS. The ratings for "American Family" were phenomenal. TV viewers watched riveted as the family's Mom and Dad, Bill and Pat Loud, went through a very nasty marriage breakup.

But even more shocking, considering the era, was the episode in which the Loud's son, Lance, came out publicly as a homosexual. The show was an instant classic. And, classically, the Loud family complained—as do many of today's reality "stars"—that the footage chosen by the producers for broadcast totally misrepresented their lives…blah, blah, blah…etc. Ten years later, in 1983, America caught up with the Loud family again in a sequel produced for HBO.

There is no question that "American Family" inspired MTV's "The Real World"—and it was widely imitated in the farthest reaches of the western world. The year after "American Family" debuted, a copycat show called "The Family" aired in the United Kingdom. And in 1992, Australian viewers were riveted by the real-life adventures of the newly rich Baker-Donaher family of Sydney, chronicled in a show called *Sylvania Waters*. Several reality shows broke through in America during the 1980s, notably "Star Search" and "Real Stories of the Highway Patrol."

But what we know today as Reality TV *really* began with "Cops." This mesmerizing breakthrough show aired in 1989, showing real-life cops catching real-life criminals in real locations like gritty urban neighborhoods, trailer parks, lonely backroads and super-highways. "Cops" had that nitty-gritty camcorder look, the *cinema verité* feel that characterizes modern Reality TV.

Another seminal show was "America's Most Wanted." The brilliant twist in this production was that it was interactive—with the audience enlisted as couch-bound detectives who helped the police track down real-life criminals. The next trail-blazer, the instant smash hit, "America's Funniest Home Videos," proved that reality can be hilarious, with average people sending producers their candid videos of kids falling off the barn roof, poodles dancing in ballerina outfits, Uncle Ed's pants falling down, etc.…

The next ratings-grabber to surf the swelling Reality TV wave was "The Jerry Springer Show," which debuted in 1991. The angle of this white-trash fest was injecting real-life drama onto the conventional TV talk-show stage—deliberately booking the guests most likely to end up beating the crap out of each other.

One of Springer's imitators was "The Jenny Jones Show," fronted by a woman who'd had a so-so career as a standup comedienne. Her name will always be associated with the very first death connected to a Reality TV show. The shocking incident sounded a warning that's all too often ignored even today by cynical, inept, or downright evil producers: be careful how you turn up the heat on those "ordinary" people…or you might end up getting some innocents burned. Here's how the fire started raging:

On a 1995 Jenny Jones show about "secret crushes," a guest named Scott Amedure—who was gay—revealed on the air that he had a secret crush on a hometown friend who was also guesting, John Schmitz. Amedure shocked the audience when he gleefully revealed he had fantasized about tying Schmitz up and staging "a whipped cream-and-champagne adventure." The studio audience screamed with laughter as Schmitz—stunned and humiliated by these unsuspected revelations—was forced to listen to his friend's fantasies. Freaked, he kept insisting as Jenny Jones and the audience roared, "I'm 100% heterosexual."

Sadly, Jenny's "joke" backfired—with terrible consequences. After returning home from the show, John Schmitz could not shake his feelings of rage and shame at being the fantasy figure in another man's homosexual reveries. Three days later, he boiled over. Barging into Scott Amedure's home, he blew him away with two point-blank shotgun blasts to the chest. Schmitz was convicted of second-degree murder, but the case was overturned. In a re-trial, however, he was convicted and sentenced to serve a 20-year prison term. Many viewers blamed the "Jenny Jones Show" for Scott Armedure's death, and felt it was a miscarriage of justice that the producers and Jenny got off...scot-free.

Then, in 1992, MTV discovered a brand-new audience for Reality TV—young people who were tiring of the network's one-note programming: a seemingly endless lineup of rock bands performing music videos. Development execs came up with a totally cool idea: making total strangers live in a house together over a long period of time, and recording whatever ensued. As they tweaked their instantly successful experiment, dubbed "The Real World," MTV pioneered many of the tried-and-true techniques that are standard in Reality TV today: trapping people in a claustrophobic environment, tweaking footage with dramatic soundtrack music, and using after-the-fact "confessionals" recorded by cast members as voice-over narration to onscreen events.

"The Real World" also pioneered the concept of competition. Contestants battled each other in an elimination contest and were booted off the show, one by one, until only the winner remained. "The Real World" still stands as the mother-lode model for today's reality shows, and many of the genre's producers got their first training there.

Looking back at the international TV landscape in the 1950s, scripted shows from the United States dominated the world's television networks, from Europe to the Far East and Australia, with shows like "Charlie's Angels," "Ben Casey," "Get Smart," and "M*A*S*H." Foreign markets just couldn't compete with American production values, so they licensed and telecast our scripted shows with American stars. But locally produced reality shows often became hugely popular because they reflected each country's culture and starred local talent. Shows like Holland's "Big Brother," Belgium's "The Mole," and Scandinavia's "Expedition Robinson" (later re-titled "Survivor") were spotted by British producers and imported to the U.K.

These shows—along with a flood of others like "Trading Spaces" and "American Idol"—were picked up and developed in the United States for major networks, but they were tailor-made for cable channels that were suddenly multiplying faster than bunny rabbits. All it takes is one cheap-to-produce Reality TV show, like Bravo's "Queer Eye for the Straight Guy," to turn around the fortunes of a cable channel.

In May 2000, the trend really took hold with the debuts of "Survivor" and "Big Brother." In 2001, a raft of Reality TV shows opened big, including "Fear Factor," "Temptation Island" and "The Mole." Then along came "Who Wants to Be a Millionaire," and it blew the doors off American TV. "Millionaire" had the format of an old-fashioned quiz show, but the feel was total reality. Instead of the breezy, chatty atmosphere of a "Family Feud" or "Wheel of Fortune," it evoked the creepy ambience of a psychological torture chamber, totally involving the studio audience and at-home "lifeline" buddies that under-the-gun contestants could telephone anywhere in the country for help.

Audiences were totally hooked. Ratings skyrocketed. The Hollywood Suits sat bolt upright in their executive suites and got on the phones, barking at the talent agents: "Send us Reality shows...now!" The reality floodgates opened and its future looked like a slam-dunk...until the most terrifying TV vision ever witnessed by mankind threatened to kill the new genre aborning: the 9/11 terrorist attack on America.

Suddenly, every TV screen in the nation lit up with images that played like an insanely surreal video game…planes slamming into the twin towers of the World Trade Center…an inferno of smoke, fire and falling bodies…the spectacular collapse of a skyscraper crashing into the screaming streets below…and all the other shared, indelible images that horrifically redefined the term "Reality TV."

On that day of hyper-reality, on 9/11, a genius of the reality genre stepped up to the plate and made broadcast history in an ad-lib performance that proved, once and for all, that he's the un-sung pioneer and innovator of America's newest art form. The curious failure of snobbish, asleep-at-the-switch historians to acknowledge this broadcasting giant and accord him the credit he's due will be corrected by the author a few chapters from now, dear Reader. It is a story that will not fail to fascinate.

But as for 9/11…the awful shock of that terror attack on national TV had pundits predicting, as pundits love to do, that the American public would no longer have the stomach to watch half-naked babes gobbling down pigs' rectums on "Fear Factor"—or care to hear a fat, flabby totally-naked homosexual man bragging that he'd won some stupid "Survivor" game by having the ingenuity to employ his rectum as a hidey-hole for forbidden matches that allowed him to light a fire. (True story, gossip fans! Watch for details in an upcoming chapter.)

Had 9/11 really killed Reality TV? That's what the experts were telling us. In a well-done overview, Washington, D.C. editor and writer Chris Wright pulled together statistics, studies and news stories that seemed to indicate a premature death for Reality TV in the wake of 9/11—including this plaintive wail from Dave Walker in the *New Orleans Picayune-Times:*

"Pundits galore have speculated that the horrible reality of that (attack) and subsequent days permanently dulled our appetite for the contrived drama, teasing sexuality and synthetic 'peril' of reality television."

Though it seemed strange that precocious "pundits galore" were betting against the so-called baser instincts of human nature, there were signs and portents of trouble in Reality-Land. Opinion-makers opined that calling someone a "Survivor" just because they'd romped around an island playing primitive man for 39 days would seem pathetic to viewers—and downright insulting to the real survivors of the savage terrorist attack on New York's World Trade Center. And, surprise, surprise! It began to look like the pundits' predictions were coming true.

Incredibly, a poll taken just a month after 9/11 showed that a whopping 83 percent of Americans were less interested in watching Reality TV after witnessing our national violation by the *jihadi* scum of Islam. And ratings seemed to prove the point. It wasn't just that viewers in the millions suddenly deserted Reality TV— long-running sitcoms like "Everybody Loves Raymond" and "Becker" suddenly got ratings *bumps* in the months after the attacks. From mid-September to late October 2001, "Friends" snagged nearly 25 percent more viewers. And while that show had been smacked down by "Survivor" the previous season, it came back and whipped the reality show, week after week, in fall 2001. Kevin Bright, the executive producer of "Friends," agreed that 9/11 had changed America's TV viewing habits dramatically. "The renewed popularity of the series was probably linked to the events on September 11. It's like going back to comfort food."

Robert Thompson, director of the Center for the Study of Popular Television at Syracuse University, told the *New York Times,* "Watching 'Friends' is like watching 'Gomer Pyle' during the Vietnam War. It was terribly comforting to watch Marines not fighting any battles. Just as it's terribly comforting to watch Ross and Rachel not mourn the loss of any friends."

It looked like a Reality TV rout. "Survivor" instantly lost a third of its audience. "The Amazing Race" debuted to major hype and critical acclaim, but immediately tanked with low ratings. Even worse, several reality shows failed completely: "Temptation Island 2," "Lost," and "The Mole 2."

Doom-and-gloom headlines tolled the death knell:

"Can Networks keep Reality Shows Afloat?"…"Will 'Survivor' Survive?" …."Suddenly, Reality TV is too…Real!"

But then, in late October 2001, a lone voice cried out for calm. *USA Today's* Robert Bianco wrote that it was tempting to lay the blame for Reality TV's sudden decline on 9/11 and "an easy argument to make, as there's no way to disprove it. But before we tackle a sociological explanation, we should first consider a simpler, ordinary TV explanation: *There were too many reality shows at once, and too many of them were lousy.* The truth is, the networks have done what they always do—take a good idea and beat us with it until we're senseless."

Entertainment Weekly weighed in, reporting that most industry insiders were blaming Reality TV's decline on "over-saturation that came when a white-hot trend coincided with a network buying frenzy—on the eve of a threatened strike by writers and actors. Poor scheduling hasn't helped."

The reality? Reality's death had been greatly exaggerated.

Its resuscitation was rapid. Ratings for the next three "Survivor" cycles kept escalating. By spring 2002, ABC's "The Bachelor" was a socko hit. MTV's "The Real World" racked up its biggest numbers ever; and that network's "The Osbournes" broke records as the highest-rated series in its history. Even more notably, "The Osbournes" was the breakthrough that kicked off the whole celeb-reality craze.

Pop Quiz: Who told Sharon and Ozzie Osbourne that they should do a reality show based on their wacky life in Beverly Hills?

Hint: The aforementioned unsung genius of reality (whose name will be revealed, as promised, in a later chapter.)

By spring 2003, Reality TV shows had captured six of the Top 20 Nielsen slots. The *New York Times* reported that "the six broadcast networks showed 14.5 hours of unscripted entertainment, representing 14 percent of their schedules…up from eight hours during the same week last year."

Suddenly—and it comes as no surprise to this grizzled journalist—the same publications that had come to bury Reality were praising its astounding resurrection. To be fair, there certainly had been a startling dip in ratings, but that could have been attributable to any of the factors mentioned above, or because the news media relentlessly kept publishing those "Dead Man Walking" headlines that probably influenced viewer turnoff. We'll never know for sure, but whatever the reason, reality suddenly came roaring back.

Oh, there were still doubters predicting the genre's ultimate demise. Editor Chris Smith chronicled this crotchety rant by the *Chicago Tribune's* Steve Johnson, datelined January 16, 2003:

"Reality is already cannibalizing itself; participants in one show admitted at the press tour to out-and-out fraud. Questions arise that the genre is inherently less valuable (in terms of advertising) to networks than more traditional television, and that, except for 'Survivor,' it has yet to (be proved) that any reality shows can endure."

WOW! Talk about a scorched-earth attack. Steve Johnson takes no prisoners and demands proof that "any reality shows can endure." Well, Steve, let me wind up my treatise on the history of Reality TV with some jaw-dropping statistics that will clarify just how astoundingly wrong you were, you poor little pundit:

In the year 1989, American television debuted just *one* unscripted show: "Cops." But in the 2005 season alone, a whopping *99 Reality TV shows premiered.*

Allow me to quote an expert, ex-MTV babe Kennedy, who fronted that network's "The Best Week Ever," and now hosts Fox's red-hot "Reality Remix TV":

"You can't escape Reality!"

* * *

Chapter *Four*

As creator and star of "American Idol"—the mega-monster smash hit that ate America and spat out the bones—Simon Cowell reigns as the uncontested King Kong of Reality TV.

Yet, before that show's debut, Cowell was a total unknown in the United States. In Great Britain, the smug Ego-Meister had earned a well-deserved reputation as a record label talent manager—or A+R man—but U.S. audiences had never heard of him until the smash debut of "Idol" in June 2002.

Incredibly, just one year later—after a rocket ride to the top of the showbiz heap—Cowell had inked a $2 million deal with Simon & Schuster to write his autobiography, titled "I Just Tell It Like It Is."

The smirking, sneering, smart-aleck Brit had proven one thing, in spades: there's big money in insulting Yanks.

Why do we love Simon Cowell in America? He arrived in this country just as American viewing audiences were clinging desperately to the still-shifting terra firma of Reality TV, embracing the new format's refreshing, warts-and-all honesty even as our airwaves sank slowly into the La Brea Tar Pits of Political Correctness. Then along came Cowell...and he went where no man, or woman, had ever gone before on national television, slicing and dicing "American Idol" contestants in a chainsaw massacre of non-PC insults, slamming them as too fat, too ugly, too gay, or just too damn hard on the ears.

In those days, even the mosh-pit of cable TV drew the line when it came to brutal personal attacks, and that includes ballsy Rosie O'Donnell, who—during her reign as daytime TV's so-called "Queen of Nice"—never once dared to reveal herself as the foul-mouthed, nasty, combat-boot-wearing bull dyke we've come to know and love. So when Cowell savagely tongue-lashed young, vulnerable amateur warblers on his sudden-death-by-karaoke spectaculars, startled folks sat straight up in their recliners, slapped their knees and yelled, *"Dang!"*

Far from being revolted by this posh-talking, sadistic alien, American audiences loved him. His like had never been seen on our TV screens, yet his supremely cheeky confidence—perhaps his very British-ness—allowed him to get away with verbal murder. For whatever reason, America quickly hiked its chairs closer to the telly, not wanting to miss a single, stroppy word of what "Simon Says."

Suddenly, Judge Cowell became hot copy in the press. Snarky journalists—led by yapping, snapping coyotes like myself, who purvey cutting-edge pop culture phenomena in gossip columns—began burnishing the legend of The Man You Love to Hate. The first item I ever published about His Honor, Judge Cowell, was datelined September 10, 2002, and summed up his persona perfectly in this headline:

"Ryan Seacrest Thinks 'American Idol' Judge Simon Cowell Keeps Giving Him The Finger!"

Here's what I wrote:

> Folks, lend me your eyes! "American Idol" co-host RYAN SEACREST—who's constantly feuding with tart-tongued SIMON COWELL—is suddenly obsessed by the suspicion that Judge Sarcastic secretly keeps flipping him the bird! Yeah, I know what you're thinking: Is Ryan NUTS?! That's why I'm asking you, my eagle-eyed readers, to watch future shows carefully—try to catch Simon flashing the one-finger salute. Ryan claims he keeps catching Simon's surreptitious digital disses from the corner of his eye. Simon always denies it, saying he was simply scratching his

ear, adjusting his cuffs, etc.—and insists Ryan's imagination is in hyper-drive!

The story captured perfectly the sly, cunning humor that underlies Cowell's trademark meanness, illustrating that he's far more than just your garden-variety viper. On the contrary, he possesses a searing intelligence and a cruel skill for ferreting out the insecurities of his targets. And once Simon's zeroed in, he slips under the skin with scalpel-like precision.

For example: How do you best drive a fussy, vain metro-sexual like Ryan Seacrest mad? Signal secretly that you're mocking him by, say, flipping him a surreptitious bird or two at odd moments; then play him like a fool by denying that you're doing any such thing. Cowell had "finger fun" with Ryan for nearly a year until the rest of the press twigged to my scoop. As I reported in April 2004:

> Congratulations to *USA Today*, *New York Post*, and *New York Daily News* for finally catching up to the SIMON COWELL "scandal" I broke over a year ago—he's repeatedly used the obscene middle-finger salute on national TV! E-mails from my readers poured in with complaints—and even onscreen photos—of the "American Idol" Judge secretly flipping viewers (or was it just RYAN SEACREST?) the bird. In September of 2002, I told Simon, "Be warned, Brit Boy—the Eyes of America are on YOU!"...Howard Stern's obscene?? Wake up, FCC!!

Busted yet unbowed, Cowell reluctantly desisted, but his relentless teasing of Ryan Seacrest never skipped a beat. His next ploy was sheer genius. In a Chinese water-torture onslaught that continues even to this day, Cowell—wielding that devastating arsenal of cutting quips, raised eyebrows and lip-curls—began to hint broadly that Ryan is gayer than springtime. In early 2003, I reported that Cowell had enjoyed a hearty laugh when they were out at a bar in artsy Laguna Beach and he caught the preening host flirting with...what he thought was a beautiful woman.

> Pitching fast and furious, RYAN SEACREST asked The Mystery Lady for a date—then suavely kissed her hand when she finally nixed his offer and split! Ryan rejoined SIMON COWELL...who

was grinning from ear to ear. "That woman you hit on is actually a man," chortled Simon. So, you're asking, HOW did Simon know this? He claims he's visited the bar before and knows the drag queen's a regular. Okay???...Okay!

Amusingly, Cowell's campaign began backfiring a bit when journalists started noticing that the pair were starting to hang out together on a regular basis. Rumors bubbled that both might be just a tad light in the loafers. Helping matters along, I began referring to the boldface "Idol" boys in print as Ryan "I'm Not Gay" Seacrest and Simon "I'm Not Either" Cowell. All of this boy-ish byplay kept "American Idol" fans in stitches. And therein lies the secret of Cowell's popularity. What saves him from being dismissed as just another vicious British boor is his instinctive, unerring showmanship. His constant teasing of Seacrest, his off-handedly chauvinistic condescension to Paula Abdul and his benign tolerance of good-natured Randy Jackson, guide the audience into connecting with the four personalities, and finally embracing them as their very own dysfunctional TV family. This is the underlying factor that defines the show's true appeal. Much more than a talent contest, "American Idol" is a riveting, rollicking soap opera that the audience controls by its phone-in votes.

Insiders are quick to point out, however, that the instantaneous clash between Cowell and Paula Abdul was not a producer-contrived feud concocted strictly for the sake of ratings. Indeed, Simon and Paula are truly a heaven-sent mismatch. The whole point of "American Idol" is sucking the audience in with raw, un-sanitized spectacle—and Cowell's avowed mission statement has always been "telling lots of useless people that they are useless." At the taping of the very first show, Paula Abdul looked stunned as Judge Cowell terrorized one contestant after another, calling them "wretched," "pathetic," "horrible." He advised one sweet young thing to hire a lawyer and sue her vocal coach. And when a brave kid had the guts to stand up to him, predicting he'd someday feel sorry for breaking everyone's heart, Cowell curtly dismissed him with, "You're a loser!"

Contestants left the stage in tears. And time after time, Paula was caught looking at her fellow judge with unmitigated disgust. After the taping ended, Cowell predicted to producers, "I think Paula is going to walk."

But Ms. Abdul was made of sterner stuff than anyone suspected. She stayed on, and more than held her own with Cowell and Seacrest, lashing back at their "boyo" behavior and crude quips. And in early 2005, published reports noted that she'd wickedly regaled star-struck first-class passengers on a Los Angeles-New York flight with the "scoop" that Simon and Ryan were locked in a gay love affair. Paula was joking, of course...or was she?

Enquiring minds *still* want to know.

In assessing why Simon Cowell stands astride Reality TV like a Colossus, reel back to the summer of 2001 and the first auditions for the British hit show "Pop Idol," the genesis for "American Idol." After a gaggle of singers had strutted their stuff, Cowell knew the show was just lying there, dead in the water. The drama, tension, entertainment value—call it what you will—was nil, null, zippo! After minimal reflection, snarky Simon instinctively put his finger smack on the success button.

"This is not like a real-life audition," he told one of the producers, according to a report by Bill Smart of the *New York Times*. "We have to actually tell the performers to their faces what we thought. We've just got to tell the boys and girls the truth. They're *rubbish.*"

Like all great ideas, it sounds almost stupidly simple. And in the hands of a less intuitive performer, it would have played as off-putting sadism. But Simon tinkled the torture keys with a light touch that delighted the American ear.

Lee Frank, head writer for Fox's "Reality Remix TV," put it this way. "What's the difference between a show like 'Star Search,' for example, and 'American Idol'? The answer is...Simon Cowell. Without him, 'Idol' would be just another 'Rock Star INXS.' It's not just personality, and it's more than his ruthlessness. When Cowell judges a performance, people may hate what he says, or applaud it—but deep in their hearts, they agree with him. They know he's always right."

And therein lies the indictment of those preening pinheads who run network television...the "weasels," as David Letterman calls them. "American Idol" was a smash hit right out of the box. The American viewing public "got" the show... immediately. Yet it was turned down by all the so-called experts at NBC, CBS, and *twice* by ABC, until Fox finally green-lighted it. So the question arises, as it always does:

Who *needs* these highly paid Hollywood/New York Suits?

Nor should Fox execs be too quick to pat themselves on the back. They were lukewarm on the project until Boss Aussie Rupert Murdoch himself ordered the network to buy the show, on the recommendation of his daughter, Elizabeth Murdoch, the founder of parent company News Corp.

The saga began with the gigantic success of the British TV show "Pop Idol" in 2001. Record producer Simon Cowell—acting as ruthlessly honest as he always did when conducting real-life auditions for his label—gave the viewing public an eye-opening lesson in how to pick talent when two "Pop Idol" finalists, both bound by tight contracts to Cowell's company, released albums that sold millions. The show's enormous success caught the attention of the American television networks. ABC, which had twice turned up its nose when offered the mega-hit reality show "Survivor," took a first look at the British "Idol," but finally passed. Why? Because so-called "music" shows like "Making the Band" and "Pop Stars" had failed. But ABC's analysis of why those bombs bombed missed the point totally. Both of the shows were about forming musical groups and striving for showbiz success. The "Idol" concept, on the other hand, was all about watching amateur vocal wannabes—most of them excruciatingly talent-less—making utter fools of themselves before millions of people…then getting sliced like so much sushi by Simon Cowell.

It was those excruciating, nail-biting auditions—not the ho-hum mechanics of forming a band and moving forward with a musical career, etc.—that nailed TV viewers to their Barca-Loungers. But ABC, like NBC and CBS, just didn't get it, so they passed.

The British producers came to America and pitched Fox. The network's initial reaction was lukewarm, but development executives left hope alive by saying they'd consider taking the show if producers could attach a sponsor willing to pay the bills. Months passed. Ratings for "Pop Idol" in Britain soared even higher. The Fox "deal" hadn't moved an inch, so the Brit producers went back to ABC. And that's when reality-programming honchos—who'd twice let "Survivor" slip through their fingers—turned thumbs-down *again.*

"Idol" lay idle...until Elizabeth Murdoch made her fated phone call to Daddy. After a brief chat with his darling daughter, media mogul Murdoch swiftly picked up his own phone, barked an order to underlings, and a deal for 15 episodes was struck, literally overnight. The British producers were thrilled. But Simon Cowell was less so when they phoned to relay what they thought was good news: Fox wanted him to appear as a judge on the American version. Cowell, who didn't have an ownership position in the show and had come along for the ride only in the hopes of signing new talent for his label, was decidedly underwhelmed. He'd taken a strong dislike to snotty American TV executives and their trademark rudeness during the initial pitch meetings for "Idol." He figured they'd insist on muzzling him and demand a tamed-down, politically correct show. Cowell was monumentally disinterested in doing any such thing.

Little did he know he had a secret, and hugely powerful, ally behind the scenes: Rupert Murdoch himself, who had warned Fox execs not to change "Idol" an iota from the way it was being presented in England. The Boss Aussie, famously suspicious of Hollywood Suits, has always believed that they constantly ruin perfectly good projects with the mind-numbing committee-think that drives creative people like Cowell insane.

Despite Murdoch's orders, however, at the very first taping of "American Idol," Cowell was handed a scripted list of "put-downs" and told they were *approved by the American producers*. He could hardly believe his eyes as he scanned the list of insipid, canned quips—hot off the computer keyboard of some hired-hand Yank joke-writer. Stunned and offended, Cowell informed the native show-runners that he had always ad-libbed his zingers, and he would continue to operate that way.

The rest, as they say, is history. The show debuted in June of 2002 and racked up through-the-roof ratings: 10 million viewers on its premiere night, and 11 million viewers the next. And right from the start, it dominated in the highly coveted 18 to 34 youth market.

The "American Idol" juggernaut rumbled out of the starting gate in a crack of thunder, and immediately began picking up speed. The show was "appointment television" on steroids. Viewers flocked to the screens like proverbial lemmings, driving ratings up, up...and away!

On a Tuesday night in February 2006, "American Idol" averaged 30 million viewers leading into President Bush's State of the Union address. During the show's finale in May, it reached a peak of 43 million viewers in its final half hour. Ryan Seacrest breathlessly boasted that 63.4 million votes had been cast in the 2005/6 season, "more than any president in the history of our country has ever received." The perky host either conveniently ignored, or (more likely) was ignorant of the fact that he was comparing apples and oranges. "American Idol" voters are allowed to cast multiple ballots, and often do, but that's a no-no at the presidential polls.

Nonetheless, the point was well taken. The face of American television would never again be the same, and Simon Cowell was now one of American television's favorite faces. He and his dysfunctional "American Idol" family became red-hot copy, achieving what my reporting staff and I call "Simon burped" status. Simply put, that's when celebrities get so hot that people are dying to read or hear anything about them, no matter how insignificant. I told my reporters: "If Simon Cowell so much as burps, I'd better know about it!"

* * *

Chapter *Five*

Over the next few years, my column served up one breathless exclusive after another about Simon Cowell, most of them based on the humor we all find in his enormous ego...stuff like:

SIMON COWELL's spitting mad at LORENZO LAMAS and his new TV show, "Are You Hot?"—apparently convinced it's a ripoff of "American Idol." Guesting on costar RYAN SEACREST's radio show, Simon snarked: "Well, if Lorenzo was on television in the 80s, he should have stayed there! He's trying to be me—and looks ridiculous in yellow sunglasses!" Sneered Ryan: "What's his show about—just looking good?" (Now, girls...!)

Near-naked "American Idol" judge SIMON COWELL nearly jumped out of his skin when he exited the shower at his mansion and faced a shocking surprise: an ambush audition by a warbling wanna-be contestant—his HOUSEMAID! Unsuspecting Judge Cowell—who'd hired the twenty-ish girl only days before—was flabbergasted when he emerged from his soak wearing nothing but a towel and found her standing in his bedroom...all sexy in tight jeans and a midriff-bearing T-shirt. Before he could say a word, Ms. Chutzpah punched "Play" on a ghetto-blaster she was toting—and started hopping around the room, vocalizing at the top of her lungs! When she'd finished, the judge swiftly delivered his verdict, bellowing "You're FIRED!" Crushed, she whined, "You mean I have no chance to be on the show?" Softy Simon sighed and—trying to be merciful—said, "No...but you can stay and clean my house." Rejoined the girl: "I'm not really a maid. I only took this job to sing for you." Snapped Simon: "In that case, pack up your things and leave!"

He's-so-vain "American Idol" star SIMON COWELL grooms his chest hair! Eeeewwwww!! Simon—whose mat would terrify a grrrl gorilla—thinks the chest thatch is absolutely un-sexy, but can't bear getting it waxed off...OWW!... So every three weeks he sneaks away to a stylist and gets his boy-bosom snipped, thinned and groomed.

When "American Idol" ringmaster SIMON COWELL showed up for a meeting at Fox Network's New York offices, he opened his briefcase—and out fell an endless cascade of tiny bottles of shampoos, creams and conditioners he'd snagged from his hotel! Sneered one exec: "What's the matter, Simon—don't we pay you enough?" Embarrassed Cowell admitted sheepishly he never can resist slipping a fat supply of freebie grooming goodies off the maids' cart!

Can you guess what single-exercise regimen SIMON COWELL follows to fight off man-boobs so he can sport those skin-tight T-shirts? (No! He does NOT bench-press RYAN SEACREST!) The American Idol star's live-in love TERRI SEYMOUR confides that "the only exercise Simon really does are ordinary push-ups"—but he flops down for the grunt-and-groans several times a day.

In November 2007, this snarky headline from British scandal sheet *News of the World* (prepare to deploy grains of salt, folks!) seemingly shattered the myth that Cowell maintains his man-bosom through ardent exercise. It screamed:

"Simon Had Boob Job!"

The story quoted Irishman Louis Walsh, a fellow judge on Cowell's "Idol"-like U.K. show "X Factor," who claims his costar "had chest implants to look butch and compares his gleaming white teeth to piano keys." Walsh, known in his native land as quite a cut-up, actually insisted that ALL his fellow judges—including Sharon Osbourne—"have new tits—and lots of other work done…Simon's definitely had a boob job!"

Was Loudmouth Louis chest kidding around? We report, you decide!

*

"American Idol" fans devoured backstage and real-life gossip about their favorite dysfunctional family—and my column never stopped feeding their appetites. Paula Abdul was a fan favorite after "Idol" re-launched her career. In 2003, Paula, who'd languished in showbiz backwaters for years since early success as a singer, re-learned the painful lesson that rising stars make oh-so-easy targets. Comedian Chris Rock, after dissing her singing career on an L.A. radio station, cruelly cracked:

"Can you believe it? Paula Abdul on 'American Idol' telling people they can't sing! …What's next? Christopher Reeve judging dancers?"

Just to make Paula feel better, I followed that item with this one:

> Cheer up, **PAULA!** Egomaniac **SIMON COWELL** admits American women are a lot tougher to impress than British birds. Simon sez a hot brunette approached him seductively at an LA bash, then "whispered in my ear slowly, 'You must have a very small d---!' I almost choked on my drink!"

Endless stories leaked from backstage about Paula's fury over what she felt was the personal nature of Simon's insults; insinuations that contestants were stupid, gay or—even worse—fat!

> Now I understand why **PAULA ABDUL** got so angry when **SIMON COWELL** told singer **VANESSA** she needed to lose a few pounds! Paula took her personal stylist to a private boutique sale— but after trying on numerous outfits, tears welled in her eyes as she wailed, "I looked terrible in everything—I'm too fat!" Her stylist

tried to reassure her, but Paula left without buying a thing—
still sobbing!

Amazingly, over time, Simon actually started getting flirty-dirty with his comely fellow judge. I duly reported:

> PAULA ABDUL might have to call for security if SIMON COWELL doesn't keep his hands off her! He's been pawing her on and off the screen, touching her and nudging her with his leg so often that fed-up Paula finally told him: "Don't touch me!" Simon Sez: "You should feel flattered."

Then things *really* heated up between ex-cheerleader Paula and Captain Cruel—and his longtime girlfriend actually got jealous:

> "It meant nothing!" SIMON COWELL said over and over to live-in love TERRI SEYMOUR after she watched that shockingly steamy kiss between Cowell and his "American Idol" costar PAULA ABDUL in a taped skit. "You don't see RANDY JACKSON doing things like that," angry Terri told him. "He's married," Simon said. Terri shot him one of those you're-approaching-the-danger-zone looks and snapped: "Exactly!"

Of all the "American Idol" regulars, Randy "Dawg" Jackson gets the least mentions in the press. The former Columbia Records exec—an accomplished musician who once played bass for the group Journey—is the show's calmest personality, affable and even-keeled; the perfect counterpoint to snarling Simon, simpering Seacrest and giggly-weepy-drama-diva Paula. Going into the 2005 season, Simon easily led the "Idol" pack in press mentions, Ryan and Paula were about neck and neck, and Randy was next to invisible. Certainly he was less visible than when he topped out at a scale-busting 329 lbs. before undergoing gastric bypass surgery in 2003.

Randy lost a whopping 100 pounds and made a triumphant appearance on good friend Oprah Winfrey's show in 2004 to show off his new shape. But soon enough the pounds started piling back on, prompting an alarmed Oprah to take action. As the *National Enquirer* reported in a follow-up story, Oprah was so worried about Randy's health that, after worried discussions with his wife, Erika, she offered to build him a $100,000 custom home gym!

Given all that, how weird is it that Randy, a guy with a family history of diabetes—and who said before his gastric bypass, "I was afraid that if I didn't get healthy and do something drastic I may not be around that long?"—just signed an endorsement deal with…*Oreo Cookies???* It certainly caught Simon by surprise. As I reported in my column:

> During a phone call to Simon Cowell in London, Ryan told his grouchy "American Idol" compadre the news that fellow judge Randy Jackson's endorsing Oreo cookies—and his kisser's plastered all over the box! Simon seemed skeptical, so after the call, Ryan personally paid for a round-trip ticket to London, then flew an assistant there to deliver a carton of Randy's Oreo's just in time for a dinner party Cowell was throwing. Aaaaaaaaw…that's so sweet!

But going into the 2005 season, the scandal meter suddenly peaked dangerously for Paula Abdul. A young male contestant who'd been booted off the show in 2003 for failing to disclose a criminal record—which included assault and resisting arrest—had suddenly surfaced with an astounding allegation:

Judge Paula Abdul had coached, coddled, cozened, cosseted—and even *cuddled* him at home in her bed.

The shocking, juicy pillow-talk tale, which broke in the *Globe* and made major headlines everywhere, was hotly denied at first. Simon Cowell staunchly defended Paula and sneered that the disgraced contestant, Corey Clark, was a lying hustler looking to sell a tell-all book. Abdul's managers called Clark "an admitted liar and opportunist who engages in unlawful activities."

Fox executives scoffed at the sensational charges, pointing out that Clark had never informed them of his allegations back in 2003. Fox network publicly pledged to investigate the charges, swiftly and thoroughly.

The gossipy scandal spread like wildfire on the Internet. Fans of the show remembered how the smirking, smarmy 22-year-old Clark had played outrageously to 42-year-old Abdul during one of his songs, even strutting up to the judges' table and seductively kissing her hand. It was right after that performance, alleged Clark, that "someone" on the show slipped him Paula's phone numbers.

Naturally enough, said Corey, he made the call, and Paula immediately sent a car that whisked him to her house. Stunned and flattered, the young singer—who'd made it as one of 12 final contestants——apparently made himself right at home in Paula's luxury pad as she gushed about his talent. They spent that first night, he claimed, discussing a strategy for winning "American Idol." Incredibly, several such meetings took place at Paula's house, said Clark. "It felt like she was hitting on me a little bit—and I liked it," he recalled.

One night, he says, Paula came up behind him, kissed him on the neck—and their affair ignited.

News organizations who claim to sneer at so-called "tabloid journalism"— embarrassed at being caught flat-footed on a must-read story about America's hottest reality show—rushed belatedly to investigate Corey Clark's claims. ABC's "Primetime Live" reported that Abdul had supplied Clark with a cell phone, and they showed viewers pages of phone records detailing calls between the aspiring singer and the celebrity judge nearly two decades his senior. One of the May-September couple's conversations, the phone records revealed, lasted a whopping 155 minutes.

According to the *Globe* story, Clark claimed that sexual encounters with Abdul occurred on numerous occasions in the guest room of her house. He disclosed that she'd paid some of his expenses and promised to invest $2 million in his career, but made him vow to keep their relationship a secret. If he ever broke silence, Paula allegedly warned Corey, she'd make things very hard for him.

"Don't screw me or you'll be sorry," Paula told him.

Talk about "Idol" gossip! Corey Clark even claimed he'd overheard former contestant Justin Guarini bragging "about having an affair with Paula." When asked why he'd waited so long to bring his sensational charges, Clark said he'd tried to achieve success in the music business on his own, but claimed "Idol" producers had spread lies about him—and actually sabotaged a deal with Jive Records. He said he'd finally come forward because he wanted to set the record straight in a book he'd written, titled "They Told Me to Tell the Truth, So.... The Sex, Lies and Paula-tics of One of America's Idols."

Summing up his new get-tough policy, Clark intoned solemnly: "I'm just cleaning up my own pathway. If that involves getting your dirt off my pathway, I'm going to do that."

Although he came off as a callow, pathetic hustler, Corey Clark loomed as a real threat to a cash-cow enterprise. Attorney Harvey Levin noted that even though "nobody's going to get prosecuted for this, I think it's highly embarrassing for Paula Abdul." But show producers and Fox executives faced a bottom line that was even more frightening. If fans suspected that "American Idol" was "fixed" in any way, they'd desert the show in droves.

Media Week TV critic Marc Berman struck terror in Fox hearts with his dire warning: "If the charges are true, this is a huge scandal that could kill 'American Idol'!"

Behind the scenes, worried producers game-planned with lawyers and PR experts. How to stop Corey? He had no solid evidence for his claims—so far, it was a he-said, she-said standoff. But the public was lapping up the juicy scandal, and Paula was on the defensive. Lacking evidence to the contrary, all she could do was deny, deny, deny the alleged affair. But how do you prove a negative? Somehow— and quickly—Paula had to make the public believe that Corey Clark's claims were ludicrous.

Finally, in an inspiration born of frustration, plucky Paula took the bull by the horns—and gored Corey! In a slick PR move, the feisty star booked herself on "Saturday Night Live," brilliantly playing the scandal for laughs. Looking ultra-sexy in a skin-tight dress and push-up bra, Paula faced the "SNL" cameras, smiled sweetly and said:

"What you're about to see is a reenactment of some of this week's biggest news stories. All of the facts have been changed to get laughs at my expense. I hope you enjoy it."

In a skit that followed, Amy Poehler—playing Judge Paula Abdul—said to the Corey Clark character after he vamped his way through a song like a pimp who believes he's got bedroom eyes: "That was wonderful! Like I rolled over and said to you this morning, you have real star quality. I'll see you at home."

The show's "Live Update" newscast featured this faux "American Idol" report:

"In a show of support on Wednesday night's program, five finalists presented Paula Abdul with two huge bouquets of flowers, and it worked—she slept with all of them."

After all the skits had ended, Paula appeared as herself and gave Amy Poehler some pointers, "Amy, you need to perfect the clap a little more—and be a lot more sexier so contestants will be willing to sleep with you."

And then, just for the record, Paula made a heartfelt pitch to the people out there in TV Land, "I do trust my fans, who can see through attempts at character as assassination—and I do trust the essential fairness of the American public."

It was game, set and match to Paula. And just to drive the point home, the season finale episode of "American Idol," featured an "SNL"-style parody skit mocking Clark's claims, in which judge Simon Cowell was alleged to be having a hot affair with…himself.

Finally, in a revelation that shocked absolutely no one—except, perhaps, the *Media Week* TV critic who'd warned that the scandal could "kill" the show—Fox announced the results of their official investigation in August 2005, and reported that they'd found absolutely no evidence to support any of Clark's claims…and Paula Abdul would therefore continue to be a judge on "American Idol."

Corey Clark's book was never published. His first record album flopped miserably, selling just 2500 copies. Just before he disappeared into richly deserved oblivion, a brief press headline revealed that he faced a year in jail and a fine of up to $150,000 after pleading guilty to violating a restraining order taken out by his ex-wife and confessing to "aggravated harassment, involving domestic violence" while on two-year probation for drug charges.

The sordid scandal was over at last. "American Idol" was—to mix a Reality TV metaphor—a "survivor."

*   *   *

Chapter *Six*

PAULA CHANNELS DEAN MARTIN.… PAULA GOES
"UU-U-UURRRPP!" …CLAY AIKEN TROLLS
BIGMUSCLE.COM AND MEETS HIS GI JOE.

Incredibly, "American Idol" ratings just kept right on rising. The audience loved the amateur-night-in-Dixie contest, just as they always had—but it soon became clear that they now loved their dysfunctional "Idol" family more than ever before. Paula's scandal hadn't come close to hurting the show—in fact, it had actually endowed her with "heat." Suddenly, Paula Abdul was more than just a has-been singer. Almost overnight, she'd morphed into a "boldface name"…a tabloid staple. Every time Judge Abdul giggled, acted ditzy or blathered nonsensically on the show, she made copy.

Playing an "Idol" contestant on "Saturday Night Live," Kevin Spacey chortled about playing up to "that Puerto Rican judge who's always drunk." Suddenly, Paula Abdul was the new Dean Martin—who, depending on whom you believed in Hollywood, was either perpetually schnockered…or hardly drank a drop. When Paula fell down in a nightclub one night, there was endless speculation in gossip columns about whether she'd been shoved, had collapsed in a drunken stupor, or simply slipped and fallen—but the answer didn't even matter that much. Suddenly, people just loved gossiping about Judge Abdul. Here's my favorite-ever item about her, published in my *Enquirer* column under this classic headline:

"Paula Abdul Treats Fan to Lunch—on Him!"

HI, I'M PAULA ABDUL OF "AMERICAN IDOL" AND...UU-U-UURRRPP!! Unless you get queasy easy, don't skip my scoop about perky Paula's airborne upchuck on a fawning fan who was thrilled at being seated next to the star on an LA-Phoenix flight. The guy gushed about how he idolizes "Idol" and Paula cheerfully chit-chatted about the show—until sudden turbulence turned her green with nausea! "Oh gosh.... You okay?... What can I do?" stammered Man Fan as Paula, frantically scrabbling for a barf bag, abruptly heaved—tossing her cookies all over them both! "OOH!" shrieked the vomit victim! Flight attendants rushed up with wet towels and poor Paula mumbled profuse apologies—even offering to pay for dry cleaning his suit! "No, no, it was just an accident," said her suddenly non-chatty seatmate—who bolted the minute the plane landed without so much as a "Buh-bye!"

As Paula's star rose, hair-gel host Ryan Seacrest was fast becoming a household name. The drumbeat of speculation about his sexuality—always a great gimmick, unless you're Tom Cruise—reached a crescendo when Jay Leno treated his "Tonight Show" audience to a side-splitting, edited videotape of Ryan interacting with a series of contestants...first, females, then males. The contrast was startling—and hilarious. The Tale of the Tape showed that whenever he faced the females, Ryan studiously kept his distance and acted quite formal. But when he interacted with male contestants, he suddenly got all up-close and touchy-feely, laughing and chattering animatedly while patting and hugging the fellas in a most familiar fashion.

And then, of course, there was Ryan's incredibly silly sign-off catch-phrase: "Seacrest.... OUT!" He finally abandoned it after endless ribbing from snarky media types like Howard Stern—and Mike Walker. I wrote in my column:

Wisecracks by SIMON COWELL and PAULA ABDUL fuel endless speculation about "American Idol" host RYAN SEACREST's sexual orientation, and here's a weird remark, right from the horse's mouth, that should keep the fun going. You be the judge, but...on his LA radio show, Seacrest—speaking of how bearded and hairy MICHAEL DOUGLAS has looked lately—made a comment I can't imagine coming from a straight guy when he declared emphatically: "I'm not into bearded men!" (Seacrest... OUT??)

And:

GAYSSIP DEPT.: Weeks ago, I reported that RYAN "I'm Not Gay" SEACREST commented on his LA radio show that MICHAEL DOUGLAS looked hairy lately—and then added: "I'm not into bearded men." In my opinion, I said, no straight guy talks that way—but I asked you to judge. Well, folks, don the black robes again and grab your gavel—Ryan just interviewed VINCE VAUGHN and gushed: "Dude, I'm totally into girls...but you're at the top of my hump island when it comes to guys!" Hump WHAAT!? Vaughn, caught off guard by the beyond-metrosexual, sex-ish remark, said: "That's like saying you don't sweat as much for a fat girl." Huh? (Just where is Hump Island, Ryan? Near Fantasy Island, no doubt! Seacrest...OUT???)

And:

RYAN SEACREST was NOT naked when he dished with Dr. McDreamy on his LA radio show, but gushed: "I'll say it on the record—you are better-looking with every year that goes by!" Dempsey stayed silent as Ryan's female sidekick sighed in disbelief, "Oh, Ryan!...Ryan did a man compliment." Dempsey finally croaked "thank you" ...and Ryan burbled: "I mean, like, straight dude to straight dude!" Then he closed the dreamy interview with, "McDreamy OUT!"

Then there was that bizarre, and obviously staged, news photo of Ryan Seacrest kissing "Desperate Housewives" star Teri Hatcher during a stroll on the beach not far from Malibu. Jay Leno immediately joked, "The rumor is that Teri Hatcher is dating Ryan Seacrest in an attempt to get George Clooney's attention. Oddly enough, Ryan is dating Teri for the exact same reason."

Seacrest, who knows there's no such thing as bad publicity, showed off his shrewd showbiz instincts in an interview with the *New York Times,* insisting that he's not gay and really doesn't mind all the ribbing—although, he claims, his friends do.

"They're always, like, 'Why don't you tell him to stop'...but I'm, like, there are worse things in the world than being a joke in a Jay Leno monologue."

Interestingly, Teri Hatcher told Oprah Winfrey on her talk show that right after the headline-making kiss, Ryan called her up and dumped her cold. Why? He told the *New York Times* that his tight schedule and overwhelming media scrutiny led him to quit Hatcher. He added, "What's wrong? It is strange, but I don't think it was a Teri Hatcher issue. It's a Ryan Seacrest issue." (Whatever *that* means. Or, do we sort of know...what it means?)

Just to prove how he loves going along with the is-he-or-isn't-he gag, Seacrest gleefully confirmed that he and Teri had started dating during an interview on Jay Leno's show. He told Jay, "She's fantastic, she's great. I think she's a beautiful woman...and she's a great dresser. *We can share jeans...it's perfect!"*

Despite all the kidding, Ryan's a well-liked member of the "Idol" family. He's spiky-haired cute, he works hard, he's eager to please—and people admire his success. At age 31, Ryan raked in major bucks from "Idol," has his own daily radio show in Southern California, hosts the nationally-syndicated radio show "American Top 40," has inked a $21 million news-casting deal with E! television, and he's host and executive producer of the legendary ABC "New Year's Eve in Times Square" show made famous by Dick Clark. And in 2007, he added another coup: hosting the Emmy Awards.

Not surprisingly, Simon Cowell takes total credit for Seacrest's success. "I gave him a personality," insists Cowell. "He was the equivalent of a non-vintage wine, cheap plonk, and now, as a result of being around me, he's become full-bodied."

Yes, it's all about Simon. He knows it, and he's not shy about it. From my column:

> When a guy stars on a show that hits a socko "30" ratings share, he's allowed to let his ego rage out of control, so don't scowl when I tell you **SIMON COWELL** keeps several big-screen TVs and computer monitors at his BevHills home blazing all day long with a screensaver photo of his favorite "Idol"—Simon Cowell!

As for the ruthless ragging Ryan endures from Simon, Paula, and the cruel likes of journalists and broadcasters, Simon says, "Ryan loves the abuse. He's like the dog in that *Garfield* comic."

So...coming full circle again to Simon Cowell...he's now the Colossus of Reality TV, moving effortlessly from success to success. With "American Idol" under his belt, he launched "American Inventor" and "America's Got Talent," which features people of any age performing in any genre—singing, dancing, magic, comedy, trapeze acts, etc. Cowell doesn't appear on the NBC show, and hired emcee powerhouse Regis Philbin to host. But why isn't the show on Fox? Incredibly, says Cowell, his network ho-hummed it—took a pass!

"Obviously, we spoke to Fox about this show," Cowell told an interviewer. "I can only guess they thought they had enough talent shows of their own. If it's popular, they won't be too happy—but that's how it goes."

Fox turned down Simon Cowell? Unbelievable? Well, not really. The old saying about showbiz was, "That's showbiz!" Today, of course, they say, "It's hard out here for a pimp!" Because if Simon Cowell can't sell a talent-based reality show, who can? After all, here's a guy who shot to the top of the America's showbiz heap by ripping us Yanks a new one—*and* making us love it. Incredibly, like Ryan Seacrest and the masochistic mutt from *Garfield*, we actually sit up and beg for more. Check out this head-shaker from my *Enquirer* column:

> Speaking of obnoxious "American Idol" stars and the women who love them...a gal working behind the counter at an LA sandwich shop refused to hand SIMON COWELL his order until he insulted her! "Oh, come on," said Cowell. "I don't want to do that—just give me my sandwich." But the babe persisted, so Cowell snapped: "Okay...I only come here because of the food, which is quite good—but the service is terrible. And your uniforms remind me of those worn in a 1960s meat-packing plant." Cowell then pointed at the woman—who had beaucoup tattoos— and said: "If you're going to litter yourself with tattoos, my dear, why not tattoo the menu on your forehead. Then I can look at you and order lunch at the same time!" As the shop's staff applauded Simon's insult, the woman said, "That's great!"—and handed over his turkey and avocado sandwich.

As I write this, ABC—which turned down Cowell and "American Idol" twice, but picked up his "American Inventor"—is still holding auditions for hundreds of wanna-be pop stars for his "American Idol" clone, now headed for a third season. When the show debuted, a network spokesman actually had the chutzpah to tell the press with a straight face, "We are not a ripoff." So what's the difference? In "Talent," 10 finalists live together, attend intensive music lessons—and finally perform in live venues, where they're judged by call-in voting from viewers.

Oh, gee…night and day, huh?

The only unanswered question in this trip to Rip-Off City is: will "American Idol" losers like William Hung, Corey Clark and Clay Aiken ever be allowed to compete? Stay tuned.

(Speaking of "Idol" gossip, by the way…after the *National Enquirer* discovered Clay Aiken trolling the Internet for gay lovers at sites like BigMuscle.com and broke the story in a seamy first-person account by ex-Green Beret John Paulus, the GI Joe he met there—some Aiken fans actually filed a lawsuit against his record label, RCA, for misrepresentation. Fearless RCA immediately postponed Aiken's Bible-thumping album until further notice!... That's showbiz, pal.)

"Idol" now runs like a well-oiled machine. They know all the tricks of their tear-jerking trade and never leave anything to chance. Consider this amazing item from my column:

> Here's an "American Idol" makeup secret: Producers confiscate all eyeliner and mascara from female guests—and not because Ryan Seacrest might need more. They don't want the gals wearing the waterproof kind—and they insist makeup artists use stuff that runs like water, because it makes them look extra-weepy when they LOSE.

In the fickle world of network TV, viewers can declare you dead in a heartbeat. It's hard to imagine "American Idol" faltering before the next decade or so—and although "American Inventor" and "America's Got Talent" are nowhere near the level of "Idol," they're holding their own nicely. Cowell's still got that magic touch—he's even got a new show in the U.K. called "X Factor," and he's even asked Paula to appear on it. But carping critics are always waiting in the wings, so Cowell works hard on keeping the quality fresh. When "American Inventor" debuted, *New York Post* TV critic David Bianculli labeled it "shamefully, or shamelessly, derivative" of Cowell's maiden show, citing this example: "One of the judges has a British accent, the judges don't always get along—and the sole woman even gets weepy sometimes."

Frankly, I loved the show in the first season. But it labors under a major weakness—there are far too many stupid inventions, compared to those that actually seem practical and, well…inventive. To borrow from the "Idol" playbook, it needs fewer William Hungs, and more Kelly Clarksons. But I laughed till I cried watching that weird Latin gentleman demonstrating to incredulous judges how his invention, "The Bladder Buddy," rescues you from discomfort when you're out in public and Nature suddenly calls—urgently.

Imagine the situation: There's no john in sight, but you've just gotta go! What to do? No problem-o, *mis amigos,* Señor Weird Latin Guy tells the judges—and then proceeds to demonstrate how Bladder Buddy brings fast, and private, relief. Unfurling what looks like a giant garment bag, El Weirdo zips himself into the thing until only his head and feet protrude. Then, as the judges' faces wrinkle in disgust, he explains—as his hands fumble visibly inside the bag—that once you're covered up, people can't see you unfurling your naughty bits. The next step, explains Señor, is to unzip a small, presumably watertight, pouch on the inside wall of your Bladder Buddy—and *let 'er rip!*

The truly priceless moment comes when the female judge recoils in horror as Weird Latin Guy then demonstrates how to use a small, crotch-shaped pouch—carefully designed, with anatomical correctness—for ladies who need to tinkle privately in public.

Stupid as it sounds, the Bladder Buddy demonstration was one of those unique moments that captured the mesmerizing magic of Reality TV—real people competing and ad-libbing in real, unscripted situations. It was truly beyond anything a dramatist or comedy writer could conceive. That's why, despite reports that crop up at regular intervals, the death of TV is greatly exaggerated. "American Inventor" may not make the cut, but this pundit predicts that the you-know-you-wanna-watch genre will outlive us all.

And so, no doubt, will Simon Cowell.

When he was asked in an interview what one luxury item he would choose to take with him if banished to a desert island, narcissistic Mr. Nasty answered, "Easy.

A mirror. It's true…because I'd miss me." As would we all, old chap…as would we all!

(As I rush toward the completion of this manuscript, one thought has sustained me through difficult moments: When the book is finally published, I think there's an excellent chance that Simon Cowell will insult it—and me. Like that mutt in the *Garfield* comic strip—and Ryan Seacrest—one can only hope…*Woof…WOOF!*)

Speaking of carping critics, Cowell's "America's Got Talent" got hammered when it debuted on NBC, and it's easy to understand why the show's premise seemed "iffy." Looser and loopier than "Idol," it showcases ordinary people, like the world's oldest male stripper, or a guy who balances a kitchen stove on his chin, plus yodelers, contortionists, hog-callers, folks who can play a harmonica even after swallowing it…whatever! Alessandra Stanley, in the *New York Times,* nailed the zeitgeist perfectly when she described "Talent" as "Idol" with its socks rolled down and belt loosened!

"…something between amateur night at the Elks Lodge and the counselor's farewell roast at summer camp! Regis Philbin is the master of ceremonies, not Ryan Seacrest, and that is another liberation: Mr. Philbin has the right vaudeville touch and is funny without trying. Mr. Seacrest tries to be funny and isn't; his efforts to goad Mr. Cowell are as painful as a child's first bow strokes on the violin. David Hasselhoff is a playful, 'Gong Show' kind of judge, and so is the pop singer Brandy. The British judge, Piers Morgan, serves as a sneering stand-in for Mr. Cowell.

"…Almost all the new reality contests include at least one British authority figure…on reality shows the British are there to heighten the coarseness of Middle America."

Methinks the lady had Simon summed up to a fare-thee-well. The *Washington Post's* TV critic, savage curmudgeon Tom Shales, agreed. He called the show's British judge Piers Morgan an "insufferable twit"—and added that "the rule has been established: to do one of these amateur-hour shows, your panel of judges must include a snotty Brit…!"

Shales dismissed Brandy as "a young singer with a look of bewilderment on her face." Then—in one of the most vicious take-downs in the history of TV criticism—Shales eviscerates hunky/drunky "Baywatch" him-bo Hasselhoff as follows:

"It could very well be that David Hasselhoff is the most pitifully indisputable imbecile on network television, even considering all the competition. One could say, of course, that Hasselhoff belongs to that campy little community of twinkling clods whose infamy is their fortune; they specialize in self-mocking shamelessness, and they go along with the joke because a parody of a career is better than no career at all.

"Hasselhoff got his start as—well, as the spawn of Satan."

Say *what?* Spawn of *what?*

Incredibly, even that wicked shot did not sate Shales' blood-lust. Having pinned The Devil's Hoff-spring with his critical pitchfork, Shales rammed home the killer point, sneering at the star's qualifications as a judge with this sarcastic flourish:

"…who indeed would recognize absolute perfection better than the man who starred in 'Baywatch'? The dolt always standing in the way, between the camera and the bathing beauties."

Hell hath no fury like a writer with a column to fill.

Interestingly, Shales was content to dismiss Piers Morgan as "an insufferable twit" without noting his lurid past in British journalism. And just to clarify quickly, before I bust a cap on Piers, the word "lurid" is not to be taken as a slur on his early days, when he pursued the…er, noble calling of gossip columnist. As it happens, I followed the career of Piers Morgan career closely—and he certainly followed mine! Why? Well, on my many trips to the United Kingdom, I would often—in that good-natured, fun-loving way of mine—twit this insufferable twit on TV and radio shows for ripping off items from my column. That didn't stop him, of course—he eventually rose to become the high-flying editor of one of Great Britain's great newspapers, the *Daily Mirror*. And, believe it or not, Morgan's magic carpet ride to the top was actually pleasing to me, in a strange way. A lesson I've often repeated to desperate young journalists teetering on the edge of temptation is this: "If you must steal, steal from the best." Week after week, year after year, my showbiz scoops show up—uncredited—in newspapers from London to Hindustan. It annoys me, yet…I feel somewhat flattered, to be honest. My peers—Piers included—know a good story when they see one, so a ripoff is also, in a way, an homage.

What Tom Shales did not reveal about Piers Morgan, in his zeal to unmask Hell's Imp Hasselhoff is that this Cowell-appointed judge, who high-handedly makes decisions on America's talent, was axed and escorted out of the *Daily Mirror* by security guards for publishing shocking, controversial photos of British GI's abusing Iraqi prisoners. Morgan staunchly defended the photos as authentic, but they turned out to be…fakes. Lousy judgment for a judge, some might say. Eh, old chap?

As for the self-replicating spore which threatens to devour Reality TV—I'm speaking of Simon Cowell, of course—he debuted yet another show on Fox called "Celebrity Duets" in the 2006 season. Tough as it is to predict these things, this columnist went out on a limb and called it "one of Simon's simply irresistible, why-didn't-I-think-of-that genius strokes!" The premise: veteran star singers like Patti LaBelle, Wynona Judd, Aaron Neville, Kenny Loggins, Dionne Warwick, Randy Travis, etc., sing duets with such non-singing celebs as Lucy "Xena" Lawless, Olympic gold medal gymnast Carly Patterson, comedian Cheech Marin, "Queer Eye" style guru Jai Rodriguez, etc. Just as in "Idol," viewers vote off one contestant each week—and the winning celeb gets $100,000 for their favorite charity. Thanks to the success of "Idol," Simon signed a hot roster of celebs for "Duets." I commented at the time: *Stop Simon before he spawns again!* In a rare setback, the show went off the air for "re-tooling." Stay tuned.

* * *

Chapter *Seven*

JENNIFER ANISTON ATTACKS REALITY TV.... "FRIEND" HATES
"AMERICAN IDOL".... BATTY OZZIE OSBOURNE KICKS A COYOTE....
BOBBY BROWN DIGS FOR WHITNEY GOLD.

In a bitter, revealing "it's-all-about-me" rant, egomaniacal TV komedy kewpie Jennifer Aniston raged in an eye-opening magazine interview that she hates, hates, hates Reality TV—and actually blames its explosive growth for the public's rabid obsession with her love life!

As Aniston sees it, her life was hijacked for a reality show she never agreed to star in when her husband, Hollywood's Hottest Hunk, dumped her, melded body and soul with The World's Hottest Woman—and was reborn as that larger-than-life tabloid entity "Brangelina!" (If there's anyone on the planet who doesn't know, that's Brad Pitt and Angelina "Hubba-Hubba" Jolie.)

Today, bitter "Friends" star Aniston abhors the medium that made her a multi-millionaire.

"I don't watch TV anymore.... Nothing!" she snarled in an interview. "I have no interest in that 'Idol' shit."

WHOA! Let the bitch-fest begin…!

"We have an obsession with Reality TV," rages Aniston. "It's the majority of television.

"What happened to a great half-hour sitcom? It's all Dancing With the Stars…Knitting With the Stars…Building a Home With Stars…Living in the Homes of Stars…And then ripping people to shreds.

"Humiliation…Degradation…What is going on? There's so much instant gratification, and we want it. It's just bizarre. I wonder if Reality TV is adding to the obsession with the rag magazines that create all those soap operas with celebrities…it's so pathetic!"

Reading between the lines of that statement, it sounds like Ms. Aniston may still have anger issues about her mother. In a nasty family feud, they stopped talking for years after Dearest Mommy wrote a "celebrity soap opera" tell-all book about…daughter Jennifer Aniston!

To be fair, Jen's paranoia is not unfounded. After Brad decamped to new squeeze Jolie, the "Friends" star squirmed uncomfortably in the media spotlight—cast as the poor little woman who'd carelessly surrendered her rich, famous and impossibly handsome husband to a sexy man-eater who was eager to bear his child.

Playing the "victim" role made Jennifer Aniston *crazy!*

"There's nothing worse," she says. "I hate it. It makes my skin crawl. *'How's Jen doing?'* Please…don't feel sorry for me. Don't make me your victim. I don't want it. I'm so tired of being part of this sick, twisted Bermuda triangle. It's just stupid. It's ridiculous.

"Unfortunately, the world is in such a state with this war and everything else—it's easier to look at the triteness of a celebrity breakup. It's like, 'Ahhh…relief.' It's an escape, rather like a daytime soap opera. There's nothing left to talk about—and I'm just sick of everything about myself. There's nothing to do about it.

"All I can do is go on with my life. It's *not a show.* It's real! And it *sucks."*

Sha-*ZAM*, girlfriend!

That angry diatribe was a key inspiration for this book, an attempt to capture the now-sprawling world of Reality TV. In all seriousness, Jennifer Aniston's heated rant stands as one of the most intelligent, coherent statements exceeding 25 words that this writer has ever heard out of the mouth of a showbiz star. Seriously.

How easy it would be to dismiss Aniston as just another whining celebrity who purrs in the spotlight's caress, but panics when it reveals warts and wrinkles. How tempting to sneer at her pouty-puss exaggeration that gossip about stars' sex lives never existed until Satan spawned Reality TV. But just this once, let us all refrain—and that includes mean old me, Mike Walker!—from taking a feel-good, slam-dunk cheap shot at Jen. Instead, let us consider seriously this star's charge that our obsession with so-called "humiliation...degradation" and "that 'Idol' shit" has transformed us into a nation of mouth-breathing knuckle-draggers.

And because adorable Jen's a celebrity, let's kick off our investigation of the charges she's leveled at Reality TV by examining shows that starred...stars! It's a perfect jumping-off point, because the sudden proliferation of celeb-reality shows really jazzed up the genre by revealing that dirty little secret known to all showbiz insiders:

Boldface Names often act like desperate, pathetic losers.

And that reminds us of...us.

*

"The Osbournes" pioneered the celeb-reality genre. A weird show about a zonked-out rocker living in Beverly Hills with his zany family, it was hilarious, shocking and fun. Here's an example of its ongoing weirdness from my *National Enquirer* column:

> **Truth is always stranger than fiction for The Osbournes! First, Sharon's beloved pooch Lulu was killed and eaten by a coyote—then their tiny dog Pipi was attacked! Furious Ozzy raced to the rescue, pried it from the coyote's jaws—then kicked the beast, sending it howling. Determined to kill the predator, Ozzy hung a poisoned chicken carcass on the back fence—but suddenly, BevHills cops rolled up! Why? A nosy neighbor had reported that "those weirdo Osbournes" were conducting "a Satanic ritual!"**

"The Osbournes" had its strangely touching moments—like the time Ozzy's teenage son Jack was caught smoking pot and defended himself by insisting he was "not addicted."

Snapped Ozzie: "You're not addicted *yet!* Look at me. Do you want to become like this? Look what can happen to you."

Speaking of dads dispensing sage advice…when Whitney Houston's notorious jailbird husband costarred with her on "Being Bobby Brown," he imparted this nugget of hard-earned wisdom to his four children: *You can never have enough guns!"*

Right on, my bruthah! Now, let me speculate that when Jennifer Aniston gets all frowny-face on our ass about the "degradation and humiliation" that defines/defiles Reality TV, she's most likely not referring to verbal head-shakers like the above. No, in her mind's eye, Jennifer is almost certainly conjuring up what aficionados rank as the *most* vomitus moments in its history.

Consider, for example, that mind-blowing scene from "Being Bobby Brown," in which the bad-boy star—over dinner with his then-wife and friends at a fine restaurant—affectionately describes digging impacted fecal matter out of his distressed Whitney's rectum with his bare hands as she exults:

"That's love…! That's *black love!"*

Then came a truly classic reality moment—Bobby actually demonstrated how he'd performed the extraction, showing which fingers he'd used. Shortly after that that riveting demonstration, Bobby topped himself when he warned a dinner guest:

"Don't smother my food with your boogies!"

Many knowledgeable experts on truly disgusting Reality TV moments point to the "The Surreal Life"—the show that forces washed-up celebrities to coexist as roommates. As one TV critic put it: "To call this show a train wreck is to insult train wrecks!"

Reality buffs will fondly recall that queasily surreal moment in the show's fourth season when a naked, drunken Verne "Mini-Me" Troyer—staggering around the shared digs like a poteen-poisoned "Twin Peaks" leprechaun—abandons a futile search for the bathroom…and urinates splashily in a hallway as the cameras roll— as do the eyes of his costars. (Just havin' a *wee wee*, as the Scots would say!)

Or how about steroid-popping baseball star José Canseco bragging to brain-dead model Caprice and his "Surreal Life" costars that he's a super-stud and "goes like a Clydesdale."

In a spinoff of that show—VH1's "Flavor of Love," hosted by the incomparable rapper Flavor Flav, there was a moment almost impossible to top for sheer shock value, when a white blonde with the cutie-pie name "Pumpkin" spat a huge lunger in the face of a tough-looking black babe…who immediately tried to beat her ass to death.

What made this moment truly classic was the camera tracking that gob of spit through the air in *slow motion!*

But just when you think Reality TV standards are totally in the toilet, someone flushes. An even more shocking moment occurred on the same show, and Flavor Flav proudly described it to the press like this: "On one of the future episodes, a girl (defecates) on my floor. I kept her around anyway, just to show everybody that accidents do happen and I can forgive."

What makes you think it was an accident, Flav?

Putting aside moments of sheer bad taste, the question is often asked about Reality TV, "How low can a show go?" Submitted, as the immortal Rod "Twilight Zone" Serling would put it, for your approval: "The Surreal Life"—which proudly touted a truly blockbuster episode that pitted Evil Bitch Omorosa of "The Apprentice" and Fruit-Loop Supermodel Janice Dickinson of "America's Top Model" against a team of folks afflicted with Down's Syndrome—in a *bowling match.*

If that's not the bottom…I challenge you to top it!

After shows like the aforementioned clicked, Reality TV really started picking up momentum. It had struck a resounding chord with fading boldface names, who immediately sensed the publicity potential and started clamoring to stage their own "Welcome to My World" reality shows. Suddenly, the dynamic shifted into hyper-weird. Instead of watching regular people striving to be celebrities on TV, viewers were treated to the bizarre spectacle of celebrities trying to convince us that they're normal folks just like anybody else; a bull-bleep premise that fooled damn near nobody.

And then…(*cue ominous organ chord….*)

…resurrected out of Hollywood's "where-are-they-now" crypts, addled wack-jobs Anna Nicole Smith and Farrah Fawcett came lurching back into the limelight like long-buried zombies answering a George Romero casting call for "Night of The Living Dead 2."

In a class of their own—over-the-hill, but not quite ripe enough for "The Surreal Life"—these eccentric, imploded bombshells amused America with their ditzy-diva shtick. The dearly-departed Anna Nicole intrigued audiences far more than Farrah, whose show ended after just a few episodes. Anna Nicole snatched the reality spotlight for more than two years. The not-as-dumb-as-she-looks blonde proved she's a shrewd promoter, building in the successful hook of a massive weight-loss campaign that worked big-time! She lost nearly 100 pounds over the course of the show—although she kept saying she'd lost "69" because it sounded sexually shocking. Anna Nicole always kept the press well-fed with provocative quotes, like this answer to an FHM interview question:

"Anna Nicole, what's the kinkiest sex you've ever had?"

"Well…a ghost would crawl up my leg and have sex with me at an apartment a long time ago in Texas. I used to think it was my boyfriend, and one day I woke up and it wasn't. It was, like, a spirit. And it…*WOO!* (miming a ghost flying from under her sheets)…went up! I was freaked out about it, but then I was, like, 'Well, you know what? He's never hurt me—and he just gave me some amazing sex, so I have no problem'…It wasn't a dream, because it was happening every night!"

Ah, for the good old days, when reality stars were anonymous nobodies. Before Farrah Fawcett's TV Land show "Chasing Farrah" even started—producers were going nuts with her trademark looney-tooney mood swings. That's why the entire first episode focused on whether Farrah even wanted to do a show! Of course, everything is grist for the mill in Reality TV Land, so opening scenes show the frazzled director pleading for her cooperation while she hems and haws.

Finally, in a bizarre move that flabbergasted the network folks, flipped-out Farrah whipped out a video camera and announced she'd consent to do the show on one condition—she'd film the crew while the crew filmed her. "Then I can keep the show honest," she babbled. Incredibly, her every wacko whim was granted. She was courted and butt-kissed as though she were still the famous, red-hot star of "Charlie's Angels" days—not the washed-up old kook she'd become.

Not surprisingly, Farrah's fiasco flopped after just one month. It was just too damn crazy even for Reality TV.

Then up popped fresher faces; newly married Jessica Simpson and Nick Lachey—she, a buxom Britney Spears wannabe…and he, a former boy-band hunk. Neither had ever been big enough to be classified even as has-beens, but they managed to launch a reality show chronicling the trials and tribulations of young, sorta-celebs settling into a brand-new marriage. Critics immediately pegged "Newlyweds" as a loser, but it became a surprise smash that lasted three seasons—thanks to huge publicity generated when Ms. Ditz famously asked Hubby if Chicken of The Sea was actually chicken; and even refused to try buffalo wings because she "doesn't eat buffalo."

Nick and Jessica went on to host a TV variety show that not only failed—it drove a wedge between them. I broke the first hint of trouble in their marriage in April 2004:

> The honeymoon's over for "Newlyweds" Jessica Simpson and Nick Lachey—insiders say the couple constantly fought on the set of their new variety show! Jessica thought Nick was hamming it up and trying to hog the limelight, and she wanted to focus more on musical acts. Nick felt Jessica was a "prude" for objecting to his foul language off-camera and told producers the show should center around comedy. Taping had to be halted several times as Jessica wailed: "I can't do this!" Stay tuned.

But Nick and Jessica's "Newlyweds" success had already triggered a brand-new stampede of stars into the reality arena.

Tommy Lee, the tattooed/pierced Mötley Crüe drummer and ex-husband of both Heather Locklear and Pamela Anderson, enrolled in NBC's "Tommy Lee Goes to College." This show proved that the lure of preening for Reality TV cameras can be a powerful aphrodisiac—even for America's supposedly dignified institutions of higher learning. My item exposed the not-so-surprising dynamic behind the show—as far as Tommy was concerned, anyway:

> ROCK & REAL DEPT.: Here's what Chancellor Harvey Perlman says about why he let NBC shoot the upcoming Reality TV show "Tommy Lee Goes to College" on the University of Nebraska at Lincoln campus: "We believe the effort will be serious," he wrote to faculty and staff, adding that the show will feature "a good message." And here's what TOMMY LEE told a source at Chicago's O'Hare Airport as he waited for a plane to his adopted alma mater: "I got to have sex with a lot of college girls!"

Then ex-"KISS" rocker Gene Simmons signed on to teach "Rock School," which was a charming show that critics loved because the flame-spitting star actually was very gentle with the young kids who were his students. Gene went on to do another reality show called "Family Jewels"—in which he all but wore an apron as he puttered around his BevHills estate and lavished love on the kids and their still-single mom, hot soft-porn icon Shannon Tweed.

Critics summed up the saccharine "Family Jewels" by bitching: Hey, Gentle Gene…stick out your tongue, or *something*, dude!

Even accused wife-killer Robert Blake aggressively shopped a celeb-reality show, but the project…er, died, so to speak. Then a genuine star—a famous, chart-topping singer—hopped the Reality TV train and quickly copped the Train Wreck Award! Pop Tart Britney Spears, flanked by slanty-hat loser/spouse Kevin Federline, signed with UPN for "Chaotic!"

The show should have been called, "SEX!!" Mostly, it featured a vapid Britney babbling incessantly about sex—asking people about their favorite sexual positions and quizzing Kevin on what makes a girl good in the sack, etc. When the shameless Bayou Bimbette appeared on the "Late Show with David Letterman" to promote "Chaotic," she and K-Fed read a Top 10 list of why viewers should tune in.

Reason No. 1? "In the season finale, you'll find out that Dave is the father of my baby—*Oops!*" Britney's show lasted just six episodes, and Dave's apparently not paying child support.

Then a Boldface Name even more notorious than Britney entered the reality arena: Paris Hilton! Her show "The Simple Life," costarring then-BFF (Best Female Friend) Nicole Richie, was a surprise sensation in its first season. The gimmick behind the show was that the two spoiled Beverly Hills brats would go into the heartland and attempt to live like normal people.

It worked out just about the way you'd expect. Paris and Nicole swooped into the American heartland like "Alien Bitches from Planet Gollywood" and—ignoring everything Captain Kirk taught us on "Star Trek"—immediately broke InterGalactic Rule #1…which bans any sexual contact with species from less-advanced civilizations. Yessir, them hi-falutin' BevHill fillies taught the young Arkansas bucks a thing or two—including the meaning of the term, "skank 'ho!"

EEee-*HAH!*

Here's my behind-the-scenes report on Whoopee-time in Hicksville:

> RIDE 'EM COWGALS! "The Simple Life" stars PARIS HILTON and NICOLE RICHIE flounced into the Arkansas heartland and rodeo-d with two high-teen local bulls—both just a smidge south of barely legal! EEE-HAH! Insiders on the TV crew called the BevHills bad girls things like "ungrateful, unapologetic, self-entitled"—and "the worst people I ever worked with!" DUH! But here's my sexy scoop: when their smitten swains dropped by the staff—after milking, or whatever—hottie heifers Paris and Nicole took turns distracting the crew as they slipped the lads into dressing rooms…and even the john!

Paris and Nicole were great role models for the local belles, who were dying to know how Hollywood gals keep their buffed, Hollywood hottie bods so super-skinny. My column revealed the diabolical secret of "The Simple Life"—the celebrity binge-and-barf technique, which I recounted at length in this book's Preface. Just to remind you briefly, it began:

> During the Arkansas sojourn of "The Simple Life," svelte-figured PARIS HILTON regularly sneaked away from the cameras to hog hearty on greasy fried foods and pizza…then dashed to the bathroom for lengthy barf-a-thons, reveal owners of two local eateries!…. "We knew to give that girl her space when she wanted bathroom time!"…BURP!….

Paris and Nicole's fish-out-of-water antics sent ratings skyrocketing, but "The Simple Life"—co-starring the entire town of Altus, Ark.—broke two local yokel hearts. In an eye-opening exclusive that illustrated how local folks are often fodder for Reality TV, the *National Enquirer* headlined:

"Paris Hilton Busts Up Childhood Sweethearts' Engagement!… Wrecks their 'Simple Life' to boost her show's ratings!"

Reporter Alan Smith wrote: "Man-eater Paris, 22, didn't even have feelings for Trae Lindley, the guy who dumped his fiancée Caroline Cains for her, but instead staged the romance to boost the show's ratings, said a source in Altus.

"At one point, Paris and Caroline nearly came to blows after the heiress and Nicole heckled her high school graduation ceremony. And when taping was finished, Paris packed her Prada bags and blew out of town like a tornado, leaving the relationship between the 19-year-old lovebirds in ruins."

After the cameras stopped rolling, handsome Arkansas teen Trae called Paris in Hollywood, but—SURPRISE!—the romance was over. Incredibly, Trae said that while he regretted breaking up with his high-school sweetie…he'd always have Paris!

"I wouldn't trade my time with Paris for anything in the world," he told the *Enquirer.*

That first season of "The Simple Life" stands as a shining example of why America loves these "ain't-celebrities-stoopid" shows. Reality fans gibbered like happy baboons when Ashton Kutcher conceived and produced "Punk'd"—which incorporated the mean-spirited, ambush-camera technique that drives modern Reality TV. "Punk'd" busted the laugh-meter with its breakthrough "watch-them-celebrities-suffer" hijinks. Ashton Kutcher, himself a celebrity and the producer of "Beauty and the Geek," chalked up huge ratings by "punk-ing" unsuspecting stars—and even making them cry—in an infinitely more vicious version of that pioneering granddaddy of Reality TV, "Candid Camera."

Wiseass Ashton shattered the "cool" of sheltered stars like Halle Berry—who freaked when she was "barred" (wink, wink!) from her own movie set; and self-styled tough-guy rocker Tommy Lee panicked when he thought he'd committed a hit-and-run! But best moment of all for jaded sadists came when Ashton punk-ed swaggering SexyBack heartthrob Justin Timberlake—who burst into tears and sobbed like a bitch when he returned home one day to discover "IRS agents" stripping his home of furniture because he "hadn't paid his back taxes."

Oh, just kidding, Justin, you little girl! STOP CRYING, FOR CHRISSAKE!

Sound like fun? Well, let's take the premise a step further: imagine the snarky thrill of punk-ing Mr. Punk'd himself! As I reported in my *Enquirer* column, Ashton's sense of humor deserted him totally when the tables were turned:

> Strolling an LA street with a pal, **ASHTON KUTCHER** flipped when two young guys came running up to him, shouting they'd just heard on the radio that wife **DEMI MOORE** had been in a horrible car accident involving a bus! Turning ghost white, the agitated star demanded, "Where did you hear it?... How long ago?" When he didn't get instant answers, Ashton really started freaking—and that's when the two punks, flashing a digital camera, admitted they were amateur video artists—and they'd just taped Mr. Punk'd being...punk'd! Exploding, Ashton screamed, "You're an ass—! That's not funny!" Retorted one guy, "But you do it all the time on your show!" Spewing unprintables, Ashton stalked off in a fury.

And when a major Hollywood star brilliantly turned the tables on smart-ass Kutcher, he didn't dare to get even the slightest bit angry—and here's why, as I reported in my column:

> Looking forward to a brief UK holiday, **ASHTON KUTCHER** ankled out of the airport terminal in London, where he was meeting up with lady love **DEMI MOORE**—and nearly fainted when a uniformed security guard grabbed him for "suspicion of drug smuggling!" White as a sheet, Ashton started babbling that he was innocent—but the color seeped back into his cheeks when galpal Demi suddenly sprang out of nowhere and giggled, "Boy...you been PUNK'D!" Turns out the guard was a phony she'd hired.

Then came my *piece de resistance!* I broke the world exclusive scoop that Ashton became the victim of an incredibly inventive prank when his cell phone was apparently hacked by two teenage techno-geeks—and his voice-mail messages started circulating on the Internet. One was an incredibly explicit, vulgar—but very sexy—message from a young lady sighing about how they'd hooked-up, had great sex...and how she hoped they'd get together for an encore performance. Suddenly, the Internet was agog. It was hilarious, but...was it real?

Sounds like a job for "SuperMike!"

I flew at the story faster than a speeding bullet—but when Ashton's handlers discovered I was investigating their bourgeoning scandal, they launched into full-alert damage control. Attempting to deflect me, they started spinning wildly, saying: "You never know—this might be a hoax we're pulling on people." Uh, huh! Nice try, fellas—but I knew in my cold reporter's heart that this was no hoax. The voice-messages sounded totally authentic, no matter how vociferously Ashton's team tried to deny it.

Supposedly, two high school kids were given Ashton's phone number by "a friend of a friend…somebody who works at MTV," and they hacked into his voicemail.

The messages they retrieved were then posted on a website called ahstonhacked.com—which was owned by a Boston man who'd met the guys while playing Xbox Live. He was quoted by UPI wire services, which repeated quotes he'd given to the *New York Daily News*, saying that he was convinced the voice-mails were real. "I can't imagine these guys would have the ability to fake it," he said. "Much easier for me to believe they stayed up all night hacking his phone."

Indeed, that version of events was a lot more believable than the spin Ashton's people were putting out—that voice-mails from several male buddies, including a "Bruce" that sounded like a dead-on Bruce Willis, were brilliantly faked by a couple of teenagers. And there was a salacious phone message from a young woman—definitely NOT Demi Moore—who purred, in steamy reminiscences, that she'd gobbled Ashton's El Gordo during a hot-sheet hotel session. She then went on to describe the star's apparatus in lustful detail.

What a great story—was it true? Punk-ster Ashton Kutcher getting punk'd by a couple of kids? As I often tell my reporters—and constantly remind myself—never fall in love with a story. If you can't stand it up, drop it. I knew I needed to dig hard to prove this one; get something solid.

And then, I lucked out.

A brief message on Kutcher's alleged voicemail had escaped the attention of journalists and fans alike, probably because they kept fast-forwarding to the naughty bits. The message was from an alleged desk clerk at a certain Las Vegas hotel, who was confirming a reservation for Kutcher, along with a confirmation number and confidential code name. I was convinced this message was authentic for two reasons: (1) punk-ass kid hackers would consider it kicks to fake a heavy-breathing girl, or imitate the voice of a celeb Kutcher pal like Bruce Willis, but fabricating a mundane message from a hotel clerk would be boring and pointless; and (2) my experience with celebrities had taught me that they often use secret code names to thwart nosy journalists.

I called the hotel and "identified" myself with the confirmation number I'd heard on the voicemail. Then I said, "I might need to change my reservation."

The girl on the other end said, "Didn't you just call and cancel this reservation an hour ago?... For Mr. Kutcher, right?"

Bada-BINGO!

The room clerk's response proved that there had been an authentic reservation under that number. It also proved that Ashton's damage-control team—even Ashton himself, perhaps—had cancelled the booking. After all, a prankster—or a nosy journalist like me—would simply ask about the reservation, not cancel it! This also proved, I realized, that Ashton's handlers were one step ahead of me—but not for long! I had tricked the hotel staffer into confirming that a reservation had been made to a confirmation number known only to Ashton Kutcher.

Then I got lucky again—and knew I'd nailed the story!

Suddenly sounding upset, the hotel clerk asked me, belatedly, for the code name. Celebs and their handlers routinely use these code names when dealing with hotels—but she had forgotten to ask me for the secret code name before she'd blurted that Kutcher had indeed made a reservation.

I'd punk-ed her, and she knew it!

She stammered, demanding to know who I was. What the hell, I thought. It's your nightmare, babe. I told her gently, "This is Mike Walker...of the *National Enquirer.*"

She gasped and hung up. It was one of those fun moments that reporters live for! Now I'd proven that the voicemail heard over the Internet truly belonged to Ashton Kutcher. I broke the exclusive in my column:

> **PUNK'D YA, KUTCHER!** Ashton Kutcher's reps deny reports that pranksters hacked his cell phone and posted his VM messages on the internet—including a salivating babe's salacious blow-by-blow of her alleged sexual encounter with Demi Moore's new

hubby! Kutcher's handlers keep crying "Hoax!"—but the messages sound authentic to me, including three from a "Bruce" who sounds a lot like BRUCE WILLIS, in this reporter's opinion. So, gossip fans, true or false? After listening to a message from a Vegas hotel confirming November 11-12 reservations for "Ashton Kutcher" in the Penthouse Suite, I phoned them. I never uttered Kutcher's name. I recited the confirmation number. "Mr. Kutcher, right?" the clerk said, then quickly stammered, "Wait…what's the code word…?" HELLO-O!

(MEMO TO ASHTON: Dude, why don't you punk Jennifer Aniston?... That would be a*wesome!!)*

* * *

Chapter *Eight*

SPACE ALIEN COMMITS MURDER! ...BLOODY CORPSE ON
CARPET TRIGGERS LAWSUIT! ...MAKEOVER HELL!

Ambush TV!

Violation of privacy!

Emotional devastation!

Deliberate infliction of pain and fear!

Isn't Reality TV GREAT?

And it's good, clean fun, mostly. But when it starts going downhill, it's a toboggan ride, with Satan at the helm.

Right, Jennifer?

On Oxygen's "Girls Behaving Badly," hottie actresses prowl the streets seeking victims ripe for "mindf****ing," as co-executive producer Barry Poznick puts it so elegantly. These happy-to-misbehave ladies pounce on male prey—who aren't aware they're secretly being videotaped—then cajole them into performing embarrassing tasks that are mainly associated with female taboos, i.e., enlisting a male mark to help search for a "dropped ovary"...or persuading him to pick up a used tampon.

Raunchy, but fun.

And MTV's "One Bad Trip" turned out to be one big hoot for...well, for the audience and the producers, at least! Using those magical hidden cameras, parents of college kids are allowed to spy on sex-drugs-rock-and-roll antics of their darling off-spring during Spring Break. Genuine shock-and-horror reactions on both sides put a slight damper on the fun for both parents and kids—but what a crackup to watch.

("WHOA!… Mom, Dad…what are you doing here? Oh, um, this is…er, Hillary and she's a…er, practicing nudist, kind of a religion thing…and she's… teaching me about it, sort of." Yeah…teaching me…*that's the ticket!*)

Sci-Fi Channel's "Scare Tactics" worked hard at keeping it real—as in, real *scary.* In one hidden-camera stunt, a stripper gets "beaten to death" at a bachelor party (WOW…talk about fun!). A partygoer who doesn't know it's all a gag is suddenly facing the very real horror of murder charges.

"We want everyone to have a good time," gushed one of the show's producers to writer Joy Press in the *Village Voice* (What a perfect name for a reporter…Joy Press!) But as Press points out in her piece, there's a problem looming for all these highly-amused, ain't-it-a-blast Reality TV producers—lawsuits. And lawsuits lead to higher insurance premiums. Studios and TV networks love the genre because it's cheap to produce, but fat payoffs from sympathetic juries can wipe out profits fast.

Consider the case of the couple who sued Ashton Kutcher and MTV because they were scared out of their wits when they walked into their Las Vegas hotel room—and found a bloody corpse on the carpet! The body, of course, was actually a fake "mutilated murder victim" planted by producers of the very aptly-titled show, "Harassment."

These lawsuits join a growing number of complaints filed against networks and TV producers by reality contestants. Shows such as "Fear Factor," "Survivor" and "Joe Millionaire" are cheaper to produce than scripted shows, but the risks involved are "real," so to speak, and they're costing producers and networks real money as lawsuits proliferate and insurance premiums rise. Shows involving hidden cameras can be particularly vulnerable because contestants don't sign release forms in advance. One fitness trainer sued PAX network after he was tricked into lying down on an X-ray conveyer belt for a "security check" at an Arizona airport before boarding a plane. The "fun" went afoul when the poor guy's leg jammed in the machine. He suffered a painful injury, and did NOT "smile" when he found out he'd been filmed for an updated version of "Candid Camera."

The Sci-Fi Channel's "Scare Tactics"—hosted by "Mean Grrrl" Shannon Doherty (inspired casting, one must admit!)—used hidden cameras to film the reactions of not-in-on-the-gag people who are suddenly confronted by horror scenarios, such as haunted houses and alien abductions. One woman—who claimed she suffered real-life trauma, and was hospitalized after witnessing "an extraterrestrial murderer"—filed a lawsuit in Los Angeles County Superior Court. She alleged that she was lured to "an exclusive Hollywood party" at a Southern California desert resort.

When the car taking her to the party "stalled" along a remote stretch at night, she was told by the people with her—who were actually actors from the show—to run for her life to escape a murderous alien attacker running amok. Escaping into a nearby canyon, she was terrified when she witnessed the "alien" commit a murder. The actors in the show, the channel that aired it, the producers or creators, and their production companies were all named in the lawsuit.

Just pranks? Harmless mind-fucking? Not to the mind of Deleese Williams, a young woman from Texas, who filed suit in Los Angeles against ABC, Disney Corp., and others—including a jolly production company that calls itself "LightHearted Entertainment"—for allegedly treating her with unspeakable cruelty after it was announced on national TV that she'd won a once-in-a-lifetime chance for an "Extreme Makeover."

The lawsuit charges that the defendants—the show's producers—set in motion a chain of events that triggered the tragic, real-life *suicide of her sister.* In blunt prose that beats the usual legal-ese, her lawyers' cry for justice outlines the shocking story of how Deleese Williams was allegedly kicked to the curb on the eve of her promised plastic surgery makeover, and told to hightail it back to Texas pronto—a vicious thing to do, considering that producers had manipulated her family, even her own husband, into mocking her physical appearance as cameras rolled.

The opening paragraphs of the lawsuit—which seeks $1 million-plus in damages for Deleese Williams, identified as "the Participant"—read like a horror tale scripted in Hell:

1. Deleese Williams is considered ugly. But Deleese and her friends and family didn't notice, or they politely pretended not to notice, choosing to see instead her gentle, trusting nature and her pleasant and sweet personality. She was a perfect candidate for ABC's Reality TV show "Extreme Makeover," which was designed to strip away the veneers that masked Deleese's physical features.

2. The show consists of on-camera interviews with the Participant and family, films of the Participant undergoing extreme cosmetic surgery, and "before" and "after" views of the Participant. The makeover is intended to provide a dramatic physical and emotional improvement, thereby removing problems and obstacles caused by physical appearance.

3. The "Extreme Makeover" people promised to make Deleese's ugly physical features match her pretty inner-self, in exchange for Deleese's agreement to allow herself, and her husband, family, friends and the world to look hard at, to see, feel, touch and acknowledge Deleese's ugliness, to talk about it, to expose it and all its aspects to the world on national television for the sake of advertising revenues and high Nielsen ratings.

4. After many weeks of agonizing interviews, filming, and preparations, finally Deleese was in Los Angeles to receive her "Extreme Makeover." But on the night before the surgery, Defendants came to her hotel and told Deleese to "go home to Texas." No warning, no apology. They had simply canceled the makeover.

5. Back in Texas, Deleese tried to hide. She and her family were devastated, humiliated, crushed, embarrassed, ashamed. Deleese's sister, Kelli, had said awful things about Deleese, thinking she was helping, as Defendants had intended. Unable to face Deleese, Kelli committed suicide. Sometimes Deleese blames herself for Kelli's death.

It's a shocking story. Here is a woman who knows she's physically unattractive in the extreme, but who's always cherished the comfort of knowing that while others might snicker and jeer, her family and her husband have steadfastly loved her for herself. She and her sister, Kelli, were devoted to each other. They'd opened a successful business together. Yet Deleese never stopped praying desperately for deliverance from the prison of her physical ugliness. Ever since she could remember, she'd dreamed of an end to the cruel sneers endured since childhood.

And then, in a moment of magic, Deleese Williams believed that salvation was finally at hand when—as an in-studio guest on the show "Life After Extreme Makeover"—a spotlight suddenly picked her out of the audience, and the show's host announced as the audience applauded:

"Deleese Williams, stand up! You are getting an 'Extreme Makeover!'… Congratulations!"

It was her dream come true. But all too soon, Deleese Williams' Hollywood miracle morphed into a horror show that's not over yet…and will re-run, over and over, long after she's had her day in court.

Typically, the nightmare began the way it often does in Reality TV—with those ubiquitous hidden cameras. Then, using trademark tricks and ruthless deception to amp up the agony and spike the ratings, the producers—experts in the arcane art of manipulating human beings like marionettes—allegedly goaded and encouraged her own family to talk about her ugliness on-camera, according to the lawsuit. And when they balked, they were told that if they didn't speak bluntly about Deleese's physical deficiencies, she'd stand no chance of winning the makeover she wanted so desperately.

In a cruel twist, the lawsuit reveals, Kelli—literally bullied into making devastating remarks about Deleese's "ugliness"—had no idea producers had put her sister into an adjoining room…where she rocked in emotional pain as she overheard every stinging insult her sister was making about her physical appearance.

Then, according to the lawsuit, LightHearted Entertainment, a.k.a. the Defendants, sent their jolly producers to Deleese's hometown of Conroe, Texas. No matter who wins this case, what you're about to read is a searing and accurate look at the unreal underbelly of how Reality TV really works.

41. Deleese and (her husband) Mike returned home to Texas, and it wasn't until January 4, 2004, that Deleese was told that a film crew would be traveling to her hometown, Conroe, Texas, to film with her family….

42. From the moment Defendants arrived on January 6, 2004, it was immediately apparent that their goal was to create extreme emotional turmoil and distress for the subjects of their cameras, Deleese and her family, and to capture that turmoil and distress with their cameras. Also apparent was the Defendant's skill, experience and ruthlessness in achieving this goal.

43. For example, Kelli, Deleese's younger sister, was the first family member to be interviewed on camera. As the interview began, Kelli tried to discuss some of Deleese's positive attributes. Defendants thwarted these attempts by peppering Kelli with questions about her childhood with the ugly Deleese. Defendants repeatedly put words in Kelli's mouth to invoke an emotional on-camera reaction. When she wasn't displaying the extreme emotion Defendants desired, Defendants turned off the camera and changed tactics. The Defendant's interviewer alternately attacked and shamed and condemned Kelli for her sometimes cruel past treatment of Deleese. When Kelli was ultimately overcome by emotion and collapsed in tears, the Defendants' film crew resumed filming and the interviewer changed to a milder approach on-camera. The diverse and sudden swings of emotion that Defendants caused were essential to the television program's success, and were achieved a by subtle and undisclosed manipulation, subterfuge, and emotional abuse.

44. While Defendants were brow beating Kelli, Deleese and her older sister Patty were in adjoining rooms. Both women could hear Kelli's interview (by Defendants' design), and Deleese was hurt and angered by what she heard. "Through all this my friends and family, who had never said anything before, have said things that made me realize that, 'Yes, I was right…and everyone did think I looked like a freak.'" The only comfort Deleese found was in the knowledge that no one would ever be able to say these things to her again. "I'm going to be pretty!" She was getting a complete "Extreme Makeover." Patty, however, was disgusted by what she believed was the Defendants' unethical and malicious treatment of Kelli, but she went along so that her sister would get the promised "Extreme Makeover."

45. Defendants informed Deleese that she would be required to leave for Los Angeles yet again, immediately upon the conclusion of this round of interviews and filming in Texas. When Deleese's nine-year-old daughter, Amanda Rose, realized that her mommy would be leaving again, she began to cry. Defendants physically restrained Deleese from comforting her daughter so that the child's tears could be filmed for television.

Shortly after Deleese arrived back in Los Angeles, she got the shocking news that producers were reneging on written and verbal contracts to award her the promised "Extreme Makeover." On just a few hours notice, she was put on a flight back to Texas. The lawsuit documents the alleged horrors that followed:

58. On January 20, 2004, Deleese came home. But it was not the same home, and she was woefully unprepared for the homecoming that awaited her. Defendants had elicited horrific, hurtful statements from virtually every member of her family, recorded them, and shown them. Everyone was waiting for the "new" Deleese. Now that she had returned in the same condition in which she had left, there were no secrets, no hidden feelings, no reward. Deleese and everyone else saw (her) as Defendants had revealed her: "Ugly." Worst of all were the comments elicited from her husband. Deleese had always believed he was the one person who only saw the beauty inside, but Defendants had successfully encouraged him to betray that sacred trust. Under the heat of Defendants' interrogation lights, he admitted her physical failings as well.

59. Deleese doesn't go out much now. She refuses to wear makeup, or style her hair, because such things cannot hide her ugliness, irrefutable proof of which was carefully captured on film and shoved in everyone's face, so that nobody could miss or hide from it.

60. Before Defendants' actions, Deleese and Mike had enjoyed an active social, sexual and married life together. They were a close couple, who spent hours talking and doing things. But since returning from Los Angeles, Deleese has withdrawn from him. They have been out together just twice. The long, intimate conversations have been replaced by periods of silence.

61. Deleese's relationship with Kelli disintegrated. They had raised their children and built a business together. Now Kelli was lost. She had been shamed and humiliated in front of the cameras, and did not forgive herself for the way she had treated Deleese—and the fact that Deleese now knew all of it. Her guilt was overwhelming her and nobody could help. Patty and Deleese tried, but Kelli would not listen to Patty, and she wouldn't let Deleese forgive her....

On May 25, 2004, just four months after Deleese returned from Los Angeles, Kelli killed herself. Deleese is now raising Kelli's two children.

In late 2006, her lawsuit against ABC-TV was settled for an undisclosed sum.

*

Lawsuits against Reality TV tell sad tales—and spell out a clear message: Caveat *emptor*. Let the buyer beware. Consider this saga of a bright new beginning that became the Hollywood ending from Hell:

Five brothers and sisters, suddenly orphaned after losing both parents, were charitably taken in by a married couple from their church. Tipped by news reports, producers from the hit Reality TV show, "Extreme Makeover: Home Edition," swooped in—and told the couple they'd rebuild their house to accommodate their newly expanded "family."

Isn't that touching? But in a nasty twist straight out of a Dickens novel, the Higgins orphans—after being showered with gifts and presented with their new mansion on the Reality TV show—ended up filing a lawsuit against the producers and the couple. Aimed at ripping the happy façade off Reality TV, it alleges fraud and breach of contract, claiming that the couple engaged in "an orchestrated campaign" to drive the youngsters out of the new home by insulting them and treating them badly.

"We were promised a home," said Charles Higgins 2, the eldest of the five siblings. "They broke that promise."

The network continued to air the episode, the lawsuit alleges, even though the siblings have been forced from the house and are effectively homeless.

"What we're really seeing is the collision between 'Reality TV' and the perception Reality TV seeks to create in the minds of the general public," said Patrick Mesisca, the Higgins' lawyer.

Filed in Los Angeles Superior Court, the lawsuit targets ABC, the program's production companies, the firm that built the house, and the couple who helped the siblings, Phil and Loki Leomiti.

A network statement said: "It is important to note that the episode was about the rebuilding of the Leomiti family's home to accommodate the inclusion of the five Higgins siblings, whom the Leomitis had invited into their lives following the death of their parents."

The Higgins family had lived together in an apartment in Downey, California, until April 2004, when their mother died of breast cancer. The father died 10 weeks later of heart failure. The Leomitis took the Higgins siblings, aged 15 to 22, into their Santa Fe Springs house in July 2004. Meanwhile, producers of "Extreme Makeover" learned of the Higgins siblings' situation from a newscast and were interested in doing an episode on them.

Crews traveled to Santa Fe Springs in February and demolished the Leomitis' house. In its place, Pardee Homes built a nine-bedroom home while show producers arranged for the siblings to receive cars, groceries, computers, stereos and gifts.

Pardee paid off the mortgage on the new house, according to the lawsuit—and the Leomitis retained the title.

Around the time the episode aired, the lawsuit claims, the youngsters were driven from the house. The Higgins' lawyer acknowledges that the siblings were never promised a house in writing. But he contends that the network's statements and actions could be considered a promise for legal purposes.

In other words, the couple got a luxurious, rebuilt house because they'd taken the orphans in and needed a bigger place—but now the orphans are out.

The suit seeks unspecified compensatory and punitive damages, and no matter how it turns out, here's the reality: It stinks.

* * *

Chapter *Nine*

TRANSVESTITE HOOKERS.... INSANE 'ROID RAGES....
SHOCKING SUICIDE TRY.... THE SCARY WORLD OF DANNY BONADUCE!

And now for something completely…different.

In 2005, VH1 debuted a debacle—a celeb-reality show so frighteningly "real" it was nearly canceled mid-run. Incredibly, VH1 executives and the show's producers were terrified that their star—steroid-snorting, rage-o-maniac Danny Bonaduce—might die on-camera.

Literally!

If ever there was a perfect candidate for a candid-camera exposé of a celebrity life that seemed to be descending inexorably into hell, it was, paradoxically, the witty, charming, glib Bonaduce, who'd wowed America playing a mischievous, red-headed moppet on the enormously popular "Partridge Family." But when the show ended, as happens so often with former child stars, whether talented or not, Danny's career spiraled downward. He was barely heard from until a shocking headline in 1988 trumpeted:

"Bonaduce Accused of Punching Out a Transvestite Hooker in Las Vegas!"

Apparently the redhead was still quite mischievous, but a moppet no longer—now he was tabloid fodder. He'd hit rock bottom after being lambasted in the press as a sexual deviate/druggie charged with committing assault. But as Danny languished in a Las Vegas jail cell, unable to think of a single friend who'd make bail for him because, as he'd later put it, "I'd burned them all too many times," he was about to make some new friends—me, and the *National Enquirer.*

On the morning after his arrest, a guard unlocked his cell door and said, "You're out of here...somebody posted bail for you." Blinking in surprise, Danny asked, "Who?" The guard shrugged and motioned him out of the cell. When they got to the reception area, Danny saw a smiling face he'd get to know a lot better over the years—and whose work he could brazenly rip off and sell for cash money!

Isn't it great to have a friend at the *National Enquirer?*

More on that later.... But on that lucky day when he walked out of the Las Vegas jail, even Danny didn't realize that he'd just scored the big break that would catapult him back into show business—and new-found success as a radio talk show host in Chicago, New York and Los Angeles. He would have laughed at the notion that he'd fall in love so fast, with a beautiful woman named Gretchen, and that he'd marry her after just one date.

So less than a year after his embarrassing arrest—and whispers about why he'd been in a close encounter with a transvestite hooker—Danny was suddenly sitting in the catbird seat again. But all too soon, the demons started whispering in his ear anew. In a pattern that would become all too familiar, Danny began to throw success away with both hands, slowly slipping back into a degenerate booze-and-drugs lifestyle.

Flash-forward to 2005: Danny and Gretchen's marriage is coming apart at the seams as he spins out of control. Yet somehow, the couple decide that inviting a VH1 camera crew into their volatile home would be a fun, rewarding idea.

The show was called "Breaking Bonaduce"...and it was a voyeur's wet dream. As the ultimate portrait of celebrity breakdown, Bonaduce set the benchmark. It's safe to say that "Breaking Bonaduce" will never be topped—unless, of course, Reality TV producers can find another star who is not only fun to watch, but is perfectly willing to die on camera. Consider this: when VH1 producers confronted Danny and told him they wanted to pull the plug because they feared he had a death wish, he responded:

"You'd have a great show if I died. I can't believe you're not willing to roll the cameras on that."

The crucial moment in "Breaking Bonaduce" occurs after several episodes establish that Danny's life has become progressively worse as he and Gretchen contemplate a divorce—not because he doesn't love her and their two children, but because the death-dealing drugs-booze-steroids cocktails he consumes drive him into near-homicidal rages that frighten everyone around him. At one point, Danny agrees to go into rehab. After his release, he hits the Hollywood streets and phones Gretchen—raging at her for hiring male strippers to perform at her 40th birthday party.

The couple exchange vicious insults, Danny slams down the phone—and explodes in typical steroid rage. He begins threatening the VH1 crew physically. He screams that he's going to Gretchen's party to assault the male strippers…and even the guests. He grows more erratic and violent. Finally, he breaks down in tears, shrieking that he's lost control…that he's going out of his mind.

Hours later, in a startling cry for help, Danny slashes his wrists.

He survives, but so does the madness. Danny even accuses the psychiatrist hired by the show, a Dr. Corgiat, of conspiring to turn his own wife against him. The doctor tells VH1 it's time to bail—that they can't just stand by and watch this man die on-camera.

*

How would Danny Bonaduce respond to Jennifer Aniston's furious attack on Reality TV? Would her angry rant that it's "humiliating…degrading" trigger steroid meltdown? That's a joke, if you know Danny. He rarely explodes when asked challenging, even antagonistic questions about his profession…or his personal peccadilloes. Here's the "Breaking Bonaduce" star's rationale—and he takes my "You Know You Want to Watch" slogan a step further when he describes his life, and why it's okay for the world to watch what's happening to him:

"I'm a car crash," he explains, "...and you have every right to slow down and watch the car crash."

Got that, Jennifer Aniston?

But seriously, folks, does watching a man's real-life spiritual death on national TV qualify as great entertainment? We're fine with watching, say, the fictional "Death of a Salesman" on "Masterpiece Theater," but why is that not only permissible, but laudable? Because, as Jen would patiently explain, art in the form of a written play is "real" in the sense that it's artistically and emotionally true to the human spirit—but this real "real" is just too damn "humiliating...degrading."

Did I get that right, Jen? (Call me.)

So...was Danny's Reality TV show "really" that bad? To recap: On "Breaking Bonaduce," the first major thing we learned was that Danny married Gretchen on the first night he met her. Well...that's touching, right? Ah, but the second revelation shared with the audience is that Danny's been embroiled in an affair with another woman—and Gretchen knows all about it!

WHOA!

Crisis! Screaming...fighting...drugs, booze, steroids...blah-blah-blah...!

Danny finally ends up in rehab. At first, he shows signs of progress. When he and his 10-year-old daughter, Isabella, finally meet for the first time in weeks, Danny vows he'll never leave her again for such a long time. And he makes a solemn vow to Gretchen that he'll become a better husband and father. But there's an underlying problem, the resident shrink points out to Danny—Gretchen doesn't speak his language, and doesn't believe him. On the verge of moving out of his home and possibly leaving his wife, Danny realizes he's actually got a great life, and it's worth keeping...but...

In the fifth episode of "Breaking Bonaduce," 10-year-old Isabella looks shocked when she sees bandages on Danny's hands and asks, "Daddy, what happened to your wrists?" Danny lies, telling her he injured himself installing windows. The truth, of course, is that Danny slashed his wrists in a desperate suicide attempt, triggered by a wild night of swilling down pills and booze, after Gretchen told him she wanted a divorce.

Fortunately—or not, depending on your appetite for raw-meat reality—before Gretchen confronted Danny about a divorce, she asked the VH1 crew to leave...and that's the only reason why her husband's attempted suicide and hospitalization didn't make it to videotape. But the cameras did capture Danny drinking himself into a rage that culminated in his shocking threat to attack a producer.

"I will cripple him for the rest of his life!" Danny screamed.

Then he made threats aimed at Gretchen, yelling, "If she doesn't get on the phone right now, *there will be no stopping me.*"

Rampaging Danny had crossed the line. The VH1 camera crew physically restrained him and told Gretchen, "This party is over. Your husband is out of his mind." The shaken, disgusted crew left. Shortly after that, Danny slashed his wrists. Gretchen's first desperate reaction to save her husband's life was to phone 911—but she thought better of it midway, and put down the phone.

Recalled Danny: "The cops showed up anyway, and I'm bleeding all over the place. I'm not being arrested but they take me to the psych ward for a mandatory lockdown."

And why did he slash his wrists? "I was trying to make a point," said Danny.

Cynics say VH1 knew the dangers of signing Danny to a Reality TV show based on his life; the history was there for anyone to read. Years of insane boozing, drug abuse—including steroids, which whipped him into frightening rages—followed by multiple arrests, and a stint in jail for beating up a transvestite hooker.

In 2005, on his TV show "The Other Half," Danny told the world how the *National Enquirer* saved his life after that incident—how we bailed him out of jail and wrote a touching story about the tragic downfall of that mop-headed, adorable kid from TV's "The Partridge Family." Incredibly, in a weird twist, that *Enquirer* story catapulted Danny back into the big time. A Chicago DJ who read it jokingly started a drive to "Feed Danny Bonaduce"—asking listeners to send in canned food for the starving "Partridge Family" bad-boy.

Within days, amused fans had dropped off a mountain of canned goods at the radio station. So the DJ sent Danny a plane ticket to Chicago, then conducted a hilarious interview with him before turning over the food. Danny was such a hit with listeners that the station gave him his own show—kicking off a radio career that lasted decades. It was during this career rebirth that Danny met Gretchen and married her after just one date.

As the years wore on, Danny became a radio gypsy, leaving Chicago for New York City, then moving on to Los Angeles. And he still made headlines that revealed his ongoing struggle with addiction. But he'd finally gone on the wagon after connecting with a TV show called "The Other Half." The show had been conceived by NBC as the male-oriented counterpart of ABC's "The View." Among the regular group of guys was Dick Clark, who constantly encouraged Danny to stay sober.

As a semi-regular on the show with my gossip reports, I ear-witnessed several of these conversations, and it was touching to observe Dick's sincere interest. I told Danny he was fortunate because Dick—who's known in Hollywood as a hard-headed businessman—is not a bleeding heart who says nice things just to hear himself talk. Dick genuinely liked Danny, and thought he was worth the trouble.

But then the dynamic changed. "The Other Half" went off the air…and Danny heard the siren song of Reality TV. He was perfect celeb-reality material; a volatile, dodgy dude who loved living in the spotlight. He'd do anything for a laugh—and VH1 knew it. Even better, in reality terms, was the trouble brewing in Danny's marriage to Gretchen. He'd had an affair, and Gretchen had just found out about it. Shortly after the show debuted, Danny fell off the wagon in spectacular fashion—binge-drinking on camera…even guzzling a bottle of vodka in one long, horrifying chug-a-lug.

Danny started taking the drug Vicodin. Then, after subjecting himself to an insanely obsessive exercise regimen, he started injecting steroids. In a shocking parallel to the comic character The Hulk, his muscles suddenly bulged alarmingly. His eyes flashed with the fires of rage. He began abusing everyone around him verbally: Gretchen, their therapist, Dr. Garry Corgiat, the VH1 crew and even the Suits.

Finally, after Danny's suicide attempt, Dr. Corgiat refused to deal with the show unless the star checked into rehab for treatment of substance abuse.

"Breaking Bonaduce" wasn't fuzzy-wuzzy Reality TV, à la "The Osbournes." There was nothing sweet and endearing about 'roid-ripped Druggy Daddy, compared to the twinkly, benign Ozzie Osbourne—a man so zonked, the story goes, that he can't remember biting a bat's head off. Danny's kids, Isabella and Dante, age 4, had become wary of their steroid-stoked father, and they sensed the tension between him and their mother.

VH1 execs took a meeting and asked themselves the burning question: "Do we pull the plug?" At that point, say insiders, the Suits literally believed Danny might hurt someone, do serious harm to himself—or even die on camera. In the filmed therapy sessions with Dr. Corgiat, which occurred twice a week in a replica of his office built on a Hollywood sound stage, the shrink challenged Danny constantly about his steroid abuse, according to a report in *New York* mag.

The good doctor also grilled Gretchen, asking if Danny had ever hit her or the children. Gretchen insisted that had never happened. Nonetheless, Dr. Corgiat became increasingly concerned. The tension built, and in the fourth episode Danny broke down in tears and told him, "I never expected any of this. I thought this would be the best thing that ever happened, because I'd have another TV show. And that made me happy. Because it's what I'm good at. But now I see that my marriage is dissolving."

Then came the ultimate shocker—Danny's suicide attempt. "That was the dealbreaker," said Jeff Olde, VH1's senior vice president of production, in a published report. "We've all worked on a lot of reality shows where a lot of people get really, really drunk and do some crazy things. But Danny's behavior was on the edge. We would not have continued shooting that show, there was no way."

Dr. Corgiat reportedly told VH1: "Danny's in a drug-induced psychosis. This is not okay. I'm not doing this—this is unethical, immoral. We need to take care of this guy."

But when Gretchen was told they were killing the show so Danny could get help, she broke down in tears—and begged them to keep filming. Gretchen knew that the only leverage she had to force Danny into rehab was to keep the family rooted in his favorite comfort zone, the one place where he always felt safe, protected: in front of TV cameras.

"Danny loves to be on TV," Gretchen told VH1. If they yanked the show, she told them, he'd fall apart and never get help. As Danny put it later, "I pushed them to film. VH1 said, 'You've gone too far. We can't film you—you're dying.' I thought, 'What are you talking about? You have a great show if I died. What's *wrong* with you, not rolling on my death?' So that surprised me."

VH1 found a rehab facility that allowed cameras—but kept fretting they'd be excoriated as typically heartless Hollywood Suits who'd ignore danger to keep a profitable show on the air. But, to be fair, the network had a co-dependent: Danny. They both wanted to stay on the air—and they did.

And incredibly, Danny got through drug and alcohol rehab, graduating with flying colors. The guy was sober—that was the good news. Then came the bad news: despite his sobriety, Danny got axed from his radio talk show on L.A.'s Star 98—a gig that paid him a reported $1 million a year. He immediately filed suit against his female co-host, Jamie White, who ragged on him ruthlessly after his departure, spewing that he'd been constantly drunk or high during their broadcasts. Then she unloaded a charge that was truly vicious—because it crossed a line I've always drawn for myself in decades of edgy, in-your-face, but-as-honest-as-I-can-make-it journalism:

NEVER HURT A CHILD!

But the nasty bitch went ahead with her on-air poison—and dragged other talent into her filthy mix, egging on a co-worker to confirm her accusation during a live broadcast. Whether Jamie White's accusation is true or not is beside the point. Hating Danny on a personal level is an issue between two adults. To publicly utter words that could forever stain the heart and soul of a child is unconscionable. Kicking Danny when he's down is one thing—dragging in his 10-year-old daughter brings new meaning to the term "media whore." After Jamie White excreted her bile on-air, I tried to reach Danny. He did not respond. In my *Enquirer* column, I wrote:

> **MEMO TO MY PAL DANNY BONADUCE:** On the "Other Half," the TV show you co-hosted with **DICK CLARK** and **MARIO LOPEZ,** you credited me and the *National Enquirer* with bailing you out of jail after you beat up that transvestite prostitute years ago— and you thanked us for jump-starting your dead career. We've been pals since, Danny, but I just heard an accusation that sickens me— and I hope it's **NOT** true. **JAMIE WHITE,** the woman who co-hosted your radio talk show on Star 98—the LA station that axed you after the drugs/booze melt-down you suffered while taping VH1's "Breaking Bonaduce"—just alleged on air that she and coworkers eyewitnessed you screaming in your little daughter's face, "You effing whore!" Please say it isn't so, Danny. Tell me your side, and I'll print it. Enquiring minds need to know, pal!...(PS: My best to **GRETCHEN.**)

*

Had the producers of "Breaking Bonaduce" consulted me, I'd have advised them—based on a lifetime of hard-earned knowledge about the celebrity psyche—to discount Danny's dramatic threats of suicide, while taking the appropriate cautions, of course. Danny's ego, and I say this in some awe, is far too powerful to countenance self-extinction. This ex-adorable-mophead is a hardy, resourceful survivor, and endlessly inventive when it comes to...re-inventing himself. Years ago, after the *Enquirer* bailed him out of jail and put him back on the front pages, I interviewed Danny—who'd just started a new talk-show career in Chicago—on my own nationally syndicated radio show. As he waxed enthusiastic about finally getting back on his feet, Danny volunteered to me and my audience that he now had a terrific, new money-making sideline—selling a showbiz gossip column in Australia.

"It's a column just like yours, Mike...in fact, it is yours," he said, brazen as brass. "I just steal your items, put my name on the column, and sell it in Australia. And they love it!"

I believe my gob-smacked response was, "Really?"

Years later, when Danny appeared on the nationally syndicated daily television series that I created and co-hosted, "National Enquirer TV," he told me he had been selling my gossip on an Aussie radio station. Once again, stunned by the guy's awesome chutzpah, I said, "Really?"

"Yeah," he responded, "and when I told them I was getting too busy to do it anymore, they sent me a bribe—a customized Harley-Davidson. Come by the house and I'll let you ride it."

Despite his volatility, Danny Bonaduce got a new ride on TV, a series on The Game Show Network called "Starface." Billed as a scandal-fest that "revels in the exploits of celebrities and features such segments as 'Mug Shots' and 'Celebrity Train Wrecks,'" it shortly went off the tracks and was cancelled. The show included, of course, hot scoops from my column in the *National Enquirer.* I still remember what Danny told me years ago:

"I only steal from the best, Mike."

* * *

Chapter *Ten*

JENNIFER ANISTON DESCRIBES LIFE: "IT SUCKS!"
...THE PRINCES OF MALIBU DO THE HOLLYWOOD HUSTLE....
DIVORCE BECOMES REALITY.

MEMO TO JENNIFER ANISTON: Chalk up the following revelation as a win for you, lady! The eternally shameless star of that legendary Celebrity Train Wreck, the "Breaking Bonaduce" show, suddenly admitted for the record that his Reality TV experience left him just a wee bit...ashamed! (Imagine! This from a man who felt no shame and even swaggered cockily at the 2007 Reality Awards Show when he smashed "Survivor" contestant Johnny Fairplay into the stage face-first, sending him into oral surgery.)

Speaking of his show, Danny told *New York Daily* News TV critic David Bianculli that "there are some regrets" about allowing cameras to record his steroid-crazed crash-and-burn, plus the near-breakup of his marriage, replete with all the sordid details of his infidelity.

Said Danny: "Up until recently, I would have said, with a straight face, that I have absolutely no regrets. On the 'Breaking Bonaduce' show, I went far enough to damage my credibility...so I do now have some regrets, and I never used to."

Hey, Jennifer Aniston! Here's an even bigger Bonaduce confession: Incredibly, Danny admits he's never had the balls to eyeball his own TV meltdown—the suicide attempt, the drug abuse, etc. "I've never seen the show...not one second of it," he admitted. "While I didn't have the wherewithal not to do it, I did have the common sense not to watch it."

That's a BIG win for Jennifer, folks. Remember her ringing indictment—that Reality TV traffics ruthlessly in "humiliation…degradation." Even brazen Bonaduce has admitted she's dead-on with her warning that you can end up paying an awful price when you allow your life to be hijacked to make entertainment for strangers. Remember Jen's own words:

"All I can do is go on with my life. It's *not a show*. It's real! And *it sucks."*

*

In the old days, people watched Ozzie and Harriet and thought, "Gee, I'd like to live that way." But as the world turned, so to speak, people began to fixate on— and even emulate—the social and professional lessons learned from Reality TV shows.

Somehow, as Jennifer Aniston laments so heart-rendingly, we just don't seem to be buying into fiction these days. The children of this Brave New Millenium want to see what's really happening. So, to achieve success in business and the boardroom, we look to Donald Trump; and for clues on how to become a superstar, we observe Simon Cowell. But when we peek vicariously at the intimate family lives of the rich and famous, we come away stunned to discover that their families can be even nuttier than ours!

So now that we've met Ozzie & Sharon, Bobby & Whitney, Danny & Gretchen, etc.—let's enjoy a self-righteous sneer at other notable celebrity-family train wrecks, shall we?

Let's start with those filthy-rich folks who self-destructed so spectacularly on Fox's short-lived Reality TV show, "Princes of Malibu": Mommy Linda Thompson, a former Miss Tennessee and long-time Elvis Presley girlfriend; Daddy (Stepdaddy, actually) David Foster, a Grammy-winning, multi-millionaire music mogul; and…their two handsome, ne'er-do-well princelings, Brandon and Brody.

Let's begin by noting that, unfair though it may be, any stereotypical assumptions you make about two guys with twee names like "Brody and Brandon" will almost certainly be right-on. The brothers were Central Casting proto-types... and that was the genesis for the "Princes of Malibu" show, which starred two real-life spoiled, model-handsome Malibu rich kids who, as they reach their early twenties, are sensing for the first time hints life—even when you're lucky enough to be living it in the fabled 'Bu—isn't always the proverbial bowl of cherries.

Brandon & Brody had tasted paradise; catered to, beloved and cozened by beautiful mom Linda—and worshipped by hordes of bikini-ed beach babes who joined them for endless slap-ass sessions in the swimming pool at their eye-popping, 22-acre estate, Villa Casablanca.

But there was a fly buzzing angrily in the boys' *la dolce vita* bouillabaisse: David Foster—the hard-driving, success-smug Lord of The Manor—brayed and bullied like a stereotypical wicked stepfather out of Central Casting, constantly nagging and castigating Brody and Brandon as idle, skirt-chasing slackers who needed discipline...and a work ethic, by God!

Linda, of course, would hear none of it. These were her darling little boys— actually, the fruit of the loins of Olympic decathlon gold medalist Bruce Jenner, who'd sired them back in the days before the bizarre facelift that made him look like a bitch. Bruce was the man Mommy had married after Elvis died—but had never played the part of Daddy in the boys' lives, according to Brody and Brandon. They were toddlers when Linda Thompson married David Foster, so they'd never really interacted with Jenner. (A shame, really, since Jenner married the ex-wife of O.J. Simpson pal and lawyer Robert Kardashian, and became stepfather to a houseful of hot daughters, including bombshell Kim Kardashian. The whole family stars in its own Reality TV show on the E! channel.)

But David Foster, de facto, was the only dad the boys had ever known. A hugely talented and successful musical entrepreneur, he was basically a good and decent man, but expected his boys—who'd dropped out of college and talked vaguely of breaking into acting, or music, or something—to hustle their lazy butts and *become* somebody! But the more Foster nagged, the angrier Linda got—and the couple had actually agreed that they were going to seek a divorce.

Into this volatile mix wandered, in the summer of 2004, a USC film student named Spencer Pratt (who now stars on the reality show "The Hills.") He'd known Brody and Brandon since his teen years, when they'd all attended the elite Crossroads School in Santa Monica. Pratt—like every breathing soul on this planet, as it sometimes seems—wanted to create and produce a blockbuster Reality TV show. He'd sketched out a proposal for following a professional surfer around the world, catching the wave of the visually beautiful sport, but showing the brutality of pro surfing competitions, the always-imminent danger of bone-busting wipeout—and the threat of death.

After videotaping a ton of footage, Pratt showed it to Fox development executives—but the dudes did not hang ten.

Pratt, needing a new plan, then gave thought to the hi-jinks he'd observed over the years at Malibu's legendary Villa Casablanca. Pratt knew the Foster family dynamic well. He was well aware of the tensions between super-rich and powerful patriarch David—with his 14 Grammy wins over a career of producing such star clients as Streisand, Jackson, Dion and Diamond—and trophy wife Linda Thompson, the unshakably charming actress with the intriguing link to the King of Rock and Roll, whose bed she'd shared in the year before he died. Add to all of this, Pratt enthused to anyone in showbiz who'd listen, a fabulous 22-acre jewel of an estate smack in the middle of Malibu—just a coke-spoon's throw from star neighbors like Britney Spears. It was perfect Reality TV!

When Pratt pitched his idea to David and Linda—who needed more fame and fortune like a hole in the head—he was thrilled, and somewhat surprised, when he got an almost instant thumbs-up. Despite the tension between Linda and David Foster, who fully intended to divorce, the embattled couple somehow came to the bizarre decision (like Danny and Gretchen) that letting cameras and a film crew invade their home on nearly a 24-hour basis was a fabulous idea because…well, who knows, it might mend the relationship (Yeah, that's the ticket!) and…and, er…well, it might be a springboard to music and acting careers for dropouts Brody and Brandon.

David Foster was desperate for the boys to make something of themselves—and they were just as anxious for a slice of the fame and fortune Hollywood kids grow up around. In their crowd of rich and famous offspring, if you aren't a star by the time you're 25, you're a near-failure.

Would-be producer Pratt's timing was perfect. Even the rich and famous get sucked in by the lure of Reality TV, and for the Fosters, it looked like win-win no matter how you sliced it. Aspiring actor Brody, 21, and Brandon, 23, a striving musician, would use the show as a springboard to the top—just as Paris Hilton, Nicole Richie and Kelly Osbourne had done before them. Brandon & Brody were the kids of Hollywood rich folks, dammit, and they just could not settle for that dreary dead-end that the rest of us know as "real" life. Brandon put it perfectly in the pilot episode of "Princes of Malibu" when he whined, "I didn't ask for this life. It was not a question, before I was born. This is my situation, and I'm doing the best I can."

So the boys sweet-talked and fast-talked already half-convinced Mommy and Step-Daddy—who wanted to help their sons battle through the too-damn-real agonies of digging out from under the born-rich syndrome. As for the...er, grownups, David and Linda Foster finally bought into the Reality TV show idea because they hoped, incredibly, that it somehow might mend their family problems.

So David helpfully suggested bringing the project to GRB Productions, which had produced A&E's bizarre celeb family show about Mafioso John Gotti's daughter Victoria and her three sons, "Growing Up Gotti." GRB loved the idea, sold it to Fox TV....

...and then the fun really began!

If you look with the jaundiced eye of a Jennifer Aniston at Reality TV shows, you eventually realize you're not watching so-called "unscripted TV" at all. It's manufactured melodrama, shaped by smart, cynical producers who are hired to create chaos by manipulating the truth of any given situation.

When these sharp-eyed manipulators noted the tension between David Foster and his sons, they did what reality producers do—they amplified and exaggerated the hell out of it! Think of a grain of truth as a grain of sand inserted into an oyster, i.e., the Foster family—in hopes of ending up with a beautiful pearl. But if your oyster is already ailing—à la the dysfunctional Fosters—all you get is one hell of an irritated oyster.

So, using the tension between slacker playboy sons and short-fused stepfather, the producers persuaded them all to stage over-the-top, outrageous stunts to juice up the show…to make it "dramatic." Not ignorant of the demands of showbiz, The Fosters & Sons played along…quite enthusiastically.

In one episode, after repeatedly threatening to throw Brody and Brandon out of his Malibu mansion, David didn't just lock the doors on them, as he might in real life. Oh, no, no, no—this was *Reality* TV. Instead, the Wicked Step-Daddy literally *bricked* up the entrances to the boys' bedrooms.

And when he had one son's car towed—an unlikely action in real life because it would have triggered World War 3 with wife Linda—David Foster took it all the way to the reality limit…and has the lad's vehicle towed ALL THE WAY TO ARIZONA!

OH, HA, HA, HA!

Reality? Here's the "real" truth: the whole damn show was a lie, start to finish. In the first place, David Foster didn't have to kick the boys out of Villa Casablanca because they *weren't living there* anymore. They'd been sharing a family home nearby. In the second place, David Foster didn't even own Villa Casablanca—he'd sold it to software mogul Larry Ellison around the time that filming started.

David and Linda were actually still living at their once and former Shangri-La, but they didn't bother to reveal that they no longer owned it, until the show debuted months later.

But here's The Big Lie—the Fosters were faking togetherness to make the show happen. The only "real" part of the show was the simmering hostility boiling under the "happy family" surface—so perfectly exploited by the ruthless-for-a-laugh producers. Incredibly—for viewers, at least—just *one* day after "Princes" premiered on national TV, the boil finally burst: Linda Thompson filed for divorce in a burst of headlines.

"The Princes of Malibu" was a total bomb. It was cancelled just 11 days after it debuted to an audience of 4.5 million—and a savaging by the press. The *National Enquirer* interviewed Foster family pal/show creator Spencer Pratt, who remarked that the clan "made the Osbournes look cuddly." Gossip columns like the *New York Post's* Page Six snarked and sneered, and David Foster—true to type to the very end—was captured on-camera exploding at an interviewer from the syndicated Hollywood fluff-a-ganza "The Insider."

David Foster never consented to an interview after the show folded, according to the *Los Angeles Times*. He did make one statement, saying that the show "exaggerated" what he called "a very real family dynamic." The show's producers—mealy-mouthing a mile-a-minute, and who in Hollywood would blame them?—told the *Times* they'd never intended for "Princes" to be taken too seriously.

"It was meant to play funny—the show is about cause and reaction. Make the jokes. People laugh." Enjoy a chuckle, folks, as we watch a humiliated family disintegrate before our TV-jaded eyes.

Oh, ha, ha, *HA!*

Nope, the producers piously insisted—they had only done what any television producers would do; use the jangly, edgy tension between Foster and his stepsons as a plot device: Spoiled Playboys vs. Embittered Super-Rich Step-Dad Who Controls the Purse-Strings! Except....

...following that scenario, isn't it kind of unlikely that cranky Step-Dad would allow Brandon and Brody—in real life, anyway—to host a drive-in movie extravaganza on their step-dad's immaculate front lawn. Wouldn't he have forbidden it, in real life, anticipating the complaints from neighbors—which actually did rain down big-time when they filmed the noisy stunt?

Hey, it's not real...it's *reality!* Like the man said, "Make the jokes...make the people laugh."

"Oh, wait a second," Jennifer Aniston might say. "Isn't that what we do in sitcoms? Whatever happened to sitcoms?"

(Er, they're all in...re-runs, Jen. Check your listings.)

And here's a final note from that creator of chaos, Spencer Pratt, the family friend who dreamed up the idea and sold it. After Linda filed for divorce, he cried crocodile tears.

"I'm crazy upset because I feel responsible in a sense. We went into this thing knowing full well how volatile the situation was in this family. I was thinking, 'What we're doing here is either going to tear this family apart...or they'll end up killing each other.'"

Hey, two tough choices, Spence—but what the hell! It's a tough job, but some reality producer's gotta do it, right?

In the aftermath of the Fosters' Great Family Adventure, Brody reportedly told mom Linda that it was a great experience, but "I really want to move on." He's taking acting lessons and going on auditions.

Brandon, while conceding that his stepfather is an angry guy with a short fuse, concedes he's still the only dad he's ever known. All things considered, they have a good relationship. He even justifies Foster's temper, "It always comes down to my mom as the final say. He was never able to have the control, so he's looked for smaller ways to feel it." Brandon's now touring the world with his band, Big Dume.

Looking back on it all, Linda Thompson makes a mighty attempt to draw a dead-eye bead on Reality TV, but she's apparently still unsure about what's really "real." She told the *Los Angeles Times:*

"You take a modicum of truth and expand upon it until it's not recognizable as the truth—which is pretty much an accurate description of what we did.

"What *is* reality? I'm still struggling with that one."

Go sit with Jennifer, hon.

In a written statement released after the debacle that ended his marriage, talented lyricist David Foster delivered the pitch-perfect last word when he said:

"The end of a relationship has three sides: his, hers…and the truth."

Put *that* to music, pal!

*

QUESTION FOR JENNIFER ANISTON: Don't you agree that Reality TV shows like "Breaking Bonaduce" and "Princes of Malibu" aid in the emotional healing of dysfunctional family "survivors" like yourself—helping you realize that you're not alone, for example? And isn't it comforting to learn that while we decide which "Friends" we'll make—no one gets to choose their family?

Before you answer, Jen—and speaking, of course, as an alleged "mommy-from-hell" victim—please accept this offer you just can't refuse: if, after reading about the "Monster Mom" in the next chapter, you still believe that yours was the worst, we'll refund the price of this book.

Fair enough, my "Friend"? By the way, did you hear that Justin Timberlake shares your disdain for "American Idol"? But even he admits he's still in that "You Know You Want To Watch" category. Justin told an interviewer, "I despise it—and yet, I'm fascinated."

You despise it, too, Jen…so you're halfway there!

* * *

Chapter *Eleven*

FUHGEDDABOUDIT!... GROWING UP GOOMBAH....
MAFIA PRINCESS CONS NY DAILY NEWS....

The gangster family chronicle "Growing Up Gotti" started life as a killer show! It debuted in 2004 and did...er, gangbusters, even though...*bada bing!*...it quickly got whacked by those *putana* TV critics.

But, hey...*FUHGEDDABOUDIT!*

The average viewer—the *paisans*, ya know what I mean?—loved this offbeat reality peek into the bizarre lifestyle of big-haired, blonde Mafia princess Victoria Gotti and her tight-knit *La Famiglia* of three hair-gelled, *bello* bam-boy-nos sired by ex-hubby Carmine Agnello, who unfortunately could not appear due to his prolonged prison incarceration on a, whaddyacallit...racketeering beef.

When the show aired, it immediately hijacked an audience of 3.2 million—a huge number for cable—proving that when it comes to killing an audience, the family that slays together, stays together!

Capish?

"Growing Up Gotti" stands as A&E's highest-rated series ever. But after its fast charge out of the starting gate, it faded before the first turn. From 3.2 million, it limped to 1.5 million in just three weeks. Still, the series lasted an astounding three seasons, despite savage reviews like this one by *Variety* critic Robert Hofler, who's lucky he didn't end up sleeping with the fishes...*ya know what I mean?*

Wrote Hofler: "A&E has the potential for a sleeper hit with its new Reality TV show 'Growing Up Gotti,' but they clearly muffed the title. 'Mommy as Monster' is closer to the target. Like so much of vintage Reality TV, the major pleasure of 'Gotti' comes in imagining what the producers did off-camera to make their subjects look like fools on-camera. The twist here: Victoria Gotti is one of the show's producers and her three teenage sons are the subjects. Imagine the Medea-like possibilities! Victoria Gotti is, of course, the best-selling author ('The Senator's Daughter'), *Star* columnist and daughter of the late mobster John 'Dapper Don' Gotti. Her former life and current appearance are so tacky in their life-affirming exuberance that even the format clichés of Reality TV never threaten to dominate this woman. Then again, she is the producer."

Bada-*boom!* Has this guy got guts, or what?

Next, Hofler put the hit out on Victoria's sons: "As for those aforementioned Gotti/Agnello boys (Carmine, John, Frank), it is clear that the current hair-gel epidemic among young men continues unabated. But that's the least of the crime: Like so many *boobousie* of the tube, they mistake air-time for fame, loudness for charm, logorrhea for wit…. It's obvious these boys need a mother to protect them from their producer. And they say Victoria Gotti's dad was a bad guy."

Bada-*bang!!*

Keep checking under the car before you hit that ignition, pal.

A&E, which prides itself on its classy profile, took heavy heat from some critics for glorifying organized crime, showcasing a foul-mouthed, dysfunctional family living in luxury on blood money made by Mafia don John Gotti.

"Growing Up Gotti" centered around Mama Gotti's "hilarious" adventures with her difficult, spoiled sons and various incompetent assistants while juggling her new job as columnist for *Star* magazine. (Full disclosure: *Star* is a celebrity-oriented magazine published by the media giant that also owns the paper I write for, the *National Enquirer*. But I have never met, or even spoken to, Victoria Gotti. *Capish?*)

Right out of the box after the show aired, "Growing Up Gotti" got slammed by Italian-American groups—who threatened a boycott of sponsors because it gave Italians a bad name.

"This show reinforces a commonly held belief that most Italian-Americans are either bums, bigots, buffoons or barely literate," said Stephen R. Aiello of the National Italian American Foundation. "Enough is enough. We'll look at the sponsors and think about a boycott."

The Order of the Sons of Italy in America reported they'd been flooded by phone calls and e-mails attacking Gotti-TV.

"The only reason A&E decided to make Victoria Gotti the star of a reality program is because she's the daughter of a man who has disgraced his family name and ethnic heritage," charged spokesperson Dona De Sanctis. "Hollywood and TV have typecast us, and keep turning mobsters into mythical figures. Tony Soprano and Victoria Gotti are not role models."

Huffed A&E: "The show is about who Victoria Gotti is—not ethnicity. She feels she's depicting a positive Italian-American role model who is a successful author, columnist and mother."

By the show's third season, much of the audience had tired of Diva Gotti's egomaniacal antics, her preening-peacock teen sons and their obscene boasting about such episodes as a specially arranged vacation with a porn star...not to mention the whole "La Dolce Vita"-meets-"Goodfellas" lifestyle at their Long Island mansion, which often looked like it needed a good dusting.

For many viewers, warm, fuzzy family feelings had chilled gradually as scary Gotti pals like teenage hood Nicholas "Fat Nick" Minucci—who made hate-crime headlines for bouncing a baseball bat off the skull of a black man as punishment for the "crime" of walking through a white neighborhood—would drop by to feast on *scungilli a la linguini,* or whatever, with his goombahs.

Going into the third season, "Growing Up Gotti" had lost a whopping 50 percent of its audience. The now-desperate diva, determined to make headlines and pump up ratings to save her show, concocted an ill-advised PR campaign that shocked even the jaded New York tabloid press—and caused her publicist to quit in disgust. On Sunday, August 21, 2005, the *New York Daily News* trumpeted:

"Victoria Gotti Exclusive:
MY BREAST CANCER ORDEAL!"

In the interview, Gotti tugged at the heartstrings of *Daily News* readers, saying that "the day I got my mammogram and the doctor told me I had breast cancer...I had a little pity party for myself and I cried all day...I lost 25 pounds...I was so exhausted, I could barely lift my arms."

WOW! Talk about reality!

Except...it wasn't real.

Just three days later, the rival *New York Post* jeered at the *Daily News* and its front-page "exclusive"—ripping into Gotti with this stop-the-presses headline:

"Gotti's Sick Cancer Sham!"

Page Six editor Richard Johnson had scooped the real story. He wrote: "Victoria Gotti never had breast cancer, as the *Daily News* reported on its front page last Sunday—nor did she ever suffer a heart attack, or earn a law degree."

The story exposed Gotti's cynical scam about supposed breast cancer. She ended up admitting to Johnson that she was "100 percent well." She said she had been diagnosed with pre-cancerous cells—a far cry from cancer. Johnson also got Gotti to admit that earlier stories she'd told the press about suffering a "heart attack" were untrue. She now called it a "heart incident."

And she admitted that she had never earned a law degree, as claimed. More than that, St. John's University, the only college Gotti's known to have attended, told Page Six, "We have no record that she graduated from St. John's."

It got even worse. Once it became crystal-clear that Gotti had cynically perpetrated a cancer scam just for publicity, reported Johnson, "Matthew Rich, her publicist of seven years, quit in disgust...because his best friend's mother had died of breast cancer, a source told Page Six. Rich was said to be revolted that Victoria would promote her third season of 'Growing Up Gotti' by making up such a tearful tall tale." Then...it got worse than worse! The *Post* revealed that just before her faux "cancer scare," Gotti had pitched another whopper to prime-time media outlets like "Dateline NBC"—claiming she was devastated because her "heart defibrillator" had been recalled suddenly by manufacturers. Gotti offered herself up for tear-jerker interviews about this latest tall tale—but only on condition that her "exclusive" would run the weekend before the season debut of "Growing Up Gotti." A "Dateline" source sniffed, "We were not interested."

The *Post's* female columnists were not amused. The day the paper exposed "Gotti's Sick Cancer Scam," Victoria exposed her breasts to one of this author's all-time favorite poison-pens, Andrea Peyser. Andrea wrote a gasp-inducing, hilarious column that began:

"Victoria Gotti unbuttoned her short-sleeved charcoal top and instructed me sternly: 'I want you to feel this.' …Standing there, nude from the waist up in her sumptuous, Old Westbury, Long Island house, Victoria is determined to make me feel her pain. 'This is my pacemaker,' she said, running my fingers over a hard item placed beneath her skin. 'This is my defibrillator and these are all the wires,' she said, tracing my hand over a spider web in her chest.

"And then she starts to cry—but her makeup doesn't run. For the cameras are on hand to work on the latest installment of 'Growing Up Gotti.'

"The show must go on. Victoria has summoned me here to, she hopes, set the record straight about her curious and seemingly ever-changing health status."

As Andrea Peyser conducted the riveting interview, Gotti—wriggling like a pinned snake—shamelessly continued her pathetic attempts at damage control.

"'It's a strange cancer,' Victoria says. Then she interrupts herself. 'Do I call it cancer? Do I not call it cancer? This is a condition best described as a condition that can lead to cancer. It's called a non-invasive cancer….'

"The beautiful timing of these revelations of her 'disease'—or is it?—on the eve of her show's opening is not lost on Victoria. 'I knew how this was going to look,' she said. 'Like I was promoting my show. What a coincidence! One day before Season Three. This is not what I wanted,' she insists."

The very next day, another of this author's fave tabloid killer-babes—*New York Post* TV critic Linda Stasi—piled onto the Mafia princess with this headline: "It's Not Cancer, Gotti—and I Should Know!"

Wrote Linda: "After a lifetime of carefully watched but suspicious mammograms, I was diagnosed with lobular carcinoma *in situ* in my right breast in 2001. I did not then, and do not now, thank God, have breast cancer. Or anything close to it. And neither does reality mother Victoria Gotti!"

Citing medical sources, Linda went on to explain that LCIS—the condition that Gotti called "breast cancer"—is not a cancer. Its presence means there is a small risk of developing breast cancer later in life. Even so, most women with LCIS do not develop breast cancer.

Gotti got slammed from all sides—next at bat were breast cancer victims. In a full-page story, the *New York Post* blasted, "Phony Illness Stirs Up Some Real Outrage for Survivors." A member of the Long Island breast cancer group "1 in 9" said it was unthinkable for anyone to use cancer as a promotional tool. "I would be sick…ill…I'm a three-time survivor. I would hope to God it's not a publicity stunt."

Incredibly, Gotti then blamed the whole brouhaha on the *New York Daily News*, claiming that after they'd "browbeaten" her into talking about her condition, they'd cynically exaggerated the seriousness of her illness. As anyone who's ever seen this strident, steam-rolling diva in action knows, nobody browbeats Victoria Gotti!

A&E, the producers of "Growing Up Gotti," refused to comment as the bad press continued. But several sources at the network, noted the *Post,* flatly denied allegations that Victoria's cancer scam was part of a public relations push for the show.

Sources who know Gotti also told the *Post* that she often exaggerates ailments. When one insider asked about a scar on her chin that looked like it was related to plastic surgery, she identified it as a scar resulting from surgery on her brain—which is, of course, quite a long way from her chin.

Shortly after that, in December, "Growing Up Gotti" was whacked, to put it in the phraseology Victoria would be familiar with as daughter of the "Dapper Don." She and her three hair-gel-loving sons, Carmine, John and Frankie, ages 20, 19 and 15, had had a pretty good run. They'd actually managed to complete 40 episodes of the show. As for Gottti, her job at *Star* magazine had ended amid acrimony, so her new mission in life became supporting her boys in various business enterprises—a tanning salon, a restaurant…and the music business.

From Page Six of the *Post,* Friday, November 18, 2005: "Victoria Gotti can't stand the fact that her son Carmine Agnello has a lousy voice. He appeared on VH1's realty show *But Can They Sing?*—along with Bai Ling, Morgan Fairchild, Antonio Sabato Jr. and several others. The idea was to see how well these celebrities did as singers. Victoria went nuts after British comedian/host Ant, who was judging, said,

'Words can't describe how I feel about that performance. You sound like a cat caught in a muffler.' She went crazy, throwing a *Sopranos*-size tantrum, according to eyewitnesses. She stormed backstage, halted production and screamed at producers to remove the offending comment from the show. When asked why she was so upset, Victoria said, 'I'm just being a mother, protecting her son.' Ant chimed in, saying 'This is not a high school play.' It was suggested that Ant be escorted to his car by security."

HEY, that's-a some feisty Mama Mia, eh?...

FUHGEDDABOUDIT, right?

Ya know what I mean?

*

In a curious, ill-conceived footnote to the exotic gangland-reality genre, HBO then lapsed into a what-the-hell-were-they-thinking moment and green-lighted "House Arrest"—a half-hour show awkwardly billed as a "docu-comedy based on reality."

Federal prosecutors were furious! The show chronicled the woes of alleged racketeer/mobster Chris Colombo, who had been arrested for racketeering and gambling in 2004, but was freed to await trial after posting $1 million bail. Colombo was placed under house arrest, had to wear an ankle bracelet, and was not allowed to travel further than the vicinity of his home in upstate New York.

But then...FUHGEDDABOUDIT! Suddenly, this guy's starring in his own reality show, with cameras following him everywhere—including to a strip joint. Bada-BING! The fuzz freaked when they witnessed Colombo getting his leg—which was all ache-y from that nasty old ankle bracelet—massaged by a topless lap-dancer, and indulging in other shenanigans. Outraged prosecutors went to a judge, insisting that the reality show was making a mockery of the bail agreement—maybe even violating it.

Next thing ya know...Bada-BOOM! HBO whacked the show after just one episode. That killed the Gangland Reality genre, and here's a prediction: its corpse will never surface again, unless....

Unless some brilliant, caring, Reality TV producer—criteria that eliminates 98 percent of the breed—conceives a show that combines the danger and drama of gang life with a heart-warming, humanitarian twist. Here's the pitch:

Our cameras take you to the mean streets of South Central Los Angeles! Suddenly, you're pimp-walkin' the 'hood with America's scariest gang-bangers—the Crips!

But don't be afraid…yet! An over-the-hill gang of do-gooder, wealthy old white dudes have volunteered to donate expertise, time and money in a community-supported effort to show real-life killah gangstah's how going straight and starting a business can keep them in the Benjamins—and out of jail. Our show would be called:

"Crips: Escape From the Hood!"

Sound crazy? In Guatemala, TV producers have actually turned the country's out-of-control street gang scourge into the plot for a reality show, putting young thugs up together in one house, then bringing in business leaders to coach them on how to launch a business from the ground up—sales, customer service, marketing, motivation. Gang members were given seed money for start-up costs, plus help and advice on how to put together a formal business plan, etc. Then they launched the pilot project—and the initial results were outstanding.

In a recent show, ten former gang members enthusiastically worked together as they launched a car-wash and a shoe repair shop. Both businesses are now up and running, and producers hope their show will inspire other gang members to turn their lives around.

But now that the reality show has ended, real life begins. The question: Can these ex-gangsters make their new businesses prosper and grow? Stay tuned for the inevitable sequel, which will ask the stay-tuned question:

Will the gangsters stay straight—or end up back on the streets, robbing and killing fellow Guatemalans? Said Sergio Guiterrez: "I know if we trust in God, he will help us. We've got a chance."

* * *

Chapter *Twelve*

DOPE-CHALLENGED AARON SORKIN DUBS
REALITY TV "CRACK".... THAT DIRTY LITTLE
REALITY SECRET CALLED FRANKEN-BYTING....
AND BEWARE THE SCARY CONFESSIONAL.

Jennifer Aniston, an inspiration for our investigation into the yin and the yang of Reality TV, just found a staunch—and formidable—ally who agrees with her ringing denunciation that, "I don't go along with that 'Idol' shit!"

Speaking at a Hollywood Television Critics Association panel to introduce the Fall 2006 shows, Aaron Sorkin—the creator of HBO's "The West Wing" and writer/executive producer of NBC's "Studio 60 on the Sunset Strip"—was asked what he thought about our new and allegedly vacuous reality-TV culture.

Responded Sorkin: "When things that are very mean-spirited and voyeuristic go on TV, I think it's [like] bad crack in the schoolyard."

The audience of journalists erupted in laughter, and the suddenly embarrassed Sorkin—who'd narrowly escaped felony charges for possession of cocaine and hallucinogenic mushrooms by entering rehab in 2001—asked himself ruefully, and rhetorically: *"Why* did I use that word?"

Despite the hilarious gaffe, Sorkin is a serious player in the world of scripted TV. And like Jennifer Aniston, he professes contempt for a genre that millions of people—not just in America, but around the world—embrace with near-fanatical enthusiasm.

The yin and the yang.

Them against…us?

Do we dismiss Aniston and Sorkin as elitist snobs? Are they just bubba-snarkin'—or should we take heed of an implicit warning in their scathing contempt?

Really…what the hell is so dangerous about Reality TV? Why are Mommy and Daddy warning us against what makes us feel so good? Sure, Shakespeare stirs our souls, makes us laugh, makes us cry…but so does "American Idol," dammit!

Just years ago, the reality genre barely existed. Then came the Big Bang…"Springer"…"Cops"…and the formidable "Survivor," still surviving after 15 seasons. It created a world…then a universe. And it's barely been explored. So let's take a voyage "Inside Reality TV." Let's explore what it is, how it's put together, and meet the professionals who create it.

First, let's break the universe down and take a look at the planets—those all-too-familiar categories that populate the genre (See how many shows you can list under each category, e.g., "Amazing Race" and "I'm a Celebrity…Get Me Out of Here!" would go under the first).

1) Help, I'm Lost!

2) Scare Me!

3) Hi, Stranger…. Let's Shack Up!

4) God, I'm Ugly!

5) Get Me Laid!

6) Take My Wife, Please!

7) Take My Kids, Please!

8) Fix My House, Please!

9) Gimme a Job!

10) Make Me a Star!

And on and on…new categories of Reality TV keep springing up. There are cops-and-robbers shows, celeb-reality shows, seduce-my-mate shows, sports shows, make-me-rich shows, fun-with-fashion shows, gay-guys-makeover-straights shows….

But what mysterious power created this universe? What are the physics that hold it together? Okay, enough of the serious scientific metaphors. Let's have some fun with this quick-and-easy multiple-choice quiz.

Question: What makes entertainment TV the planet's hottest new entertainment phenomenon? 1. People are so hot to whore themselves out for 15 minutes of fame they'll do or say *anything* to get on Reality TV. 2. EVERYBODY loves watching Fame Whores acting like idiots. 3….

Ah, *fuhgeddaboudit!* There is no "3." The answer, of course, is *all* of the above. Even in fun, it's impossible to invent semi-plausible answers to the question that wouldn't fool anyone for even a minute—with the possible exception of, say, Jessica Simpson, Britney Spears, K-Fed or Paris Hilton.

The author is tempted, at this point, to launch into painful erudition explaining the Faustian legend and other sinister deals struck by avaricious network Suits, but let's keep it simple: Reality TV is a perfect devil's bargain, driven by greed and raging egos. Producers and networks want cheap shows, so they whisper seductively of fame, which…*who knows?*…might lead to fortune. Average Joes and Average Janes want cheap thrills, so they figure, "Hey, what the hell?"…then happily humiliate themselves for that all-too-brief, but golden moment in the spotlight. It's worse than karaoke—Satan's most diabolical invention.

ATTENTION, PLEASE, READ CAREFULLY: Just in case the news hasn't reached you folks out there in Television Land, let me make it crystal clear…. Nine times out of ten, *you won't get paid a dime* to be a contestant or participant on a Reality TV show—unless, of course, you're Jessica Simpson, Britney Spears, K-Fed or Paris. In fact, you'll be damn lucky if your giddy little ego trip doesn't end up actually *costing* you money. One young woman who appeared on ABC's "Hooking Up" complained: "None of us were compensated for being contestants, but the worst part was that producers refused to pay for anything. One time we were filming in a New York bar and they didn't even offer us a drink. They never picked up a tab. Not a single drink, dinner or cab fare. They paid for nothing during the taping of the show, which stretched over several months. Not makeup, not hair, not wardrobe. I was stunned by how cheap they were."

Despite that, she admitted, "It was fun being followed around by cameras, but at the end of it I felt exploited—taken advantage of. But…would I do it again? Yes, I would."

Read that last sentence again, carefully. (I'll wait.)

Okay, got the picture? The point is, you can't spell reality without "real," folks. As in "real" people. People just like you—and Yours Truly, of course. The name of the game is gettin' screwed and LOVIN' IT!

And here's consolation for Average Joes and Average Janes: Please know that you're not alone when it comes to getting screwed in Reality TV—or, as we call it in Hollywood, the Wal-Mart of Showbiz. Your fellow screw-ee's are the one thousand-plus writers, editors and producers who often work 18 hour days, who have no health care or pension benefits, and can be fired at an instant's notice. It's slave labor, pure and simple, and the TV networks get away with exploiting these creative people, who are often viewed as drones, because they can pay exactly what they want to pay for a show—and not one damn penny more. Networks make insulting lowball offers to production companies with no qualms because they know there's always a crowd of heavy-breathing competitors ready to play ball for peanuts.

These down-trodden producers work like mules to keep you entertained. Quoting ubiquitous "Swan" producer Rebecca Hertz, who also worked on the WB's "Big Man on Campus": "I'd often wrap at 1 a.m. and need to be on another shoot at 8 a.m. Post-production…was even worse. On a crash schedule, there'd be a day editor and a night editor, but only one producer. I'd be there from 10 a.m. to 4 a.m.— and then have to go back. It would be dawn, and I'd be going home."

Reality TV writer-producer Todd Sharp, the father of two, told the *New York Times* that between jobs on these shows, he becomes completely demoralized. "I can't keep doing this much longer if the conditions don't improve," he says. "I can't see the end of the road for me. I just hobble in." Worse, he adds, "You're working years and years and you're not putting anything away."

Sounds like a lousy job, doesn't it? Long hours, low pay—and not much fun. But it gets even worse....

The Writers Guild is filing suit to stop this exploitation, but don't hold your breath. And just to play devil's advocate for the networks, workers in showbiz usually end up, sooner or later, earning what they're really worth—even though no one in Reality TV wants to admit that. "Writers" who work on Reality TV shows earn anywhere from $1200 a week to $2500 a week. That's less than writers on scripted dramas and comedy shows earn because Reality TV writers aren't really writers, in the strictest sense of the word—which is something else they don't want to admit. But listen to what the marketplace says: by comparison, the minimum Writers Guild rate for a writer on a primetime 13-week scripted show is a hefty $3477 per week. If you get a gig writing comedy for Jay Leno's *Tonight Show*, the rewards get truly insane—up to $15,000 per week.

Now let's repeat again, for emphasis, the mantra that workers in showbiz *usually end up earning what they're really worth*. Any writer familiar with both writing techniques will tell you that creating a script for a finely-honed drama, or comedy, demands far higher creative skill than batting out storylines about contestants who are forced to gobble hog guts...or let spiders crawl over their naked bodies...or who get nailed into a coffin for the night.

Yeah, it's a dirty job, but somebody's damn well gotta do it—that's the bottom line. In Hollywood, anyone wearing a "WILL WORK FOR FOOD" sign is either homeless, or a Reality TV writer. Trust me when I tell you that studios and production companies will never fret about finding journeymen capable of cranking out what the genre requires. And why do you think the studios and networks didn't fight harder to avert the 2007 Writers Guild strike? Because the Suits know there are non-Guild writers who can cross the picket lines and whip up cheap Reality TV shows until the WGA throws in the towel.

Once the strike is over, if the Writers Guild fails in its fight to force moguls to throw oppressed reality writer/prisoners heftier crusts of bread, the desperate clatter of tin cups banging against cell bars will become even more deafening. But that won't scare the screws…er, Suits, who guard the Big House known as TinselTown.

Actually, pay scales aren't the worst issue, according to David Young, the organizing director for the Writers Guild, who's championing the cause of the downtrodden Reality TV workers. "It's a burnout lifestyle. Sometimes it pays okay. A lot of times it doesn't. There are no benefits. It requires people to work on compressed schedules. Something will be supposed to take 16 to 20 weeks, and then they hear the network wants it in 12 weeks."

David Rupel, a veteran Reality TV producer of such shows as "Big Brother" and "Temptation Island," talks of how NBC would suddenly decide, at the last-minute, to extend the length of a 60-minute show. Explained Rupel: "A week before they would say, 'We want it to be 90 minutes'—and you would have to work seven days a week to do that. But my paycheck didn't change. They think of us as filler."

Yet, Rupel points out, "When NBC was super-sizing 'Friends' and 'Will and Grace,' they had to pay everybody extra money."

Getting the picture, reality fans? The networks, according to this expert who knows the game, do not value writing for Reality TV as highly as writing for scripted shows like "Friends," "Will and Grace," "The Sopranos," etc. Speaking for exploited Reality TV writers, one of their number groused to an interviewer: "We have to take all the little bits and give it a clear story arc, give it a structure out of what in reality might be a big mess. That, to me, is writing."

AUTHOR'S NOTE: That, to me, is shaping events, dude. It's a skill, certainly, but nothing akin to creating characters and events from scratch on a blank page.

In fact, one of the most creative aspects of so-called "writing" on Reality TV shows is that dirty little secret called, "Franken-byting." This is the practice of creating lies by editing words and phrases spoken by contestants so that the person is made to say something they never said at all. Franken-byting! Such a lovely word, created from "Frankenstein"—as in "a monster manipulated by its ruthless creator"—and "byte," as in sound-byte, the TV industry term for a brief recorded statement. Now that's *writing!* But what exactly does the term mean?

Imagine for a moment that you're a Reality TV show producer/writer and your "stars"—who are operating under the delusion that they should be keeping it "real"—just aren't delivering the bright, jazzy, sexy, emotional quotes you need to make a socko show. One ex-"Bachelor" staffer revealed in an interview that when you're working for "desperate people who had to deliver a story in a few days," you don't let facts get in the way of "creating" a good story.

So what's the first rule of showbiz? Showbiz comes *first!* If you're a Reality TV writer/producer, you dish up some phony drama by tweaking the dialogue with tried-and-true tricks, so….

…it's Franken-byte time! You lock yourself in an editing bay with a skilled editor, then run through all the video footage of the person whose dialogue you want to change. Then listen carefully until you find the words you need from statements they've made in various takes. You re-record the words, stitch them together and…Yes, Master!…you've invented an even-juicier "reality," you sneaky little Franken-byte-er!

Freelance reality show editor Jeff Bartsch, who worked on the NBC series "Blind Date," admitted to an interviewer that his bosses often ordered him to steam up the action through creative editing. "You can really take something black—and make it white!"

Rebecca Hertz, a producer on Fox's makeover show, "The Swan," admits that she manipulated a statement by the loving husband of the show's first winner, Rachel Love-Fraser. Even though the man raved about how beautiful his wife is, Hertz expertly twisted his words for shock value. "I cut it down to him saying she looks average…so he sounded mean and horrible. He was furious." More to the point, so was his devastated wife—and that's the nitty-gritty. Reality TV loves steam, but the slam-dunk it's looking for is sweat and tears.

Here's another slick industry trick: if you still can't extract the word, or phrase, that will allow you to manipulate reality, or you need to make it appear that your reality stars are about to either beat each other up, or fall into bed together, just conduct what's called a "confessional." Here's how it works:

Imagine that your "star" is an Islamic terrorist, and you are not allowed to resort to physical torture, but can force him to endure ruthless, endless interrogation until exhaustion and/or frustration finally makes him volunteer the response you want. By badgering your subject with the same questions, over and over, you'll get different words and phrases to use in your Franken-byte-ing fun. You'll elicit a wide range of emotions and, hopefully screams, tears and revelations about kinky sexual fantasies, bomb plots, or whatever!

On the MTV series "Laguna Beach," a fascinating love triangle among hot babes L.C. and Kristin, and handsome dude Stephen, had viewers riveted—but insiders reveal that their strictly platonic relationships only appeared to be hot and sexy, thanks to camera magic and creative editing.

Sometimes, all it takes is the right—or, wrong—sound effect. "Joe Millionaire" contestant Sarah Kozer exploded after discovering that wily producers had deceptively jazzed up a scene where she and bachelor Evan Marriott took a walk behind some trees. Although absolutely nothing improper took place, Kozer insists, suggestive sounds were added to make it seem as if the couple had indulged in oral sex. Kozer also alleged that the producers added faux sizzle to another scene by inserting the phrase, "It's better if we're lying down!"—which was actually dialogue she'd uttered earlier—thereby creating a sexual context where none had existed.

It's not always necessary to change a word or add a sound to mislead your TV audience—you can simply take an existing scene and insert it out of context. Anyone who ever watched "The Amazing Race" remembers allegedly nasty-ass contestant Jonathan Baker, who forged a reputation as one of Reality TV's most notorious villains. Scene after scene showed Baker brow-beating and screaming at his *Playboy* model wife Victoria, infuriating co-contestants, and antagonizing the natives of every nation the show traveled through.

Baker claims he was victimized by the producers, who resorted to various tricks designed to create what Reality TV loves: a villain who's fun to hate. He points to a shocking example of out-of-context editing in a scene where a taxi driver, apparently tired of Baker's bad manners, orders him out of the cab. In fact, says Baker, the cab had been in an accident and could no longer be driven, which is why he was asked to find another cabbie.

"I got the worst rap of anyone in reality television ever," rages Baker.

"Apprentice 4" contestant Mark Garrison complained to an interviewer that producers made him look like a real yo-yo—by showing him playing with a yo-yo during an important presentation made by his team. In reality, the yo-yo scene was shot at another time, then inserted into the presentation scene to create maximum embarrassment for Mark.

WOW! How's that for ripping the lid off Reality TV, folks? Are you shocked? Horrified? Do you now believe that every network and every big-shot creator of Reality TV—movers and shakers like Mark Burnett, Mike Weiss, Andrew Glassman, Mike Darnell, David Martin, etc.—are villains who cynically cheat the audience that feeds them? Let me repeat the mantra I cited at the beginning of this book—the catch-phrase written for "National Enquirer TV," the show I created:

You *Know* You Want To Watch!

Don't kid a kidder! Every single one of you out there in Reality TV-Land knows darn well what's going on—although you might not admit it, even to yourself. Oh, not the details, perhaps. It's like they say about sausage…you love eating it, but you just don't want to think about how it's made. Remember my caveat, friends…*caveat emptor.*

We have met The Boss, and s/he is You!

If you didn't want these folks to put on a show unless it was "real" to the highest journalistic standards, you'd reach for that remote control quicker than a Texas rattler crossing a hot rock, as Dan Rather might say. Showbiz is God, and must be served.

* * *

Chapter *Thirteen*

BLOWING THE LID OFF "FAKE" REALITY TV....
"QUEER EYE" SCRIPT IS THE SMOKING GUN....
ONE MAN'S POIGNANT STRUGGLE TO GIVE UP HAIR POMADE!

Years ago, I started reading a sharp, funny young *Time* magazine columnist named Joel Stein. Joel's the best kind of writer, someone who makes you think while you laugh, which I find is a lot tougher than walking and chewing gum at the same time...and I think Paris Hilton would agree. Joel now toils at the *Los Angeles Times,* which published a column he'd written a while back about how Reality TV isn't as real as audiences think. Joel even produced a "smoking gun"—or, "the Pentagon Papers," as he puts it—a hush-hush script from "Queer Eye for the Straight Guy" which proves that reality's really tightly scripted, i.e., unreal.

I interviewed Joel about his take on Reality TV, and it seems he's changed his mind since he wrote the fascinating column excerpted below. Today, Joel says:

"Take 'The Simple Life.' When I watch it, I know that every move was carefully scripted in advance and virtually nothing is ad-lib...but I don't care. I still like it. When you look at the success of the writer James T. Frey, who got whipped by Oprah for partly fictionalizing his memoirs, or the case of writer J.T. Leroy, who turns out to be the alter ego of another person, and that so-called 15-year-old 'Lonely Girl' on the Internet, I think people accept all that stuff now. They're more likely to accept altered reality."

This from the guy who fearlessly blew the lid off "fake" Reality TV? Here's Joel's earlier *Los Angeles Times* column, followed by an actual excerpt from his mysteriously acquired "Queer Eye" script:

"We all figured some of it was fake: Joe Millionaire's slurping make-out noises, the depth of the relationship between Brigitte Nielsen and Flavor Flav, Jessica Simpson's breasts. And 'reality' was always a misnomer for shows that involve Donald Trump or people on desert islands. But these shows purporting to be unadulterated documentaries are unreal in a more obvious way: They are secretly crafted in advance by writers. And I've got the entertainment equivalent of the Pentagon Papers to prove it. Maybe more like the equivalent of the photo with President Bush holding the fake Thanksgiving turkey in Iraq, but still, they are definitely papers.

"Many of the shows that supposedly follow the real lives of real people are really scripted by real writers, many of whom were unemployed because their sitcoms got replaced by reality programs. So reality shows are just sitcoms starring good-looking people instead of hot actresses and the fat, ugly guys who play their husbands. That's why they're 50% more entertaining.

"Through sources I cannot reveal but would definitely not go to jail to protect, I got hold of a 19-page, single-spaced outline of an upcoming episode of 'Queer Eye for the Straight Guy.' Every moment is planned in advance, including a few specific lines for the straight guy to deliver, which Bravo says is not unusual for any reality show. It's something that people in Hollywood know and think is no big deal...."

Ready to watch the lid blown off the Dream Factory, folks?

(The script Joel Stein snatched from somewhere tells the touching story of Patrick Mullare, a pomaded "guido" who lost 100 pounds and lives in his parents' home. The "Queer Eye" guys give him a makeover, introducing him to the wonders of hair gel, and throw a party where he will hopefully meet the girl of his dreams.) Writes Stein:

"Then there's 'a funny moment' where Patrick, after showering, slips back to his pre-queerified self and almost uses hair gel. The final page of the script is Nora Ephron-worthy."

Here it is, folks, one man's "real" life, as jazzed by writers:

*

#150 - Queer Eye for the Straight Guy

Patrick Mullare

Second Draft/Stanzler/Sorenson

THE SET-UP

PROFILE: Patrick Mullare is a 21 year old senior at Hofstra University. When you first meet him you are struck by the fact that he seems much older. He was born and raised on Long Island, and exudes the tough working class edge one would expect from a character on the Sopranos, his all time favorite show. His Mother has worked for the NYPD for 30 years and his father has a metal shop, a business he started in 1958. His parents are older, Mr. Mullare is 68, Mrs. Mullare is 77, and they have been married 40 years. Patrick had an older brother who died when he was a young boy, so he feels very responsible for his parents, works for his father and is expected to take over the family business. He also lives in the basement of their home instead of on campus, because he feels they need him. In the last 4 years he has lost over 100 lbs. "1/3 of myself" he is proud to say. The extra weight coupled with Scoliosis, a medical condition that causes a lateral curvature of the spine, made High School emotionally difficult for him. He dealt with it by becoming the class clown. He would develop crushes on girls only to be hurt and rejected. The "new" Patrick still carries that pain around. He is still the life of the party, confident, and handsome, but has trouble opening up and trusting that he won't be rejected. He plans on spending second semester in Italy this year, a life long dream. He wants to experience the world, be more open to girls, learn to accept who he is now, and trust people's intentions but needs help taking the first steps.

THE ENDING

EXT. DOCK Patrick's friends have arrived and are helping themselves to wine and beer when Patrick walks up. Everyone is thrilled to see him again and in total shock at his appearance, which he handles all graciously. Patrick serves the grilled fish to his friends from college who compliment him on his appearance and the party. We see Patrick walk over to see him and possibly show interest in him, as he is irresistible. Still Patrick keeps looking down the street…will the girl from the bar come? He sees nothing. We see his parents spying from the front window, his Mother is out of control. Again, down the street, nothing.

Patrick is disappointed and turns back to his guests, cracks a couple jokes, ye old class clown. Over his shoulder a set of car headlights appear and get continuously closer until the car stops. She gets out of the car, Patrick hasn't noticed, she taps him on the shoulder. While we know he is dying inside, on the outside, he is cool as a cucumber, and thrilled to death that she came. He invites her in to see his new place, she accepts, and they walk off into the proverbial sunset. Our fingers are crossed for our boy. Fade out....

Bada-BING! You're *busted*, Reality TV. But wait...I've interrupted a poignant reaction by the irrepressible Joel Stein:

"I never thought a man could cry while reading a reality show script about another man's struggle to lay off pomade...."

Stein points out that the fine-tuned scripting of reality is not confined to "Queer Eye" productions:

"Producer Matt Swanson says that when Ozzy threw a block of wood over a fence and shattered the window of his noisy neighbors during the first season of 'The Osbournes,' it was just a sound effect and a phony reaction shot. We wanted to believe so badly in Reality TV that we believed a man so feeble he can no longer remember whether or not he ate a live bat could somehow throw like Curt Schilling.

"'The Simple Life' is so unreal that people who produce the show refer to it as a 'hybrid sitcom' or a 'soft-scripted show,' a fact Fox does not deny. This fall, when the entire season's gimmick was that Hilton and Richie slept in trailer parks, they checked into hotels all but two nights.

"In an upcoming episode, I found out, Hilton and Richie tell some kids that the best present for their daddy is to get him laid by their mom. So the women go to a bar to score some condoms. The producers had pre-interviewed a guy in a baseball cap who would agree to take them to his apartment to give them some rubbers. But the ever-confused Hilton and Richie went up to the wrong guy, who, not surprisingly, happily agreed to take them to his place.

"The producers, however, yelled, 'Cut,' confusing everyone in the bar, who thought they were at a reality show taping. Then Hilton and Richie started the scene again and approached the baseball-cap guy, because the producers had already lighted his apartment. It seems they had momentarily forgotten how effectively Hilton can act in night vision."

Stein's conclusion:

"Once you find out reality stars actually need help to be that dumb, they somehow stop being entertaining. We wanted to believe reality shows were real because they made us feel like other people's lives were more messed up than our own. Though that may not be true, at least we know that without writers they're just as boring as we are."

Judging by the comments Joel made in our interview, he's changed his mind about not finding reality stars entertaining if they need help being dumb. He now, as pointed out at the beginning of this chapter, happily watches Paris Hilton, even knowing that she's an invention conceived in a writer's brain and birthed on-camera.

That's *hot!*

Speaking of "Queer Eye," this hilarious story made the lead item in my column:

> Fuhggedaboudit! In what's gotta be the dumbest freakin' move ever made by Reality TV, those "QUEER EYE FOR THE STRAIGHT GUY" queens suddenly invaded "The Sopranos" and—with cameras crankin'—chirped cheerily at hairy-bear boss-man James Gandolfini: "HI, there! Ready for your makeover?" That's when all HELL broke loose, say insiders. Turning bright red with anger, Gandolfini snarled, "Get the F*** away from me!" When the message didn't immediately register in the Queer Qar, Gandolfini exploded! "WHO THE F*** LET YOU IN HERE?" he shouted. "TURN THOSE F****N' CAMERAS OFF...NOW!"

Finally reacting to their star's outrage at the on-set ambush, "Soprano's" producers who'd allowed the "Queer Eye" invasion thinking Gandolfini would be amused—quickly started shooing the Gay Gang toward the exit. Boss of all Bosses stormed off to his dressing room, fuming, and refused to return until he'd been assured there wasn't a Queer Eye in sight.

By the way, Joel Stein, you're not the only guy who can dig up "smoking guns." Here comes a hot pistol that'll blow your mind!

* * *

Chapter *Fourteen*

SKANKY HANKY-PANKY!... DUMB GIRLS GET IT
IN THE EAR.... HOW CANDID IS "CANDID"?

Earlier in this book, the Reality TV show "Girls Behaving Badly" was described as "happy-to-misbehave ladies [who] pounce on male prey—who aren't aware they're secretly being videotaped—then cajole them into performing embarrassing tasks that are mainly associated with female taboos, i.e., enlisting a male mark to help search for a 'dropped ovary'...or persuading him to pick up a used tampon."

It's okay for a hidden-camera show like "Girls" to be somewhat scripted—they're creating specific scenarios that their unsuspecting victims, or "marks," need to understand clearly. Otherwise, the mark might not react the way you want him to. Having said that, you'd think that the "Girls"—aspiring actresses—could ad-lib their dialogue, at least to some extent. Instead, as you'll see from this revealing script that I just happened to...er, find on a sidewalk in...er, Burbank, every single word is scripted.

In conversations with one of Hollywood's most knowledgeable writer-producers—a "Mr. X," who worked on this production—he told me:

"Mike, we actually had IFB's—those little earphones you see news-anchors wear—stuck in the girls' ears. They were hidden by hair and makeup. We couldn't trust these ladies to remember anything.... I would actually feed the funny lines right into their ears while they were on camera. One of the 'Girls'—Melissa Howard, who'd become a big star on MTV's The Real World—was supposed to be real funny, but she couldn't ad-lib a burp after a chili-dog. I had to write lines—then actually say them in her ear because she couldn't remember them.

"That was bad enough, but the real phony-baloney action comes when the marks finally are filmed with their genuine 'candid camera' reaction. But 'genuine' or not, if we didn't like it, we'd make them do it over again—our way. First, we'd come running up and tell them they'd been filmed by a hidden camera—and then we'd just lie and tell them that the microphone didn't work...or the camera glitched...whatever...and we'd ask them to perform their 'candid' reaction all over again. But this time, we'd juice it up—and ask them to say lines that we'd written so we could get the reaction we wanted—not their true reaction.

"Strangely enough, no one ever objected. After the girls told the marks they'd been pranked by 'Girls Behaving Badly,' producers would come running up and say to the mark: 'That was GREAT...just great. But we had a technical malfunction and the shot was ruined, so...could you do it all over again. Just act surprised like you did before...only this time, instead of saying X, would you say Y and Z instead. It's funnier that way, don't you think? And you want to look good on camera for the folks back home, right?'

"Then I'd tell the crew: 'Places everybody...we're going again.'

"And we'd do two or three different takes sometimes, until we got the so-called 'candid' reaction we wanted. Is it honest? No, but does anyone care? Audiences want entertainment, and we deliver it. And, by the way, saying a writer has scruples is the same as saying they're unemployed. If I won't do it, if I insist that reality must be real, a hundred other producers will happily take my place."

And why is Mr. X making this dramatic confession now?

"Because I frankly was sickened by the way we tortured some of these so-called 'marks'—the real people we preyed on. Fun is fun, but as you read this script, keep in mind that it caused one mark to flee, hysterically crying once she understood that we were screwing with her—and potentially ruining her business; it ruthlessly coaxed a school teacher to come out of the gay closet in a dream analysis prank; it badgered a kindly old newspaper editor into signing a release, and it caused an intensely shy guy to pee his pants in a prank where he's accused of making passes at men in a cafe.

"I'm not saying this is typical of Reality TV. But it happened, and I'll never feel good about it."

So here's the script, which is quite entertaining to read—or not. It's your choice. Scripts can be difficult to get through. Just glancing at few sections will give you the general idea of how brazen the manipulation can be. Or you can ignore the whole damn thing and just take my word for it. But careful perusal should be more rewarding now that you know what to look for, Reality TV fan. Do you feel shocked? Cheated? Or are you okay with manipulated reality, if it makes you laugh? Read on…and look for the "Note from Mr. X" toward the end!

(By the way, I have no idea how the show actually looked when it finally aired. It may vary from the script below. The point of this smoking gun is to prove that Reality TV is often scripted TV—the only difference being that it uses so-called "real" people, and manipulates "reality" any damn way it wants!) Here it is. [Drum roll!] The piece de resistance….

GIRLS BEHAVING BADLY

Title/#: "Beard and Groom" (F)/ #3005
Team: Loretta Swit/(Faith)
Talent: Kira
Shoot Date: TBA
Location: TBA
Call Time: TBA
TRT: 3 Minutes
Version: 7/28/03 3:22 PM; FINAL REVISION

INTRO #1: Multiple marks.

KIRA
(to camera)
We all have that girlfriend who can't see that her boyfriend
is gay. You know, kind of like how your grandmother thinks

KIRA

(Continued)

that Siegfried and Roy are just really good friends. Well,
what about the woman who hasn't the slightest notion that
her fiancé is as queer as Richard Chamberlain at a
"Golden Girls" reunion? Do you tell her that she's about to
marry a Mary? Watch what happens as we ask a few wedding
coordinators to help me and my flaming fiancé in this prank
we call, "Beard and Groom."

INTRO #2: One mark.

KIRA

(to camera)

We all have that girlfriend who can't see that her boyfriend
is gay. You know, kind of like how your grandmother
thinks that Siegfried and Roy are just really good friends.
Well, what about the girl who has no idea that her fiancé is as
queer as Richard Chamberlain at a "Golden Girls" reunion?
Do you tell her that she's about to marry a Mary? Watch
what happens as we ask this wedding coordinator to help
me and my flaming fiancé in this prank we call,
"Beard and Groom."

INTRO #3: Abridged, multiple marks.

KIRA

(to camera)

We all have that girlfriend who can't see that her
boyfriend is gay. Well, what about the woman who hasn't
the slightest notion that her fiancé is as queer as
Richard Chamberlain at a "Golden Girls" reunion?
Do you tell her that she's about to marry a Mary? Watch
what happens as we ask a few wedding coordinators to
help me and my flaming fiancé in this prank we call,
"Beard and Groom."

SET-UP:

Wedding planner/Photographer (mark) meets with our bride, Kira, and her outrageously gay fiancé at the Pickwick to go over wedding details. To the mark's astonishment, Kira has no clue that her betrothed is flaming. Mark witnesses the best man be egregiously affectionate with the groom—in Kira's absence. Kira then returns and asks the mark her/his opinion of the fiancé.

IDEAL MARKS:

If multiple marks:

- A super gay guy who is likely to tell Kira that her boyfriend is bent
- An older, conservative woman
- A younger, hip woman

SCENARIO #1

BEATS:

1. The mark is sitting with Kira at the Pickwick to discuss wedding plans. The groom ("David") arrives a minute later.

   a) Kira: "Oh here's my sweetie!" To mark: "This is my fiancé David."

   b) (The mark reacts, e.g., she/he introduces her/himself.)

   c) David: "Sorry I'm late; my Pilates class ran long." To mark: "Gotta look good on my big day, you know."

   d) David to Kira: "Sweetie, I signed you up for some private sessions this month—so your body is worthy of that exquisite dress we got you."

   e) Kira to mark: "How amazing is he?! Most guys don't want to have anything to do with the bride's dress, but David designed mine! It's got an empire waist [she pronounces it like "Empire State Building"]."

   f) David interrupts: "Empire [he pronounces it the haute couture way, "ahm-PEER"]." To the mark: "It's fabulous: cut on the bias, silk charmeuse…god, I want it!"

   g) (The mark reacts.)

2. The trio discusses "the look of the wedding."

   a) Kira: "Before we get into the details, we just want to ask you your opinion about how we want the reception to look. We were thinking some fall colors. What do you think?"

   b) (The mark reacts.)

   c) David: "It's really important to me that it have a real autumnal feel. That's most flattering for me—I see burnt pumpkin, aubergine, you know?"

   d) (The mark reacts)

3. Kira, David, and mark discuss hors d'oeuvres.

   a) Kira: "Oh, and we want lots of appetizers at the reception."

   b) David: "No, sweetie, we want lots of amuse-bouche." To the mark: "You know what that is, right?"

   c) (The mark reacts; most certainly she/he doesn't know)

   d) David explains, slightly exasperated: "It's French for 'mouth amusement'; it's very wee servings of complex hors d'oeuvres. The petite size is perfect: you get a taste but you don't have all those empty calories."

   e) (The mark reacts.)

4. The troika discusses the cake.

   a) Kira (to David): "Sweetie, let's tell her/him what we want for the cake! We really want it to be yummy." David (to mark): "I really want it to be low-carb. Does the Zone make wedding cakes?"

   b) (The mark reacts.)

   c) David (to mark): "I feel very strongly about fondant. It's seamless and I love the porcelain finish it has."

   a. Kira to David: "I really love buttercream though, honey."

   b. David to Kira: "I told you: there is buttercream. You have to crumb-coat the layers with buttercream before the fondant is placed on the cake."

   d) David (to mark): "So we need to make sure the humidity level is set in the reception room or the fondant will weep."

   e) (The mark reacts.)

    f) Kira to mark: "And we want lots of layers."

        a. David to Kira: "Bup, bup, bup.... Tiers, darling. Every tier will have 2 layers."

        b. David to mark: "I don't know how she'd throw this wedding without me."

5. Kira's cell phone rings. She steps out to talk with her mother.

a) Kira answers her phone. To mark: "Excuse me, it's my mom. I'll be right back."

b) As she walks out…MARK SPECIFIC:

    a. [If mark is a woman] Kira to David: "Now behave yourself while I'm gone!"

    b. [If mark is a man] Kira to David: "You guys can talk about the bachelor party while I'm gone—wink, wink."

6. Best Man, "Sebastian," enters with swatches for David.

    a) Sebastian (to David): "Hey, girl, here are those swatches." Sebastian kisses David right on the lips. For a kinda long time.

    b) David introduces Sebastian as his best man to the mark.

    c) (The mark reacts, e.g., introduces her/himself.)

    d) David hands swatches to mark. "Be an angel and look through these? They're for the bridesmaid's dresses. I'm partial to the pewter, but Kira— mind-bogglingly—loves the cordovan."

    e) (The mark reacts.)

    f) While mark looks at swatches, Sebastian and David bitch banter:

        a. Sebastian to David: "Thanks for calling last night, bitch. You should have been there. Marcos was doing some fierce dancing."

        b. David to Sebastian: "Was he wearing his hottie jeans?"

        c. Sebastian to David: "That's all he was wearing…I've gotta run—I've got softball practice in 15 minutes."

        d. David to Sebastian: "I'll walk you out."

        e. Sebastian to David: "What a gentleman!"

7. Kira returns. IF MARK IS A WOMAN:

    a) Kira hugs Sebastian.

b) Sebastian and David exit.

c) Kira: "How cute is the best man!?"

d) (The mark reacts.)

e) Kira: "I totally saw him giving you the eye."

f) (The mark reacts.)

g) Kira: "No, I have such a good sense about these things—female intuition! I definitely picked up on his vibe. Are you single? Because Sebastian never has a girlfriend."

h) (The mark reacts.)

ALT. Kira returns. IF MARK IS A MAN:

a) Kira hugs Sebastian.

b) Sebastian and David exit.

c) Kira: "How cute is the best man!?"

d) (The mark reacts.)

e) Kira: "He never has a girlfriend. I just don't understand it. I so wanna find a great girl for him…do you know anyone?"

f) (The mark reacts.)

SCENARIO #2

BEATS:

1. The mark, (a photographer), is sitting with Kira at the Pickwick to discuss wedding plans. The groom ("David") arrives a minute later.

   a) Kira: "Oh here's my sweetie!" To mark: "This is my fiancé David."

   b) (The mark reacts, e.g., she/he introduces her/himself.)

   c) David: "Sorry I'm late; my Pilates class ran long." To mark: "Gotta look good on my big day, you know."

   d) David to Kira: "Sweetie, I signed you up for some private sessions this month—so your body is worthy of that exquisite dress we got you."

   e) Kira to mark: "How amazing is he?! Most guys don't want to have anything to do with the bride's dress, but David designed mine! It's got an empire waist [she pronounces it like "Empire State Building"]

f) David interrupts: "Empire [he pronounces it the haute couture way, 'ahm-PEER']." To the mark: "It's fabulous: cut on the bias, silk charmeuse... god, I want it!"

g) (The mark reacts.)

2. The trio discusses "the look of the wedding."

a) Kira: "Before we get into specific set-ups, let's talk about the overall look of the wedding. We were thinking fall colors. How will that photograph?"

b) (The mark reacts.)

c) David: "It's really important to me that it have a real autumnal feel. That's most flattering for me—I see burnt pumpkin, aubergine, you know?"

d) (The mark reacts.)

3. Kira, David, and the mark discuss black and white versus color film.

a) Kira: "Now, I want to make sure you take some black and white pictures as well. Okay?"

b) (Mark reacts)

c) David: "Don't forget Sepia, honey. The tone of nostalgia...nes pa?"

d) (Mark reacts)

e) David: "And I want events covered simultaneously in the three milieus. So there's a picture of me coming down the aisle in black and white and then pow! Like Judy in the Wizard of Oz—Technicolor! Understand?"

f) (The mark reacts.)

g) David: "And then the sepia, like those heartbreaking photos that fall out of hope chests when you go antiqueing. I want to look at those and just cry."

h) (Mark reacts.)

4. The troika discusses the posed pictures.

a) Kira (to David): "Now, as far as the pictures of the wedding party, David has such a neat idea. Tell him honey."

b) David: "Right after the ceremony we shoot out the families. Chop, chop. Understand?

c) (The mark reacts.)

d) David (to mark): "Except for my grande aunt Lorna. She's a lady and requires all the attention due to a woman of her stature."

e) (Mark reacts.)

f) David: "Then when that's done, we want to do some set-ups with me and the groomsmen and Kira and her bridesmaids recreating "romance through the ages." Do you see where I'm going?"

g) (Mark reacts.)

h) Kira: "So the girls and I will change into different outfits like Greek Goddesses, Princesses, and Pin-up girls."

i) David: "And the guys will be Gladiators, Musketeers and Sailors. Isn't that precious?"

j) (Mark reacts.)

5. Kira's cell phone rings. She steps out to talk with her mother.

c) Kira answers her phone. To mark: "Excuse me, it's my mom. I'll be right back."

d) As she walks out…MARK SPECIFIC:

   a. [If mark is a woman] Kira to David: "Now behave yourself while I'm gone!"

   b. [If mark is a man] Kira to David: "You guys can talk about the bachelor party while I'm gone—wink, wink."

6. Best Man, "Sebastian," enters with swatches for David.

g) Sebastian (to David): "Hey, girl, here are those swatches." Sebastian kisses David right on the lips. For a kinda long time.

h) David introduces Sebastian as his best man to the mark.

i) (The mark reacts, e.g., introduces her/himself.)

j) David hands swatches to mark. "Be an angel and look through these? They're for the brides maid's dresses. I'm partial to the pewter, but Kira—mind-bogglingly—loves the cordovan."

k) (The mark reacts.)

l) While mark looks at swatches, Sebastian and David bitch banter:

   a. Sebastian to David: "Thanks for calling last night, bitch. You should have been there. Marcos was doing some fierce dancing."

   b. David to Sebastian: "Was he wearing his hottie jeans?"

   c. Sebastian to David: "That's all he was wearing…I've gotta run—I've got softball practice in 15 minutes."

   d. David to Sebastian: "I'll walk you out."

   e. Sebastian to David: "What a gentleman!"

7. Kira returns. IF MARK IS A WOMAN:

   i) Kira hugs Sebastian.

   j) Sebastian and David exit.

   k) Kira: "How cute is the best man!?"

   l) (The mark reacts.)

   m) Kira: "I totally saw him giving you the eye."

   n) (The mark reacts.)

   o) Kira: "No, I have such a good sense about these things—female intuition! I definitely picked up on his vibe. Are you single? Because Sebastian never has a girlfriend."

   p) (The mark reacts.)

   ALT. Kira returns. IF MARK IS A MAN:

   g) Kira hugs Sebastian.

   h) Sebastian and David exit.

   i) Kira: "How cute is the best man!?"

   j) (The mark reacts.)

   k) Kira: "He never has a girlfriend. I just don't understand it. I so wanna find a great girl for him…do you know anyone?"

   l) (The mark reacts.)

REVEAL:

8. Kira solicits the mark's opinion of her relationship.

a) Kira: "So what do you think of my future husband? I just feel so lucky. He wants to be so involved in planning the wedding, you know?"

b) (The mark reacts.)

c) Kira: "I am so excited for our honeymoon—we're going to Fire Island." She gets girly-conspiratorial: "I have been saving myself for him and he's never even pressured me once!"

d) (The mark reacts.)

e) Kira: "Okay, tell me honestly, you were with them alone...were they talking about the bachelor party? I am dying to know what they're doing—are they going to a strip club? They love that movie 'Showgirls.'"

f) (The mark reacts.)

g) Kira: "I just know they're going to a strip club to have fun. They'll just be a bunch of boys behaving badly, for a change. (Pause.) Because you've just been pranked by Girls Behaving Badly."

REACTIONS WANTED:

"I've never met a groom who was so obsessed with a wedding."

"I couldn't believe you didn't know he was gay!"

"I didn't know if I should tell you that you were about to marry a gay guy."

"I've never seen a groom kiss his best man on the lips."

"I couldn't believe that you thought those guys would be going to a strip club."

(NOTE TO READERS FROM MR. X: If the producers didn't like the mark's "candid" reactions, this is where we'd suddenly appear and confront him—persuading him to change his natural, honest reaction to another "candid" scenario that we'd dream up. It's a dirty job, but we do it for you, the fans. Honest!)

POST QUESTIONS: (Have marks answer questions in complete sentences)

"Take us through what just happened."

"Was this the most demanding groom you've ever met?"

"Why didn't you tell her that her fiancé was gay?"

"When did you think something might be up?"

MY FAVORITES:

"My favorite was when he started showing me swatches."

"I loved it when he was explaining the intricacies of cake decorating."

"I almost started to laugh when you tried to set me up with the best man."

"My favorite was when you told me that you've never had sex."

*

That's our smoking gun, dear readers. Hey, you don't think "Candid Camera" did this phony-baloney stuff...do you?

* * *

Chapter *Fifteen*

JUDGING THE BABES WITH THE DONALD....
ICE-T ON OMAROSA: "THAT BITCH IS NOT SUPPOSED TO BE FAMOUS!"
...MARTHA STEWART, TRUMP'S OTHER BITCH.

In 1999, I created and launched a national news-magazine show called "National Enquirer TV." It opened to great ratings, ran for two years, then crashed and burned after a round of bizarre, Byzantine backstage back-stabbings that I'll reveal in my memoirs—if ever I write them—under the chapter headed: "My Whiz-Bang-*Crash* Adventures as a TV Creator-Producer/Host/Hollywood Victim."

I mention the TV show because it's my opinion—although I'll never know for sure—that it got nudged into existence with a little help from a friend: Reality TV giant Donald Trump, the flamboyant tycoon who's so skilled at self-promotion that he ignored all the snarky giggles about his over-teased tresses and actually transformed them into a trademark image. He's also a natural storyteller, who transformed the dry world of business into a cliff-hanger competition called "The Apprentice"—the Reality TV show that had America biting its nails and parroting The Donald's dreaded kiss-off:

"You're fired!"

*

The Year: 1999.

The Scene: Tropicana Hotel, Las Vegas.

The Event: Miss Hawaiian Tropic Beauty Contest.

Among the celebrity judges saddled that year with the serious task of ogling beautiful girls for three days, then picking out a winner, were Donald Trump and me…your humble author.

I'd been invited to judge the Miss Hawaiian Tropic contest many times, and always accepted because (1) who can resist looking at pretty girls on parade? And (2) it's a great event that's never failed to generate hot celebrity stories and photos for my column. That year, as I recall, I arrived late for the first day of judging, thanks to a delayed flight from Los Angeles. A Hawaiian Tropic rep rushed me to the giant pool/patio of The Tropicana as the roll call of judges was announced, and I heard on the loudspeaker:

"Judge Mike Walker?... Is Mike here?"

I slipped into my seat poolside, joining 20-odd fellow celebrity judges, and waved my hand at the emcee, who announced: "Judge Walker has arrived. We'll begin the Bathing Suit Competition in just a moment."

From behind me, I heard the voice of a top MGM executive who, like practically every red-blooded male I know, had kept begging me to finagle him a slot as a judge. I'd responded to the arm-twist, mainly because MGM was this close to green-lighting "National Enquirer TV"—the show that I'd created—and I wanted to keep this guy sweet.

"Hey, Mike…look," he stage-whispered, very excited. "Donald Trump is trying to get your attention."

I looked up and saw The Donald, seated across the pool in the overflow crowd of celebrity judges, Hawaiian Tropic corporate types, ex-beauty queens, etc. He was waving and laughing, and he yelled something at me that got lost in all the hubbub. I waved back, signaling that I couldn't hear him. He yelled again, louder. I heard something about "…the 'Geraldo' show…!" I shrugged and pointed helplessly to my ears. He signaled back that he'd catch me later.

Then everyone snapped to attention as about 40 beautiful contestants started parading around the pool for our approval. From past experience, I knew I'd better start making notes on my clipboard. I take my bathing beauty judging duties seriously, believe it or not. You've got to take notes and pay attention if you want to be fair to all the young ladies who'd worked so hard to dazzle us.

Just the week before, on one of my regular weekly appearances on the old "Geraldo" TV show, I'd cracked up the audience when I told them solemnly: "Folks, serving as a judge for the Miss Hawaiian Tropic beauty pageant is a tough job—but somebody's got to do it. I try never to forget that my country has been very good to me…so if I can give something back by helping young American women realize their dreams, I'm proud and happy to do it."

It got a big laugh…or, should I say jeers? People are so damn cynical!

After the swimsuit competition that day, the judges were excused. Later that night, Hawaiian Tropic mogul Ron Rice threw a by-invitation-only luau in the sprawling pool/patio. About 45 minutes after the bash kicked into high gear, I was standing with my MGM executive/pal enjoying a Mai Tai. Suddenly, there was a hubbub at the entrance about 100 feet away. Donald Trump had arrived, trailing a huge entourage of hangers-on, flunkies, and hot-looking women.

"Wow! It's Trump," gushed the MGM mogul.

Just moments before, he'd wondered aloud for the 10th time if Trump would attend—and had mentioned, also for the 10th time, how impressed he was that I was "friends" with the Donald.

"We're a bit more than acquaintances, but hardly what I'd call 'friends,'" I told him—but I noted that my MGM pal had taken on that blank look Hollywood execs get when they're not listening to you. Never forget this immutable rule:

Once a studio Suit makes up his/her mind, they are unshakable. So as far as this guy was concerned:

Mike Walker + Donald Trump = Friends!

"Hey, aren't you going to ask Trump what he was trying to say to you out by the pool today?" he asked anxiously, eyes riveted on his idol.

I sighed. "Yeah, I'll ask him…if I run into him later. What you want me to do, man—summon Donald Trump?"

Just then, one of those perfectly timed moments occurred. Trump, the tallest guy at the party with the exception of madman Dennis Rodman, peered out over the crowd. He turned in my direction, and—despite the distance between us—I somehow caught his eye. Immediately, Trump turned sharply and strode straight toward us, his entourage scurrying to catch up.

"How the *hell* are you?" he bellowed.

In a moment, The Donald covered the distance between us and said, "I was trying to tell you at the pool that I caught you on the 'Geraldo' show the other day, and you were hilarious with that stuff about being a Hawaiian Tropic judge. And when you told that story about Roseanne Barr and Tom Arnold doing the wild thing under that restaurant table, I just couldn't stop laughing."

Then Trump turned to the MGM guy and enthused, "Mike always cracks me up."

It was like…a thunder-crack. SHA-ZAM! Trump had spoken!!

I quickly made introductions, and MGM Guy burbled: "That's why my company, MGM, is starring Mike in his own show next season."

Trump shook his hand and said, "It's about time. I've always said Mike should have his own show."

WHOA!

The Donald and MGM Guy schmoozed for a moment or two about their mutual Hollywood bigshot friends, then tycoon and entourage sailed back into the party. Starry-eyed MGM Guy said it again: "Wow!"

It was like Hare had just met Krishna.

Later, I said to him: "You know, Trump's the guy you should sign up for a show. No matter what it costs…and believe me, it'll cost! But look how he sucks all the air out of a room. People can't take their eyes off the guy."

We chatted briefly about what kind of TV show Trump could possibly do, agreeing that we couldn't quite see him hosting a standard talk show—unless, of course, he repeatedly interviewed himself.

"That won't work! It's got to be all 'The Donald'…all the time," I said.

"You're right about that," said the TV executive. "He could do a business show, but there's no big money in that. And that wouldn't interest him, or us. I'm going to think about it, though."

Incredible, isn't it? Just goes to prove that showbiz—like many things in life—is really all about timing. At that moment, TV's reality era hadn't yet kicked into high gear. And even if "The Apprentice" creator Mark Burnett had been standing there with us, I wonder if he'd have had the vision to cast Trump as a TV Svengali for future business tycoons.

About 10 minutes after this "Trump Encounter of the First Kind," MGM Guy stopped at a pay phone near the bar, called his studio boss at home and gushed like a schoolgirl:

"Mike just introduced me to Donald Trump…. No, *really!*… Yeah, they're like old *friends!*"

Raising my eyes to Heaven, I silently thanked its Hollywood Division. This was buzz you couldn't buy.

MGM Guy and I spent a great couple of days in Las Vegas. At one point, we dropped into the MGM Grand Hotel and he pointed up toward the giant panoramic TV screens that girdle the lobby and said: "You'll be up there when *your* show starts, Mike." I felt that warm glow you rarely experience in the chilly TV biz, and said: "From your lips to God's ear, my friend."

God was listening. Two weeks later, my TV show was green-lighted. A year after that, I stood in that same lobby again and saw my smiling kisser flashing over and over on that MGM Grand panoramic screen. A few years after that, Donald Trump—who'd loaned me the hot glow of his celebrity at the precise moment I'd needed it—got his own TV show green-lighted.

"The Apprentice" won big ratings fast. Not surprisingly, Trump was hardly humble about it. After two seasons—and the failures of several mogul-wannabe imitators—Trump unabashedly trumpeted that while Reality TV might not have been invented strictly to showcase his talents, it should have been. He declared to one reporter:

"Obviously, *people like Trump.* There have been 15 copies of 'The Apprentice': Tommy Hilfiger, Mark Cuban, Richard Branson, Martha Stewart…and all of them failed."

Relishing his rep as a no-holds-barred scrapper—and proving he knows exactly what human impulses drive the reality genre—The Donald came out punching for the second season of "The Apprentice" and bragged: "It's more brutal. It's more vicious. It's just better."

But was it, really? After all, the show's first season had been pretty darn brutal and vicious. It had snagged huge ratings and major headlines, thanks largely to a lucky casting coup that yielded a scary, secret weapon: what every reality show producer prays for—a villain you love to hate. And this villain even came complete with a snotty "Cruella DeVille"-type name:

Ladies and gentlemen, "The Apprentice" proudly presents Omarosa Manigault-Stallworth—the witch/bitch voted in a poll commissioned by *TV Guide* and Bravo as the "most hated reality star of all times"—by far!

(Just behind Omarosa in the most-hated category were such legendary creeps as "Survivor" conniver Richard Hatch, the pudgy queen who'd traded his island for a four-year stretch in the pen; obnoxious Puck from the "Real World" series; and that astoundingly off-key warbler from "American Idol," William Hung.)

To give Omarosa her due, her name still is a household word, even among those who never watched her on "The Apprentice." She'll always be remembered as the evil bitch who ignited an ugly racial firestorm after Trump bounced her from "The Apprentice" with his trademark phrase, "You're fired!"

Just days later, Omarosa, who's black, appeared on "The View" and claimed that white contestant Ereka Vetrini had called her the "N" word during the taping of the show.

She told Star Jones: "I had never been called that in my life. It was just one of the worst moments of my experience on that show. It was three o'clock in the morning. She was drunk. But it is still unforgivable."

Although Omarosa refused to name the contestant, there was no doubt she was referring to Ereka. The two had fought viciously on the show, and in one nasty blowup, Omarosa had screamed at Ereka, "You are emotionally unstable."

After both were fired from the show, Omarosa dropped her vicious racial bombshell. The next day, Ereka appeared on TV's Fox News Channel to defend herself, saying: "Mark Burnett, the producer, reviewed all the tapes and found nothing at all. Think about it this way—we are on tape 24/7."

Trump was furious.

"To have brought something like this up at a late date…it is not on camera, everybody else denies it ever took place…you know, that is really sad," he said.

Elizabeth Hasselbeck, a co-host on "The View," reported that she'd spoken to Burnett about Omarosa's accusation. "He told me he could not confirm that anywhere on the footage is Ereka using the 'N' word. It's not there." Even though Omarosa had acted like an evil and aggressive witch on the show, no one could fathom the motivation behind this ugly attack.

Why did she do it? An investigation by the *Enquirer* revealed that the ruthless, 30-year-old ex-beauty queen and former Clinton White House worker, had a secret plan. An insider from her home turf in Ohio, who's well-versed in local politics, said: "There's been some scuttlebutt in the local community that Omarosa wanted to ride the coattails of the popular 'Apprentice' show into a possible political run. And maybe to gain extra headlines and an advantage of publicity, she dropped this bombshell that she was racially discriminated against on the show by a fellow contestant who uttered the 'N' word against her. This is the last thing a consultant would tell her to do—by stating what appears to be a bold-faced lie, she's just giving ammunition to a future political opponent."

The plot thickened when a TV insider reported, "Omarosa has been having meetings with talk show execs about the possibility of her own talk show. Should she nail a show, it could earn her millions."

If that was Omarosa's ploy, it backfired badly. Niger Innis, national spokesperson for the Congress of Racial Equality told the *Enquirer*: "The race card, quite frankly, is overused. And it's a shame that someone would try to enhance their own stardom by employing this tactic."

National Enquirer reporters were told by a source close to TV talk queen Oprah Winfrey that "Oprah says Omarosa's claims, if untrue, belittle the real racism black people experience."

But nobody put it down-and-dirtier than rapper Ice-T. "I'll tell you who I don't like—Omarosa," the "Law and Order: SVU" star told a *New York Daily News* columnist. "That bitch is not supposed to be famous. Being somebody in the business, you have a lot of admiration for people because you know how hard they work. But certain people, you're just like, what the f*** has that ho' done?"

Told that many others agreed with him, Ice-T—whose real name is Tracy Marrow—added: "Yeah, well, I'm at the top of the list. Give me the gun."

Told of Ice-T's attack, Omarosa—who'd gone on to star on "The Surreal Life"—snarled, "Tracy sold out his rap career to go play a cop on the show because his last album tanked. You're supposed to be hard-core, rapping about killing and pimpin' ho's, and you go and play a cop? He sold out. Real hip-hop artists, the ones that are true to the art form, do not resort to playa'-hating!"

Classic Omorosa venom—spat straight from the snake's mouth! Ms. Playa' proudly plays cheerleader for killa' pimp rappers, but sneers at law and order. And Omorosa's claim that she was a high-level political consultant during Bill Clinton's White House days?

"That's a flat-out lie," a former co-worker told *Star* magazine. Omarosa worked in an entry-level position, sending out form letters saying that Vice President Al Gore would not be able to attend a function. Said another coworker: "It wasn't rocket science. It was fairly routine, but she didn't do it and caused problems."

Lightning rarely strikes twice—but Donald Trump truly felt the burn when he faced another, far more formidable she-devil: Inmate 55170-054…a.k.a. Martha Stewart, lean and mean after a stint in federal prison. With Trump's approval, Mark Burnett had signed the Domestic Diva to star in her own version of "The Apprentice."

Eager to jump-start her sputtering business empire after an embarrassing conviction for conspiracy and obstruction of justice in stock-trading, Martha leaped at the chance—then played it really stupid by attempting to bury Donald Trump.

It was one of those unbelievable stories that are my stock in trade; the kind that turn out to be absolutely true. I blew the whistle on Martha in my column of September 26, 2005, telling readers:

> **Ex-con Martha Stewart's suddenly snippy about sharing the Apprentice spotlight with that franchise's larger-them-life star, Donald Trump—refusing to appear with him in TV interviews! "I don't need him to get people to tune in—my name is big enough," ranted the diva, who insisted on flying solo on a "Today" show segment she'd been scheduled to do with Trump! The Donald's annoyed because he bent over backward to help Martha out, only to be elbowed aside. Now Martha will promote her show alone— but Trump's made it clear he won't be around to pick up the pieces if she bombs!**

The weird, behind-the-scenes feud was apparently instigated by Martha for the usual lunatic reason—her out-of-control ego. To truly understand the socio-pathic megalomania that drives this woman, consider the words she used to describe herself when asked by Queen of America Oprah Winfrey, "How has the way you think about yourself brought you to this point in your life?" Here is Martha Stewart's chilling self-assessment:

"I can almost bend steel with my mind. I can bend anything if I try hard enough. I can make myself do almost anything. But you can get too strong like that, so you have to be careful. You have to temper your strength...I'm even physically stronger than I have to be."

SuperWoman's strength was apparently not equal to the task of busting the bars of her jail cell—or maybe she was having far too much fun to leave. At any rate, she started flexing her muscles the minute she'd served her time—looking to kick her some tycoon butt!

As the weird Stewart-Trump feud raged on, Martha played politics...but The Donald played to the people. For TV audiences who watched both shows, it gradually became a case of, "hated her...loved him." The next words Martha heard were, "You're fired." And my column scooped the world with this exclusive replay of the delicious denouement scene between the warring moguls:

> Just after NBC axed her Apprentice-clone, a raging Martha Stewart stormed into Donald Trump's office, barged in on a meeting he was holding and read the too-cool-for-school tycoon the RIOT act, sources say—screaming that her cancellation was his fault because he'd trashed her show to the press! Say WHAT?? Hey, Mean Girl...it was you who told *Fortune* magazine: "I thought I was replacing The Donald. It was even discussed that I would be firing him on the first show!"... As my column reported weeks ago...prophetically: "Trump's made it clear he won't be around to pick up the pieces if she bombs!" Well...BOMBS AWAY! Trump reacted to Martha's office invasion with a big grin—then he told off Domestic Diva, down-and-dirty: Her show was canceled because it stunk!

Then Trump blew Martha right off her broom with a nasty public letter that read, in part: "Dear Martha…it's about time you started taking responsibility for your failed version of 'The Apprentice.' Your performance was terrible…I knew it would fail as soon as I first saw it—and your own low ratings bore me out…. Despite this, I did nothing but positively promote you. Your only response to your failed show was that, 'I thought that I was supposed to fire Donald Trump!' You knew this was not true—NBC would never fire me when 'The Apprentice' was, for a good period of time, the number one show on television…. Essentially, you made this firing up, just as you made up your sell order for ImClone. The only difference is— that was more obvious. Putting your show on the air was a mistake for everybody…!"

So much for newly lean-and-mean Martha, who immediately reached for the comfort food. Staggered by her prime-time failure, Trump's savage public dissing, and lousy ratings for her syndicated TV show "Martha," Domestic Diva yum-yum-yummed—porking on the entire 25 pounds she'd lost after months of eating those balanced jailhouse meals. One insider told a reporter: "Martha always eats when she's troubled, and many of her post-prison dreams have been cruelly dashed. Her consolation was tucking into the rich foods and wines she'd missed so much behind bars. The only place she fulfilled her dream of growing bigger is around the waist."

And now, for immediate release to all media, here is my public Letter to Martha:

Dear Martha…. The moral of the story: never, ever cross The Donald. Play fair with him, he'll play fair with you. Remember the last line in that open letter he wrote to you? It was, "In any event, my great loyalty to you has gone totally unappreciated!" Martha, you repaid The Donald's loyalty with treachery. Allow me to illustrate how you should treat a person who has shown you kindness. Remember my touching tale about how Trump treated me like a superstar exactly when I needed it? Well, shortly after you got yours, ma'am, I published the following item in my column, and—unless you're even further around the bend than many of us suspect—it should need no explanation. I wrote:

**I've done my share of celebrity-bashing, but even I'm shocked
by the evil, unprincipled and vicious attack on DONALD**

TRUMP's new bride MELANIA in a column written by some harpy named Lindor Reynolds in the Winnipeg Free Press up Canada way. It began: "Donald Trump and his strumpet will be married today...." then it went on to refer to the happy couple as "Trump and his little doxy"! If your dictionary's not handy, the definition of both "strumpet" and "doxy" is...prostitute. (If I remember correctly, Webster's dictionary defines "Lindor Reynolds" as..."bitch" and "media whore.")

And, Martha...just in case you're thinking that I'm getting overly dewy-eyed about Trump—especially after admitting that I'm not absolutely sure his star intervention helped get my TV show greenlighted—I ran into MGM Guy a few months back and, as we chatted about old times, I asked him if introducing him to Donald Trump that night in Las Vegas had helped get me my TV show. His response:

"It didn't hurt."

So why—when a guy helps a convicted criminal like you land a national TV show like "The Apprentice"—would you stab the poor sucker in the back? Why not support him when you get the chance?

It couldn't hurt.

* * *

Chapter *Sixteen*

THE KING OF ALL REALITY.... GETTING ANAL ABOUT SECRETS.... RAGGING ON BABA BOO-EY.

Nothing warms a reporter's cold heart like stumbling across a story everyone else has missed, and here's a mind-blower: In the millions of words written about reality programming, showbiz journalists and other so-called "experts" *never* credit the star who—to use an appropriately ribald analogy—spread his creative seed and fertilized the long-fallow reality genre, literally nurturing it to new life.

This often-imitated performance genius, with his killer instinct for keeping it real and edgy, almost single-handedly supercharged the reality genre and fueled its now-phenomenal popularity—but it's been a well-kept secret until now. Quite a glaring omission, when you consider the evidence, and usually I'd be the first to charge that it's attributable to the prejudiced, snotty media wonks who tend to dismiss him as a vulgar pop culture phenomenon.

But…that's just not true.

The real reason this entertainment monolith has never been crowned King Of All Reality is even more amazing: it's at least partly because *he himself* has never claimed credit for reality's rebirth—even though he's famously prone to taking credit for just about everything. So brace yourselves, pop *kulturatti:* the next screams you hear will be the media "experts" I've scooped yet again, decrying my sanity. But for you—all the millions of radio and TV fans who use their eyes and ears, who have no media axes to grind—there will be no great surprise as I break the world-exclusive "news" that history's longest-running, overall highest-rated, and arguably most brilliant, reality show of all time is…(drum roll, please)….

"The Howard Stern Show."

In more than two decades of producing his unique brand of radio—then creating innovative TV shows for the New Jersey-based WWOR Super-station, E! channel and "In Demand"—Howard Stern made headlines as a controversial, ground-breaking entertainer; but recognition of his seminal contribution to defining the Reality TV genre is long-overdue.

Some might say, *"Say what?...* Stern's just a friggin' Shock Jock! Whaddya mean, "reality" pioneer? Or are you just kissin' his butt, Walker, because you're on his show every Friday?"

For the record, the Author hereby discloses his appearances as a regular weekly guest on Stern's show since 1996—playing my ever-popular guess-the-phony-item Celebrity Gossip Game. But no friendship, professional or otherwise, will ever deter me from being an in-your-face reporter. Howard Stern has never paid me a dime. I'm just telling it like it is…keeping it "real," so to speak. And those who are well-acquainted with Howard's on-air persona know, as I've stipulated, that he loves taking credit for just about everything and anything that falls within his purview—or even comes within shouting distance of his damn purview, which is a loosely defined and ever-expanding universe that once encompassed most of Planet Earth until it lifted off into space, where Howard now apparently lives aboard a satellite called Sirius.

Howard directly inspired "The Osbournes," "The Anna Nicole Smith Show" and "That's Hot," starring Lorenzo Lamas, to name just three…and there are probably more. But I've got even better evidence, so read on.

Now, knowing Howard, chances are he may be pissed that I'm breaking a story *even* he missed. Why? Because he could have been bragging about it all these years! That's why I decided not to interview Howard for this book. Remember, he loves taking credit, right? So while he'd acknowledge that my book was finally breaking the news that he had pioneered reality…he'd then point out that because he's been the King of All Media for years, and because that title, de facto, would technically include Reality TV, he'd just taken the credit for granted all these years. But hey, Howard's also a very loyal guy, so I know he'll plug my book on his show. And then, of course, he'll take the credit for making it a bestseller. The important point of this rambling diatribe, folks, is that I wanted to make sure that you and Howard will read my bombshell revelation at the same time.

So…let me state it again for the record:

Howard Stern is the Leonardo Da Vinci of the reality genre. Where he led, TV followed. There would be no Simon Cowell or "American Idol" without Howard Stern.

Chew on *that,* Jennifer Aniston!

Question: What defines Howard Stern as a genius of the reality genre— whether it be radio or TV? To illustrate, let's conjure up a real event shared by all Americans; the shocking image that flashes in our collective minds the instant it's mentioned:

9/11!

Critic Michael Hiltzik got it exactly right in his *LA Times* blog when he wrote:

"Let's not forget that one of the most extraordinary radio broadcasts of all time was the Howard Stern show of September 11, 2001. I heard it years later, broadcast as a rerun. Nothing delivers the immediacy of that awful morning as the way Stern and his goofballs reported the events downtown to each other, in sudden shocked seriousness and absolutely genuine dismay and fear, knowing no more than the rest of us, all in real time. You want reality programming? This was so real it's hard to listen to without breaking into a sweat."

How did Howard Stern rise to that occasion so swiftly, so expertly? Did you really believe he was nothing more than a Shock Jock? Here was proof that Howard had been creating and honing a unique brand of reality broadcasting. By 9/11, he'd mastered it, according to Hiltzik and other critics who praised his work on that fateful day.

Speaking, as Hiltzik puts it, of "breaking into a sweat" when confronted by Howard Stern-style reality, I will never forget the morning I phoned in to his radio show for my regular Friday morning gig many years ago—and was accorded the rare privilege of sharing a stunningly intimate revelation about the sex life of the host and his then-wife, Alison. As I recall it, the conversation went something like this:

HS: Mike, I could hardly wait for you to call in because…well, you're a good friend, and I just want to share something special that happened between me and Alison last night…something very private that nobody knows about yet…and I want you to be the first….

MW: Howard, I'm honored, of course…but, er, does your lovely wife know that you're about to disclose this private moment, whatever it is?… I mean, women can get sensitive about their privacy, and….

HS: Mike, here it is…. Last night, for the first time in our marriage, Alison and I had…anal sex!

WHOA!

My strangled reaction was lost amidst wild whoops that broke out in the studio as co-host Robin Quivers and The Howard Stern Players gasped, giggled…and screamed. Howard, unperturbed, continued on…describing to me exactly how and where (it was in the master bathroom, if I recall correctly) that this mind-boggling moment occurred. I clearly remember that he began by saying, "What made it work perfectly is that I'm so tall. So, Mike, here's how I did it. First, I told Alison to…!"

It was like a scene out of Howard's biopic, "Private Parts," where Alison recoils when she hears her husband discussing her tragic miscarriage on his national radio show. As Howard continued his excruciatingly detailed description of their master bathroom encounter, I remember thinking, "Alison's phone must be ringing off the hook this very minute."

Question: Did Howard and Alison really do the deed? Or was Howard putting me on?

Like millions of shocked fans listening that day, I'll never know for sure. And therein lies the fascination of the best reality shows. All you really know—or think you know—is that the characters are real people in a real-life setting. Supposedly, there is no script. But in reality, just as in real life, there are no guarantees.

Quoting Michael Hiltzik again: "On a normal day one never could tell how much of the Stern show was truly spontaneous. The regular psychodramas featuring the staff ganging up one another, complaining about each others' laziness, stupidity, even poor personal hygiene, may have been scripted to within an inch of their lives, or they may have been as genuine as the cloudbursts within a big family. It certainly sounded real, but that might merely signify how good they were at their jobs."

Take it from me. It *was* real. Always.

After years of kicking around the radio business, Stern's big breakthrough into the national consciousness really occurred in the early '90s. Years before I started appearing on the show, I was a regular listener who—like the upwards of 18 million people who tuned in during the morning commute—arrived at work and schmoozed with colleagues about whatever outrageousness had occurred on that morning's show. As a fan of talk radio—but never dreaming then that someday I'd host my own nationally syndicated radio show—I endlessly attempted to analyze the reasons behind Howard's near-addictive appeal, arguing against those dim-bulbs who airily insisted that his success was based solely on his Shock Jock persona and raunchier-than-thou, damn-near-dirty material that made him the FCC's favorite whipping boy. Non-fans would sneer, "He's a potty-mouth, an arrested adolescent…a former geek who's living out a fantasy of meeting porn stars and lesbians."

It was true to a degree, of course. And sometimes, while defending Howard, I'd get defensive. (Hey, who you calling a knuckle-dragging mouth-breather, punk?) Sure, I listened to Howard's outrageous potty-talk, but it was often funny, inventive and edgy…and I figured, okay…so what? Yet I sensed there was more to it…that Howard had me hooked on some deeper level I couldn't quite comprehend. Now, let me state for the record that I bow to no man when it comes to curiosity about the sex lives of lesbians—especially the ones I report on in Hollywood—nor do I pretend that I'm a high-minded NPR listener. But endless, witless potty-talk bores me—and most people, I think—so there had to be a reason why millions of us reacted to Howard with such…well, affection, really. He inspired not only that, but deep loyalty as well. But why? Howard had many imitators in those days, yet I rarely tuned them in after an initial listen. I'd switch these sophomoric cretins on occasionally, but only as relief from Howard's increasingly lengthy commercial breaks. And I learned that other fans did the same thing. And then, one fine morning…I finally got it.

I remember the moment well. But here's what led up to it: Over the course of listening through the mid-'90s, I'd grown frustrated with Howard for interrupting what I called "the fun stuff" far too frequently; he'd be ranting about Kathy Lee Gifford's stupidity, or coaxing heir-head Tori Spelling into admitting she stashes vibrators in her nightstand—then he'd suddenly side-track into what I considered to be time-wasting, hokey-jokey insider jibber-jabber with his show regulars about their off-air "real" lives. I dismissed this blah-blah-blah as "filler"—it was just the whole gang vamping and chewing up airtime in between comedy bits, interviews, gossip, weird phone calls and all the other "good stuff." And hey, who could blame them? Try doing up to six hours of radio, day after day.

But somehow I felt short-changed when, for example, Howard would goad Stuttering John and Jackie "The Joke Man" Martling into rehashing some stupid argument they'd had at lunch the day before; or when he'd lead his regulars and the Wack Pack in a jeering discourse about how producer Garry "BaBa Booey" Delabate lets his wife pussy-whip and berate him when he works late...blah, blah, blah. I'd fret impatiently. Come on, guys! Let's play "The Vomit Game"—or "Point Out a Jew!"

Howard presided as ringmaster during these free-wheeling, intramural bitch-fests. He did his thing skillfully, probing for everyone's weak spots. He'd crack the whip and lash his crew into spilling the most outrageous revelations about innermost feelings and disgusting habits, etc.—like Robin admitting that she never farted in her clothes. She'd go into the john, remove skirt and panties, cut the cheese and rejoin the show.

Howard would let the conversations run on and on—not necessarily playing it for laughs, either, because it often got uncomfortably cruel. He'd ruthlessly expose the foibles, fears and fantasies of his sidekicks. Robin Quivers, Fred Norris, Ralph, John, Jackie the Joke Man, et al, noisily took sides in arguments that routinely rose to the level of near-hysteria. I amused myself by guessing how each of them would react to often brutal attacks or dare-ya challenges. Like the time Howard asked Jackie if he'd let a 300-pound guy listener gobble a marshmallow out of his butt. I guessed wrong on that one. Jackie acquiesced. He squealed like the guy in "Deliverance" and jumped three feet in the air when he felt Fattie's tongue where no guy's tongue should go, but he allowed it. As for the 300-pound guy—Mister, you're a true super-fan. In that same week, Howard casually mentioned something about his indigestion—and Robin blurted out that she'd been cleansing her insides with regular colonics. Howard then put a doctor on the air, who told Robin the real reason she had the colonics was because her father had subjected her to sexual abuse as a child—as she'd revealed in her autobio. Robin went NUTS on the guy! That same week, I heard Howard's longtime sidekick, soundman Fred Norris, rage that he was quitting the show because Howard intruded too deeply into his personal life, dragging his wife's name into arguments. Wow? Was Fred kidding? It sounded so damn real. I got pretty good at guessing how these characters would react to attacks and pressure situations visited on them by their sometimes sadistic boss because I'd come to know them quite well, listening on a daily basis. But often, they'd surprise me, as even your closest friends can. One thing I know for a fact: These insult-driven, free-wheeling conversations were definitely unscripted! I know it because…well, knowing inside stuff is my job. Even the first time I heard them, however, they had that unpredictable, natural feel of conversations you have in real-life relationships.

But therein lay the crux of my annoyance when I first began to listen regularly! Who the hell needs to hear real-life chit chat on radio, I thought? We get more than enough of that crap in real life, right? Yet, day after day I kept listening. I didn't turn off or tune out.

And then, one morning, as I floated up out of confused dreams in a Manhattan hotel room, the bedside clock-radio—set by a maid or a previous guest—clicked on, and the "Howard Stern Show" suddenly blared. I listened, halfway to wakefulness, then seemed to drift out-of-body, rising above the chatter….

…And then I was looking down into the studio…there was Howard, ragging on Baba Boo-ey…Fred was threatening to quit again…. Stuttering John was baiting him from the sidelines, chuckling evilly…and Robin, shrill and impatient, exasperated by it all….

Right then, my subconscious suddenly got the message and blurted it to my brain: "You are *hooked*, sucker!"

Finally, I had the answer to why I was so totally engaged with this show. In an instant, all the annoyance I'd felt about Howard allowing—even encouraging—those "time-wasting" personal digressions that interrupted the "professional" flow of comedy, interviews, gossip, and sex-driven hi-jinks just…disappeared. Instead, I was listening, mesmerized, to this highly dysfunctional family I'd come to know so well, nattering endlessly about insider crap that should have bored me to death. But it didn't. Not anymore. And I suddenly realized that Howard Stern and his weird band of diverse personalities had sneaked up on me, infiltrating my psyche like no other program before or since.

Without quite knowing how or when it had happened, I'd become an adoptee. Howard's dysfunctional family was now…my family. I was a part of it; it was a part of me. I was hooked. And I knew why:

Because *nothing* makes you more nuts than family! For better or for worse, love them or hate them, your family members are your major relationships. They make you feel things you never feel, even when witnessing the interactions of people embroiled in their own relationships. And try as you might, you cannot ignore family. Run to the ends of the earth to avoid them, but sooner or later they will resurface in your life; and your soul will resonate to frustration and resignation like that embodied in this famous dialogue by Al Pacino in "The Godfather":

"Just when I thought I was out, they pull me back in!"

Here is a mantra that you can repeat if ever you feel guilty about indulging in the addictive pleasures of Reality TV:

The study of character is the greatest form of human entertainment.

Never forget that statement! In fact, repeat it twice, right now, and you'll never forget it. (You too, Jennifer Aniston.) It will help you to understand yourself better; explain why you make certain choices in the arts and entertainment.

The study of character is the greatest form of human entertainment.

Not an original thought, to be sure. But take it from me, journalist, author, broadcaster and gossip columnist—and other fabled storytellers like Isaac Bashevis Singer, Shakespeare, Aristophanes…and the first caveman who hosted a campfire talk-fest, probably on the very night fire was discovered. Each of us has profited from the knowledge that character, not action, drives the creative train.

After all, to use "The Godfather" as an example, the film didn't capture the world's imagination because it featured gangsters shooting, stabbing and garroting rival hoods. And it wasn't the twists and turns of its exciting plot—like the Hollywood big-shot waking up with a bloody horse's head—that ranked it as a serious contender for Best Movie of All Time. Everyone knows that the enormous appeal of "The Godfather" was rooted, not in its depiction of chilling violence, but in the totally believable way its unforgettable characters interacted in that most personal of human relationships: family.

"The Godfather" is simply "Father Knows Best"—with machine guns and switchblades.

* * *

Chapter *Seventeen*

WHO CARES IF THE BUTLER DID IT?.... CONDOM ON A BANANA.... THE GOSSIP GAME BEGINS.

Think of character, and its paramount importance, this way: there are only seven basic plots in literature, the experts tell us, so what is the unique trigger that can suddenly conjure up the emotional memory of a novel you read years ago? Was it the shock ending, revealing that "the butler did it"? No! Plot points, no matter how clever, don't drive that in-your-gut recall of a novel you wanted never to end, and now suddenly want to read again. It's those unforgettable characters. They drew you inexorably into relationships with other fascinating characters. And they left an imprint on your soul. You know these characters. Even though they're imaginary, they're real because you know them, accept them, feel them. Your imprint is on their soul. They are, in a sense, a co-creation by the author and you. They're part of your extended family, now and forever.

Reality TV's mortal enemy, Jennifer Aniston, snarls, "I *hate* that 'Idol' shit!"

Then she whines, "Don't hijack my life…!"

Please don't be afraid, Jen. Just repeat that mantra again…the one I told you to memorize. In fact, let's all repeat it along with Jennifer. Ready?

The study of character is the greatest form of human entertainment.

There! Feel better, Jen? And now do you "get" that "Idol shit"? It's all about unscripted characters and their relationships. That's why we watch Reality TV. Simple as that. And that's how I—and millions of Americans, even fans of "Friends"—got hooked by the trail-blazing show that pioneered the reality trend that ate TV: "The Howard Stern Show"! This performance genius captured reality entertainment's potential like none of his predecessors—not "Candid Camera" or "Wanted" or "Cops" or "America's Funniest Home Videos."

And it's far from certain that Howard consciously knew what he was doing, except in the most instinctive showman's way. After assembling an unforgettable lineup of diverse personalities, Howard interacted with them, carefully molding them into distinct characters, creating back-stories for them, dubbing them with descriptive names. He was a genius at discovering what unique traits made each one of his menagerie fascinating. He flew by the seat of his pants, and you could feel it. It was ad lib, edgy, dangerous. But over time, his team streamlined into a well-oiled machine—an intriguing lineup of offbeat personalities who were "real people" first, and performers second; co-host Robin Quivers, Jackie "The Joke Man" Martling, Artie Lange, Fred Norris, Ralph, Wood-Ye, Elephant Boy, Stuttering John, producer Gary "BaBa Boo-ey" Delabate, Crazy Cabbie, King of All Blacks, Jeff the Drunk, Beetlejuice, Crackhead Bob, Hank the Angry Drunken Dwarf, John the Stutterer, Sal the Stockbroker, Wendy the Retard, Ralph, High-Pitch Eric, etc. Then there were the regular guests like comedian Gilbert Gottfried, lawyer Dominic Barbara, and—coming aboard for a regular Friday stint that began on April 11, 1996—me! An online blog by some geek who's recorded the doings on Howard's show over the years sounded singularly unimpressed:

Mike Walker, Gossip Dude. 4-11-96. Gossip on the Howard Stern show? That's right. Howard had this guy call in to play a little contest. Mike Walker, whose[sic] on Geraldo Rivera's TV show, phoned in with a bunch of gossip—and the crew had to pick which story was the fake one. No one got the correct answer. Howard wants to make this a regular thing. Something like a game show. Is this something we need? Who knows....

Well, it's 11 years later, and I'm still doing the Howard Stern show every week. The show hasn't changed all that much. But the show has changed us—and our entertainment habits. Today, Reality TV rules. Oh, we haven't done away with beautiful people like Jennifer Aniston, preening in perfect makeup and speaking brilliantly-scripted dialogue. They can still be seen and enjoyed in the movies and at live theater, and that's good. Movies get us out of the house, and as for the theater…well, one always needs a place to wear one's furs, doesn't one, dahling?

But TV? We like our TV raw…with some fava beans *and a nice Chianti!* We enjoy none-too-pretty non-actors, people who look like us, ad-libbing in situations ruthlessly designed to be stressful or laugh-inducing by semi-sadistic Reality TV producers—doing it the way Howard Stern taught them as they listened to his pioneering radio reality show. Remember, Howard's trademark move was insistent, avuncular bullying of his non-actor characters—inexperienced interns who started at interns' pay—and forcing them to interplay.

It wasn't always pretty. But it was always fun. And challenging. Famed Sunset Strip prostitute Divine Brown, who became a household name after she got caught nibbling movie star Hugh Grant, once dropped into Howard's studio—and he asked how long it took her to put a condom on a client. "Three seconds," said Divine. Flippantly…or confidently? Howard immediately whipped out a banana and a condom. Handing them to her, he said:

"I'll count…One Alligator…Two Alligators…Three Alligators…*WHOA!*… She did it!"

Always expect the unexpected challenge. That's the secret that Reality TV learned from Howard Stern.

One other unique approach set the stage for the Stern show's groundbreaking success: there was no plot, no underlying moral, no important message. This was not "Ozzie and Harriet," "Leave It to Beaver" or "The Brady Bunch." You never listened to Stern in the hope that you'd learn anything valuable, in the usual sense—even though you often did. But education was not the point. The point was…engagement. What you were listening to, and what you were subtly encouraged to join, and enjoy vicariously, was a real family—not scripted figments of a writer's imagination—a family meeting and interacting Monday through Friday as they engaged in the messy business of earning a living, chasing their dreams, getting some fun out of life, and—last, but not least—getting laid! Sound familiar? Isn't that kinda what we all do? Every day?

Why, we're just like them "real people" on those really real reality shows.

Question: are "real people" still real when they leave reality shows? Are they still, in other words, just as they appeared to be on TV? Did they grow and change permanently? Or do they change back into their real selves somehow when they rejoin us in the reality they left behind—the "really real" reality, so to speak?

(What the *hell* did I just say? Where is Rod Serling when you really need him?)

Actually, in Hollywood, there exists a strange colony of ex-contestants from reality shows who've taken up residence and are trying to break into "real" show business—or latch onto another reality show. They've even got a sort of headquarters where you can find them—the Saddle Ranch Chop House on the Sunset Strip, which hires ex-reality contestants as waiters so that *touristas* from Kansas and Poughkeepsie can wander in and squeal, "OMIGOD, weren't you Ellie on 'Bug Island'?"

To answer my bizarre question: The reality stars I've met seem to be somewhat like the characters you saw on TV, but not completely so. The longer you're on a reality show, the more it can define you. The only famous example I know personally is Stuttering John because—for a decade—John always phoned me at 5:30 a.m. to make sure I was awake and coherent for my early-morning Stern stints. Then, in a shocker that made national headlines, John suddenly quit Howard Stern to join Jay Leno's players on the "Tonight Show." But, in the opinion of many, he immediately lost the identity Stern had given him—and couldn't readily assume another.

Fish-out-of-water John was no longer Stuttering John—first, he actually had to lose his stutter. That's because Jay's staff had made the lunatic decision that a guy who stutters…are you ready?…would be the perfect choice as the show's announcer.

It got worse. Here's the real scoop: The "Tonight" staff and Jay Leno wanted to steal Stuttering John—not as a dime-a-dozen announcer, but as a well-known performer who'd bring the stodgy show a much-needed reality feel, street cred and also, hopefully, younger viewers. What made the whole brouhaha so ironic was that Howard had repeatedly accused Jay of ripping off his show's most classic bit—sending Stuttering John to infiltrate red-carpet functions and stick pins in celebrities during their phoniest moments, asking embarrassing questions about their sex lives, their disgusting habits, or why their breasts were sagging (a question he actually posed to aging sexbomb Raquel Welch).

For "Tonight Show" viewers unfamiliar with Stern's show, Jay ripped off the "Stuttering John" character when he hired that fat, effeminate kid that he'd send to celeb functions to ask silly questions—not the tough, jaw-dropping kind John was famous for delivering.

When Stern found out Leno had hired John behind his back, he went berserk on the air: "How much more material are you going to take from me?... You wanted a guy associated with my show because you can't get 18- to 25-year-old men. To an 18- to-25-year-old male, Jay Leno is gay. He might as well put a dress on.... I told him everyone in the business is talking about how transparent and lame and gay you are, and that you can't even develop your own people."

Stern has frequently confronted Leno about stealing routines from his show over the years, but he says the "Tonight Show" host always reacted to the charge "like a whining bitch." Sneered Stern, "He'd say, 'Steve Allen did all that stuff.' Jay Leno is a bankrupt comedian."

Even Leno's "Jay Walking" bit mimicked Stern's long-time gimmick of sending regulars out to do live bits with people on the street; like asking homeless guys questions about current events and history. But it was Stuttering John who'd trademarked those edgy celebrity-ambush "interviews," in which he'd confront Chevy Chase for example, and ask, "Are you wearing your toupee?" Or accost aging actress Mary Tyler Moore and scream, "How bad was menopause?" He once famously asked O.J. Simpson lawyer Johnny Cochran: "Would you let your daughter date O.J.?" And an all-time favorite was Stuttering John sticking a micro-phone in the face of baseball legend Ted Williams and asking: "Did you ever fart in the catcher's face?"

Whenever Stuttering John showed up, stars would scurry like cockroaches exposed to light. Even so-called comedians got caught with their ad-libs down. Highly offended un-funnyman Chevy Chase's grim, lumpen response to John's silly "toupee" question was an unsmiling, "How about I arrange to have Howard's dental bill suddenly go up?"

Here, for the first time, is the real story of what really happened behind the scenes on the "Tonight Show," culled from my insider sources—and the bizarre chain of events and misinformation that led to the hiring of Stuttering John. It all began when a higher-up caught John's appearance on the reality show, "I'm a Celebrity, Get Me Out Of Here!" John had made some sensitive moves, like befriending the terrified Melissa Rivers, daughter of comedienne Joan Rivers, and that impressed this lofty Suit—who then learned that Stuttering John was the guy from the Stern show who did those hilarious on-the-street ambushes.

"Oh, he does those? Great...he can do on-the-street bits on our show."

Somehow, it had escaped the notice of this over-paid exec that John did not actually write these bits. Moreover, John—a nice guy with a pleasant personality—was, as anyone who listened to Howard Stern knew, definitely not a quick ad-libber who was great at tossing the conversational ball back and forth. After all, he *stuttered!* Under normal circumstances, John's hiring might have undergone more thorough discussion at NBC, but now there was a hush-hush need for speed. Sources say the writers on the show had begun to abhor bandleader Kevin Eubanks—who looks all smiley and laid-backed on camera, but is said to be surly and resistant to suggestions about how to interact with Jay on the air. It wasn't working with Kevin, so it was decided to seek out a new hire, someone capable of kibitzing on the couch with Jay.

"No one wanted to give Kevin one more minutes of airtime than absolutely necessary," said an insider. The show's announcer at the time, Ed Hall, was a nice guy and competent, but he was considered too white-bread to achieve the edgy, youthful feel Jay and his staff wanted.

It wasn't until Jay hired Stuttering John away from Howard Stern—triggering a vicious showbiz feud—that the "Tonight Show" discovered the misconceptions about their hot new hire. When Stuttering John came aboard, he worked hard, as he always does. He eliminated his stutter and did an amazing job at announcing the show. But the first few times they put "John Melendez" on the couch to trade witty chitchat and banter with Jay about subjects young and hip, the experienced older comedian discovered what Howard could have told him—John's a smart guy who can carry on an interesting conversation, but he is not a scintillating raconteur, nor is he particularly funny. John cracked Stern's fans up because he had brass balls and dared to confront anybody on earth.

So, Leno went back to bouncing off Kevin Eubanks. The writers then sent John out to do man-in-the-street bits, but were frustrated when the bits didn't catch fire. John's ad-lib conversations with ordinary people were pleasant, but flat.

Leno was furious. "Why didn't we find out that he never wrote all those phony questions he asked celebrities," raged the host. His highly-paid writing staff rolled their eyes and avoided looking at the higher-up who'd been so high on hijacking John from Stern.

Jay had hired Stuttering John to beef up the reality feel he keeps trying for on the "Tonight Show" with bits like "The Photo Booth" and "The Newscaster in the Gas Pump." But John, whose pugnacious personality worked perfectly in the rough and tumble, boys-locker-room atmosphere at the Stern show—and who even came off funny at times with his sneering putdowns—was the proverbial fish out of water in Jay's buttoned-down world of slick comedy penned by slick writers. After awhile, John's profile on the show was lowered. He still did the announcing and physical comedy bits, but he was no longer the "reality" guy.

Meanwhile, Howard still rants about how he hates Jay—castigating him as "a robot." He does not hate John, as he's pointed out over and over. But John was a valuable "reality" character he'd invented for his show, and Howard's only cavil is that John should have given him a chance to match Leno's offer. He likes John and wishes him well—but Howard is Howard. If Jay ever boots John off the "Tonight Show," Howard will make great radio fun out of savaging his old sidekick and telling him, "I told you so."

"Today, everyone in the business knows a mistake was made in hiring John for the 'Tonight Show'," said a veteran comedy writer and producer. "One of Leno's people saw John on that 'celebrity survivor' reality show, and thought he was warm and spontaneous. Leno was looking for somebody who had authentic 'street' feel— and who could bounce off him on the air. Branford Marsalis was always unwilling to do it, and Kevin Eubanks is just plain dull. Stuttering John looked perfect.

"But what everyone forgot what was…there is no such person as 'Stuttering John.' There's a guy named John Melendez, who became the character shaped by the genius of Howard Stern. Stern has always said he doesn't like slick, scripted material. He believes the best way to find humor is in the spontaneous actions of regular people. He believes in finding characters, hiring them and forcing them to find authentic humor by reacting with other personalities—also characters shaped by Howard.

"Once Stuttering John was yanked out of the Stern aquarium, he began flopping around and gasping for air. He's not an actor. None of them are—Robin, Gary, Fred, Sal the Stockbroker, Richard, Benji, and the rest. The one exception is Artie Lange. And there's always a new set of characters. They drift in and out of the show. The one constant is Robin Quivers. She's the mother figure, the Florence Henderson. Everyone, Howard included, relates to Robin.

"But Howard uses them all for his own purposes. The theory that he pioneered this whole craze for Reality TV sounds perfectly accurate. I worked in TV most of my adult life, and his work has always inspired me. But I've never heard of him getting the credit for starting this Reality TV thing—even from people in our business who should know better."

So, let's review, shall we? Pay attention back there, Jennifer! Reality TV is not unscripted TV…it's engineered melodrama. What drives it is that we all have relationships, but we are always yearning for others.

So first we look to people in the news—famous people. They might be politicians, businessmen, fashion designers, racecar drivers, athletes—but more often it's show business personalities. Why? They're sexier, and they earn big bucks doing things all of us secretly believe we can do. We sing in the shower, speak dialogue into the mirror, fool around with a musical instrument—and we actually believe that with one lucky break, we could be singers, actors, rock stars.

Another reason why show business personalities get most of our attention is because they're easier for us to check up on. How often can you find a business tycoon like Warren Buffett, or a fashion guru like Ralph Lauren on TV? But we know we're going to see Tom Cruise, Johnny Depp, Kiera Knightley, Renée Zellweger or Lindsay Lohan…on Leno, Letterman or Larry King. We can always find Oprah, Ellen DeGeneres and Tyra Banks on their own TV shows. We like watching these glittering people, and not only because we want to emulate them. We're curious about celebrity relationships, whether it's between two of our favorite local newscasters, or Tom and Katie, or Brad and Angelina, or—I didn't forget you, Jen!—

Vince Vaughn and Jennifer Aniston. When we're coping with our own real-life issues, it's fascinating to observe that (1) celebs have the same problems we do, and (2) they have a whole lot of trouble solving their own problems.

We watch how these envied people cope. We try to copy their successes—and learn from their failures. And, let's be honest…it's so soul-satisfying to see these celebrities making mistakes, then confessing their own fallibility. It's not just that we're being mean. What's always fascinating is watching someone dig hard to get at the truth. And that's what Howard Stern always did, day after day, on his radio show. For nearly six hours a day, five days a week, Stern showed his great instinct for finding out why things worked or didn't work. He wanted to know why some people were smart, and others were stupid. He wanted to understand the impulses that drive people to do insane things.

It's riveting, for instance, to watch a driven personality like Danny Bonaduce search for the truth that always seems to elude him. Danny understands that life is full of drama and danger. His instinct is to use that to make good TV. He lives, as he's admitted, only to be on TV. He doesn't consider his life to be a real life, unless others are watching it. Danny will even create drama to make his TV show successful. He doesn't care what's real, or what's contrived. To him, it all adds up to the same thing. Pour on the pressure, interact with the personalities around you…and dig for the truth. That's why he's great as a great reality show producer—and a wreck of a human being.

On his show, Howard Stern emphasized everyone's relationships. And when someone screwed up he jumped on them. As a listener, I often found him to be a bully. I'd think, where is the bit? Why is that funny? Are we going for comedy here? Isn't that the point of the show?

Then came the epiphany, that moment of hindsight when I realized Stern was a genius, flying by the seat of his pants and creating something new that changed the world of entertainment. He spawned Reality TV. As for Reality Radio, he owns it. He was brilliant at drawing characters out, defining and polishing them. And these characters have become household words famous in their own right—Robin, BaBa Boo-ey, Stuttering John, Artie, Fred, and so many others. These sidekicks became as important as Jason Alexander was to the Seinfeld show. Howard even creates characters from the regular guests on his show. If you go to Wikipedia, the free Internet encyclopedia, you will see my name on the list of regular performers on the Howard Stern show. There's even a list of recorded bits used over and over that are familiar to listeners. Mine are: "Hey, how about a reach-around?" and "Ha, Ha...WHOA!"

When I walk down the street, people often shout these lines out to me. Or they'll walk up and laugh about the bits where Howard's elves have chopped up my recorded voice to create hilarious phone calls to: a guy named 'Howard,' a porn shop, a Chinese restaurant, etc. So even though I had a highly-defined character as a journalist, author and gossip columnist for the *National Enquirer* before I ever appeared on the show, Howard still delved into my character, re-defining and polishing. He even re-defined himself.

Said critic Hiltzik: "There was a lot of armchair analysis in the press about the secrets of his success. One constant in the discussion was his rigorously monogamous relationship with his wife, Alison. It was said—and it was true—that the conservatism of his domestic life was what enabled him to be so raunchy on the air. The constant leering and slavering over naked women and porn stars would be too scary and odious for listeners to accept if they thought he was really acting out all these verbal impulses.

"And it was true: the corny jejunity of his home life reduced all the wild talk to just banter. It secured Stern's role as an everyman, because every man deep down ogles and fantasizes about porn stars but doesn't touch.... Then he and Alison divorced. During the happy-marriage years, the story line was that if they ever broke up the change in his image would destroy his popularity. It sounds right and at some level he must have believed it, because he promptly entered into another monogamous relationship, although this time with a glamorous model. To hear him discuss it on the air, it was a marriage in all but name, and he hadn't changed."

That's just Howard re-defining himself. He never quits.

It's what makes him a genius.

* * *

Chapter *Eighteen*

ATTENTION, CONTESTANTS: YOU'D BETTER BE HOT!...
A DEAL WITH THE DEVIL.... DON'T OVERSTAY YOUR 15 MINUTES.

It's the cliché scene of the American Dream—small-town boy or girl hops a bus and heads for Hollywood, full of hope and just *knowing* they're destined for fame and fortune on the silver screen, the stage...or TV, at least.

Then, all too often, they run smack into that other cliché—Hollywood as the Boulevard of Broken Dreams.

Truth be told, youngsters from towns small or big aren't quite as naïve as they used to be. They watch TV, read Mike Walker in the *National Enquirer,* surf the Internet...and they know that 99 out of 100 dreamers never achieve that Gollywood happy ending. But hope springs eternal in the human soul. And the major sucker-bait that puts optimistic grins on those wannabe kissers is the hottest new game in town: Reality TV. Here's the message that's so irresistibly alluring:

Forget the talent, kid—we want *real* people...who look hot...and who don't mind looking *dumb* on national television.

So...you still want to know how to land a role on Reality TV? Take it from a two-time "Survivor" contestant who knows the ropes:

RULE #1: IT ALWAYS HELPS TO BE GOOD-LOOKING.

At the turn of the millennium, Rob Cesternino, a handsome young college student, became obsessed with the suddenly burgeoning genre known as reality television…"so much so that I actually wrote my senior thesis on the subject," he recalls. "And when I graduated, I sent an application to CBS to land a slot on 'Big Brother.' I got a response and went through a long application process. And finally, I was called to New York—which wasn't far away from the small town where I lived, Wantagh, Long Island."

Rob grins at the memory: "It was the most exciting adventure of my young life. I met with all the casting people and actually had a meeting with the legendary Les Moonves, the head of the CBS network. What a thrill! Now I knew they really liked me. They don't trot you in front of the Big Man unless they're serious.

"And then I got the telephone call that crushed me. It was just, 'Sorry, can't use you.' I was devastated. I'd just gotten my first real-life lesson in showbiz: never count on anything until the deal is signed. But two months later, I got my second showbiz lesson: when lightning finally strikes, it's the sweetest business in the world. CBS telephoned and asked me to come in again. They told me, "You weren't right for 'Big Brother,' but we'd love to have you for 'Survivor.'

"The next thing I knew, I was in the jungle—and on top of the world. I was a contestant on 'Survivor: Amazon (Season 6).'"

Incredibly, Rob Cesternino ended the game in third place. Even more incredibly, the producers liked him so much they immediately picked him for "Survivor: All-Stars," which aired in 2004. He didn't win the $1 million prize that time either, but host Jeff Probst gave him the supreme compliment, singling out Rob "the smartest player to never win Survivor."

And suddenly, it was all over. After two exciting seasons on the hottest Reality TV show, Rob—a face recognizable by millions—was just another face in the crowd, hustling to make a living. He sensed he could use his new-found knowledge somehow…but how? After a few false starts, here's what Rob learned:

RULE #2: DON'T WASTE A SECOND! IT'S FATAL TO OVERSTAY YOUR 15 MINUTES OF FAME.

Things move fast for reality stars. They get famous quickly, and they're forgotten just as quickly. So make the most of your time in the sun. Today, Rob produces movies and TV. And he's got specific tips on how to achieve success if you decide you love showbiz.

"The best advice I can give anybody who's interested in showbiz and/or Reality TV is get in the door however you can—I did it by becoming a Reality TV contestant—then absorb knowledge like a sponge, and make connections. Then be realistic. Look at the jobs you might be able to do, then go for something that might have longevity—there's no long-term career in being a reality show contestant. I was damn lucky to do 'Survivor' not once, but twice. But I don't think it was just luck that got me onto the show. I studied it all the time, even when I was back in college. You've always got to research what you're interested in doing. Knowledge is power, always.

"The first time I actually saw 'Survivor' was in 2002—and I was riveted. I'd always been a fan of game shows, but this was a game show with real drama to it. This wasn't about someone winning a washing machine. This was a life-or-death struggle, and the winner was going to get $1 million for surviving. I was fascinated, immediately. And then I heard that they were casting for 'Survivor: The Australian Outback (Season 2).' I wanted to get on that show no matter what, and I knew what I had to do: make an audition tape."

Here's where many inexperienced young people get stymied, says Cesternino. Everyone has access to a video camera, but how do you make an audition tape that will grab the attention of busy, jaded casting directors?

"There are two kinds of people that get cast on reality television shows—good-looking people and interesting people. I was in the latter category. If you're a good-looking person, your row is going to be much easier to hoe: just jump in front of the camera in skimpy clothes, prove that you can speak English, and mail in your tape. Sooner or later, a casting person will be calling you for an interview.

"If your selling point is that you're an interesting personality, make the job easy for the casting director and tell them why, briefly and specifically. Sit down and carefully compose a one-sentence description of yourself. It may not be easy to do, but it's crucial. Cut to the chase and describe yourself succinctly—and dramatically.

If they don't see you as a clear-cut character, it's harder for them to find a role for you. If you're the handsome firefighter type, or more of a country bumpkin, make that character come across.

"The producers have got to know who you are—right away. Don't waste time on small talk and hellos—just give them that one-sentence description of who you are and project that right into the camera. Next, tell them interesting things about yourself. Maybe it's things about your job, or maybe it's your hobby—whatever it is, you need a hook or a gimmick. Make them thinks it's worth their time and money to fly you out and look you over.

"Don't be afraid to do something offbeat or a little crazy. If you're a casting director looking at 3000 tapes in an afternoon, it takes something memorable to catch your eye. Make a funny face, do celebrity imitations, sing a quick snatch of a funny song…anything to rise above the noise. Be interesting, be wacky, or be drop-dead gorgeous…but catch the casting director's eye quickly.

"If you're lucky, you'll get a call to attend a semi-final interview—which in the bigger-budget shows, means showing up with two hundred or so other possibles in a central area like New York. And don't expect them to pay your way at this stage. After you pass this hurdle, they'll start paying your way. In my case, the 'Survivor' producers brought a bunch of us to Los Angeles, where they poked us and prodded us, did various interviews and screenings, conducted physical examinations and psychological testing." A brand-new study, the first of its kind, reveals the most desirable quality for making it big in either "legitimate" showbiz or Reality TV: narcissism. Dr. Drew Pinsky, USC Clinical Professor of Psychiatry and host of the long-running show "Love Line," authored the study with another USC professor. It found that of all celebrities, across the board—movies stars, musicians, singers—*the most narcissistic group is reality television stars*. It's also the least talented or skilled group. The study shows that females rate higher in narcissism than males, therefore…"Female reality show contestants are off the chart," said Dr. Pinsky.

After alpha-narcissist Rob got his personal green-light from executive producer Mark Burnett and CBS boss Les Moonves for "Survivor 6," he and his co-contestants jetted off to the Amazon jungle. In weeks of battling for the $1 million prize, Rob made it all the way to the last episode, where rival Jenna won the final

Challenge and helped vote him out of the game. Jenna went home with the million-dollar jackpot, but Rob got a consolation prize.

"I was asked to come to New York for what they call the 'up-fronts,' where the networks present their new shows to the advertisers. The minute I got there I knew something was up, because a bunch of other famous 'Survivor' contestants were there, like Richard Hatch and Rudy, the Navy SEAL. That's when they suddenly announced they were going to do a show called 'Survivor: All-Stars.' It was amazing, exciting, like a whirlwind. I'd just done my first season on a reality show, and immediately I been picked for another season.

"Here I was, a young guy from Long Island, hanging out with famous people like Mark Burnett and Jeff Probst, and a guy who told me he was a big fan of mine—Phil Rosenthal, the executive producer of 'Everybody Loves Raymond.' I was so thrilled when Phil asked Mark, 'Is Rob going to be on "Survivor: All-Stars?"' I will never forget Mark's answer: 'Is the Pope Polish?'

"It wasn't so great, of course, when—months later—I got voted off that show, too. But I still landed on my feet. Even if you're voted off 'Survivor,' you get some prize money. It wasn't a ton of dough, but it was enough for me to leave my job. Then I got lucky. Through all the contacts I'd made, I wound up in Los Angeles, hooked up with a partner, and became a producer. So far we've made a movie called 'The Scorned' and we sold a series to E! called 'Kill Reality.'"

Interestingly, Rob first found work after "Survivor" with a company that operated a website called Fishbowl, designed to capitalize on the semi-famous faces of people who'd been contestants on reality shows.

Said Rob: "It was called that because people who appear on reality shows really do live in a fishbowl. At first, the business plan was to capitalize on what we thought was going to be a seller's market. People may not realize it, but reality contestants are like paper plates: you use them once, then throw them out. But it's also true that the networks spend a lot of money making these people into famous faces, spending millions of dollars promoting them everywhere.

"We thought we could recycle reality stars—use them in other projects, promote them for endorsements, product lines, personal appearances, acting gigs, etc. We had only moderate success; we made a movie with a group of these people with familiar names and faces. Don't forget that many of these people are more famous than legitimate, low-level actors in legitimate show business.

"But here's what's interesting about people who are interesting enough to get on reality shows: frankly, some of them are real-life disasters. The over-the-top qualities that attracted casting directors and amused the audience often don't work well in real life. They can come across as really weird. If you see someone acting like a psychopath on scripted TV, it's called acting. If you see someone acting like a psychopath on Reality TV, chances are they really are psychopaths—and not the kind of people you want to do business with. They tend not to get up early in the morning or make careful life plans. Many are very unprofessional. They don't show up to jobs on time and tend to bite the hand that feeds them. Often, they are their own worst enemies.

"And there's another problem: there's a stigma attached to these people in Hollywood. Quite frankly, they are often looked down upon. It's not always true, but it's there. You can have all the talent in the world, but if you have that reality show stink on you, they don't want to touch you."

Ordinary people who star on reality shows often are content to return home, pick up their day-to-day lives and nurture the happy memories of their brief brush with fame. But Rob, like many ex-contestants, fell in love with show business and joined what's become a fast-growing colony of ex-reality stars who've settled in Hollywood. That means more competition, but Rob thrived and climbed a few rungs up the ladder by using the same techniques that attracted heavy hitters like Mark Burnett and Les Moonves.

"Whatever you want to do in life, you've got to pursue it with passion and great curiosity. That's how to succeed. I made it my business to know everything I could possibly know about 'Survivor' before I even tried to get on the show. It's preparation, then knowing how to present yourself. And it's important to research who the players are before you make your move to apply. It's just like the Boy Scouts—be prepared...for anything."

RULE #3: UNDERSTAND THAT REALITY SHOWS ARE LIKE LIFE: GREAT FUN UNTIL TROUBLE SMACKS YOU IN THE FACE.

"Reality TV producers want to keep you off balance," said Rob. "Their job is to put you in trouble—fast—so the first thing they'll do when filming begins is drown you in lots of alcohol. They want to get you drunk and crazy. The very nature of reality shows is to put people in situations that are outside of their element; then make them lose their inhibitions and their logical reasoning.

"On shows like 'Survivor' and 'Big Brother,' people are isolated and start out cool, calm and collected. Then the producers put alcohol into the equation, all hell breaks loose. Everybody gets horny—and what do you get? Nine times out of ten, great television! Make no mistake about it: producers want sexual tension. They want people to hook up on these shows. So they insert alcohol, that great social lubricant, into the mix. And if you think I'm exaggerating, here's the proof:

"As a 'Survivor contestant,' when you arrive at your wilderness destination, you don't have food or water laid in for you—but there is a supply of *condoms*.

"That sounds terrible to some people, but I think it's perfectly reasonable and fair for producers to make the most entertaining television they can. Remember, they're not breaking any laws supplying contestants with alcohol—everyone on these shows is of legal age."

How about contestants who complain in the press that they've ended up looking bad on these shows—and blame unethical tactics, like "franken-byting" or trick editing?

"I think that a lot of people who go on these reality shows are very quick to take all the credit for their talent when they end up looking good," said Rob. "But when they look bad, they blame the show, the producers, and dishonest editing. That's my point: be prepared. Everyone who goes on these shows should now know exactly what to expect. This is not the year 2000! Back then, the average person didn't yet understand what the reality game was all about. Now, thanks to intense media coverage and behind-the-scenes exposés, *everyone* knows what to expect as a contestant. You go in knowing the rules.

"Sure, there are producers that cross the line. But wrongdoing can occur in any business, not just reality television. Let me put it like this: it's kind of a deal with the devil. You are trading your right to privacy when you sign on and make the bargain for 15 minutes of fame. In that social and legal contract, you know full well there's a chance you could end up looking bad. When you sign those hundreds of sheets of waivers, that's what you're signing away. And I think reality producers are within their rights to show whatever they want to show—even if that's pushing the boundaries of good taste."

* * *

Chapter *Nineteen*

REAL SEX...MORE REAL SEX...EVEN MORE REAL SEX.

SEX! Now that I have your attention...!

That line is the oldest joke in the world, but it always works. Why? Because it perfectly describes the primal urge that drives us. It's the one thing we can never get enough of, and "Survivor" star Rob Cesternino, a Reality TV expert, offers this uncensored advice on how to impress producers on your first face-to-face audition:

"The thing they're dying to hear when you walk into that room is, 'I'm horny, I'm promiscuous...I want to get laid.' Anything concerning sex will make their eyes light up. They're looking for young hot people who want to have sex—that's their #1 candidate every time. And if a female happens to whip her top off, they'll be thrilled to pieces—because that means she's uninhibited, daring and serious about making great TV."

Once you're actually on the show, producers will quickly introduce what Rob calls the "social lubricant" so indispensable to making a great reality show: alcohol. You'll only see hints of sex while cameras are rolling, says Rob, "but the shenanigans really begin once the cameras are turned off."

How wild does it get? "INXS: Rockstar" got "pretty wild sometimes," said a source close to the show. "There was a party going on at that house every week after the show. Lots of alcohol flowing....people winding up in each other's beds."

On reality shows, nearly everything is filmed, even the social gatherings. But on "Rockstar," the contestants had hammered out a deal with the producers.

"It was agreed there would be absolutely no filming at these parties—because the producers were at the parties, too," said the source. "None of them wanted to be caught on camera, because there were instances of producers joining in the sexy action—partaking, so to speak. To put it in a less elegant way, there was a lot of screwing going—including talk of a three-some.

"But it wasn't just the sex—these parties got out-of-control crazy! There was a birthday party held for the winner of the first season at the magnificent home that had been rented for the production. The dining room was particularly beautiful, exquisitely decorated with spectacular, near-priceless antique furniture, tapestries, carpets and cabinetry. As the booze flowed, everybody started burning off excess energy, ending up in the showers together or actually running around the property naked—male and female. In fact, on the show's website, you get a hint of the action from footage of one of the guys—and later, one of the girls—streaking across the property for the cameras.

"But things really got out of control. All of a sudden, a stupid food fight started—like something out of 'Animal House.' It was disgusting. Birthday Boy and everyone else started flinging birthday cake all over everything in that exquisite dining room. What a mess! These so-called reality 'stars' showed a total disregard for their surroundings, lots of damage was done—and plenty of payoffs had to be made."

Rob Cesternino actually named names...well, one name.

"I don't mind telling you that the king of reality star hookups is the star of 'Survivor: Pearl Island'—Johnny Fairplay. (Note: The guy Danny Bonaduce body-slammed onstage at the 2007 Reality TV Awards show.) Fans will remember Johnny as they guy who played the sympathy card to gain an advantage by telling co-contestants his grandmother had died—which absolutely was not true. Johnny's the bad-boy rock star of Reality TV, the biggest party animal—and he's racked up more reality babes than anyone in the business. No one else even comes close. And I'd better stop naming names, before I get in trouble.

"Look, it's in the atmosphere. It's exciting. Everybody's hormones are jumping...and the adrenaline's pumping because your 15 minutes of fame are just beginning, so that leads to sex. But some people use sex to gain tactical advantages in the game. After all, Reality TV shows are a microcosm of real life, where people use sex to get ahead all the time."

So, dude…was "Survivor" insane, or what?

"Actually, on a show like 'Survivor,' even though people might be running around half-naked, sex is often the last thing on the contestants' minds. Sure, there's a lot of late-night snuggling, spooning and hugging. But nobody is really getting down and dirty…because everyone really *is* dirty. Or should I say filthy? There's an incredible lack of hygiene—you can go 30 days without showering or brushing your teeth. Think about it. My girlfriend doesn't want to have sex unless she's showered that day, so just imagine how the girls on 'Survivor' feel. Trust me, it's not a pretty picture.

"The easiest show to have sex on is 'Big Brother!' You're in a house, you've got beds and showers. There was actual intercourse on 'Big Brother 4,' when a guy and a girl got pretty drunk at about 3 in the morning and wound up having sex. It was the night before somebody was due to be voted out—and as luck would have it, she got voted out of the house. So they showed her having sex under the bedclothes on national television, and it was horrible—because her dad was there to see it. A family member is always invited when you're due to be voted off, and her dad showed up. Imagine how embarrassing that was for that poor girl."

It got much more embarrassing for a young female contestant on the British version of "Big Brother" when she had full-on sex in a hot tub—and her parents were actually asked to view the tape and comment on it for a national magazine.

Producers want to supercharge their shows with sex—but in America, it's got to be sneaky. The sex is implied and rarely gets raunchy—although there have been scenes, à la "Big Brother 4," showing couples writhing under sheets while supposedly doing the nasty.

Contrast that with Great Britain's version of "Big Brother." In their steamiest show ever, a beautiful black nurse from Zimbabwe named Makosi, and a white Brit bloke named Anthony, writhed naked in a swimming pool, fondled each other intimately, and then—ignoring the cameras and open-mouthed fellow house-mates—had full-on sexual intercourse.

Gorgeous Makosi made headlines in the British press when she confessed that she'd had an orgasm—not that there'd been much doubt. Photos showed her moment of unmistakable ecstasy with Anthony—not to mention her joyful dalliance with a pretty blonde female housemate named Orlaith.

Most American viewers have no experience of just how shocking and in-your-face British TV can get, so—as a public service for serious reality fans—here's a…er, blow-by-blow, minute-by-minute account of Ms. Makosi's immortal TV reality encounter, as published in a leading British magazine under the headline:

JUST HOW FAR DID THEY GO?

10:50 p.m. Makosi and Orlaith are in the pool and start caressing each other's breasts.

10:59 p.m. Anthony gets in the pool and starts snogging (kissing) first Makosi, then Orlaith.

11:05 p.m. Makosi gyrates her bottom against Anthony's naughty bits before kissing him again. Anthony, Makosi and Orlaith get it on for the next four minutes before they get out of the pool and run around virtually naked.

11:19 p.m. Makosi and Orlaith kiss while Anthony stands behind them. Orlaith raises up out of the water as if she's having sex. Anthony begs for a snog and they have another three-way grope.

11:24 p.m. Orlaith gropes Anthony's crotch before he encourages her to stimulate herself using the emission vents in the pool. Anthony licks Orlaith's boobs.

11:27 p.m. (Housemate) Kemal has now got into the pool and he, Makosi and Anthony are totally naked after removing their underwear. Orlaith still has her thong on. Makosi, Anthony and Orlaith are still snogging each other.

11:44 p.m. Housemate Craig joins the crowd in the pool and he and Orlaith start kissing. Orlaith and Makosi put on a show for the boys, kissing and groping each other.

12:02 a.m. Anthony and Makosi kiss against the side of the pool. Kemal, Orlaith and Craig get out as the pair appear to be now having sex. Craig remarks, "Oh my God, that's not necessary."

In what might be termed an "anti-climax" ten minutes later, Makosi and Orlaith go back to being naughty girls together. A stunned Craig is heard saying, "I can't believe it."

Blimey!

Those Brits are real goers, know what I mean…know what I mean?? (Wink wink, nudge nudge.) And now for something completely different…and I do mean *completely!*

On a U.K. reality show called "Sex Inspectors," the buff and attractive Tracey Cox, a no-nonsense body language coach who's fronted fitness and makeover shows on BBC, actually watches couples having live sex on camera—then offers tips, toys and advice. The *Observer's* Liz Hoggard wrote, "Tracey Cox is reading me a text message she received at the hairdresser's this morning: 'Hi, Tracey, I wanted to say thanks for how much you helped me. I can now have orgasms lying on my back…life is a lot easier. Lots of love, Charlotte.'

"Heavens. Of course it's all in a day's work for a sex therapist. And Cox, the best-selling author of 'Hot Sex and Supersex,' and a former editor of *Australian Cosmopolitan,* is fantastically unshockable. The unusual thing is that TV viewers will also get the chance to watch Charlotte, 30, from Essex, refine her orgasm technique on Channel 4 in two weeks' time."

Bloody 'ell! Wink, wink, nudge nudge. Take that, you bluestocking Americans! Cox doesn't deny it's all pretty shocking. "Even I, who talk about sex for a living, found it rather extraordinary sitting there and watching real people have sex," she admits. "Usually when I do TV, I'm in this zen space. I offer advice, then the couples go away and try it out. So the first time I watched the footage, I went, 'Oh my God.' The director teases me that I'm the only sexpert she knows who has to be warned when there's sex about to come up on screen. She kept saying, 'Could you look a little bit less prudish?' Eventually I thought, 'Oh come on, I'm doing a job, just calm down and watch it.'"

It's the logical extension of the reality makeover show. We've done property, plastic surgery, food, love, money—why not sex?

In the *Observer,* Hoggard defends the show: "'Sex Inspectors' is beautifully shot, full of color and humor. This isn't a porn show by another name. As Cox explains: 'I asked the director two questions, "Will it be tacky?", and she said, "No." And I said, "Will we be allowed to fail?", and she said, "Yes." Which after working in America for nine months on the U.S. version of "Would Like To Meet" was so refreshing. I thought if we can fail and they're real people it will be OK.'

"The couples, who range from late twenties to late thirties, are all in long-term relationships ('Since we started we've had three marriages and a baby,' says Cox excitedly). Yes, there is a car-crash element of: 'Ohmigod I can't believe you're admitting that on national TV.' But what's clear is how unhappy sexual dysfunction is making the couples—and how important it is to sort it out. And it's amazing how a little role-play can perk up a marriage. 'People have the best sex after fancy dress parties,' Cox confides."

Aha! That might explain the origin of that old come-on: "There's a party in my pants, and you're invited!"

How have U.K. audiences reacted to "Sex Inspectors," a show that's somewhat shocking even by British standards? "I can see why people have had a knee-jerk reaction to it," Cox acknowledges, "Because it's not sex—It's real sex. If you watch a porn movie, no one even blinks. We see far more sex on any TV program after 9 p.m. The reason why it's so shocking is it's people like you and I. You look at them and think, 'That's probably what I look like in bed.'"

Still, prim and proper persons on both sides of the pond might well ask the question, "Aren't you a bit ashamed?" What's the real purpose, outside of titillation, of knowing what real people do in bed?

Oh, puh-leeze! What's the real purpose of asking for a real purpose other than titillation. Human beings are sexually curious. There, you prudes…I've said it. Surprised, anyone? Sex fuels the engine of Reality TV. Right, Paris Hilton?

DUH!… *Hellooooo!*

Exactly! If we weren't titillated by real people having sex—and pity us poor Americans, who have to make do watching bedsheets twitch—we could rent porn or watch the fictional "Sex and the City." "Sex Inspectors" is fascinating because it uses real people. But is it ethical to show people talking about their problems on camera? Shouldn't they be consulting a therapist? Will they be damaged long-term? Or even split up?

Says Cox: "All the people who went on it knew what they were up for, they had a personality that could cope, and they quite liked the fact that the rest of Britain would be watching. The joy of these couples is they really want to help other people. When Charlotte learned that other women have problems climaxing, she was like, 'Right, I was made to feel so upset by this, I want everyone to bloody know the truth.' She was on a bit of a crusade. I think for a lot of the couples, there was a sense of giving something back. By not going to a therapist, they're actually able to help other people.

"I completely and utterly believe in [the show]. Forty per cent of us are dissatisfied with our sex life, we've got a 50 per cent divorce rate, everybody, but everybody, is having affairs...because we've got unreal expectations. We get to dispel all those sexual myths, so you don't feel so bad about yourself, and offer practical tips that do really work. And unlike most sex shows with an educational slant, it's not anti-men—to be honest I think women should act more like men when it comes to sex."

Blimey! Cheers to that, luv! And have you tried selling your show to America? Sadly, we Yanks are way behind the sexual curve. Jack Nicholson once put it: "In America, you can't show a breast being fondled, but you can film one being cut off."

And while we're comparing Reality TV sex overseas, here's a Japanese show that's not quite ready for American prime time—"Shinjuku Nozoki Beya," or "Shinjuku Peep Room." (Remember what I told you in Chapter 1, fans—it's all about voyeurism!) The show is a red-hot ratings smash on Paradise TV, Japan's prime purveyor of puerile porn, according to the magazine Asahi Geino. (Calling it the "prime purveyor" implies there's plenty of "puerile porn" on Japanese TV.) "Peep Room" is a Reality TV show where cameras surreptitiously record a young woman living alone in an apartment in Tokyo's hip Shinjuku district.

It's a four-hour, live-to-air weekly show—and not staged in any way, say producers. They offer young girls the chance to live free in the apartment for one month. The girls don't know where the cameras are located, and they can be switched on remotely. Because Japan has a strict legal ban on displaying genitalia, the main problem for producers is being really careful about camera angles because the show goes to air live—so anything can happen.

Many of the young women who take the deal figure it's a perfect way to come to the big city and find a job while living rent-free. And they're not shy about the viewing audience peeping at their sexual high jinks.

"I'm surprised just how brazen some of these supposedly average types have gotten up to," said a spokesman for Paradise TV. "What's really shocked me has been the onanism. I had no idea there were so many different ways that women are able to get themselves off. Some girls just use their fingers like normal, while others prefer rubbing up against a pillow and still more give the [porno] actresses a run for their money by using vibrators or rotors. We have put more cameras in for the new version of the show, so I think viewers can expect some good stuff."

Like any live TV show, "Shinjuku Nozoki Beya" has had its share of unexpected, off-the-wall occurrences. Staffers can make a phone call to the occupant if necessary, advising her to be just a tad more decorous—and make sure that blankets are covering up the naughty bits.

But it's not all fun and games. Viewers are always taking a gamble because reality can be boring. One episode of "Shinjuku Nozoki Beya" focused on a woman sleeping for four hours after she'd come down with a bad cold. Now that Paradise TV can be viewed over the Internet or on cell phones in Japan, producers are planning programs that encourage more viewer participation.

"We're thinking of 'Shinjuku Misshitsu Nama Hoso' ['Live Broadcast from Shinjuku's Secret Room'] which will have girls responding in real time to viewers' requests for such acts as masturbation or simply showering," said the Paradise spokesman. "Another idea we've got is 'Mayonaka no Shinjuku Nanpa Sex Nama Chukei' ('Late Night Shinjuku One Night Stand Broadcast') where we go out on the streets of Shinjuku on a Friday night after the trains have stopped running to pick up a stranded girl for sex."

Meanwhile, back in America…where the blankets *always* cover the naughty bits, we get Reality TV shows that aren't even conducive to sexual shenanigans. Said "Survivor" star Rob: "On 'The Amazing Race,' you're running around so much, who has time for sex? The show with the most sex going on is almost certainly MTV's 'The Real World.' Reality TV's female equivalent of Johnny Fairplay is probably Trishelle, who starred in the Las Vegas season of 'The Real World.' But contrary to popular belief—in this country, anyway—reality stars aren't having non-stop sex, because there's simply no privacy. Cameras are running, and most people aren't anxious to be seen having sex on television.

"That's probably why it's memorable when anything does happen. A scene every reality fan remembers is from 'Joe Millionaire,' where Evan Marriott sneaks off into the bushes with contestant Sarah Kozer—and the audience heard slurping sounds suggesting that she was giving him oral sex. Sarah has accused the producers of dubbing in those sounds…but Evan has never commented one way or the other."

One of the hottest reality show debuts ever, "Joe Millionaire" went on the air in 2003. The premise was fascinating: 20 women were vying for the hand of a multi-millionaire named "Evan Warner." Actually, the women were being hoaxed by Evan Marriott, a $19,000-a-year construction worker—and part-time underwear model. What the cameras never revealed was the behind-the-scenes scandal that rocked the show and threatened to finish it. The *National Enquirer* revealed that an ugly controversy began after Evan and one of the contestants kept sneaking away from the other women for hour-long hook-ups. A source reported that when a few other contestants cornered the woman and asked where they disappeared to, she talked about giving Evan sexual favors in exchange for his promise that she wouldn't be cut from the show.

Within minutes, Evan's sex scandal reached all the girls—and they were furious. Some were so angry they threatened to walk off the show unless producers immediately addressed the issue. The brouhaha finally died down when Evan and the woman made efforts to convince both contestants and producers that nothing sexual had occurred between them and that she had simply been joking about their sexual quid pro quo. "But nobody on the set really believed them," said show insiders.

Richard Hatch, the often-naked arch-villain of "Survivor," once got involved in an alleged "real sex" incident that blew up into a claim of sexual harassment. Said Rob: "There was a big scandal when contestant Susan Hawk accused Richard of rubbing his private parts up against her during one of the challenges. She threatened to sue him, and they had to be separated for the remainder of the show."

Asked what it was like meeting the notorious Hatch on "Survivor: All-Stars," Rob chuckled and gave up this truly "ass-stounding" scoop: "Richard was a trip, man. On that show the producers make a big deal about us all having to learn how to make fire in the wilderness before going on the show. They warned us that they weren't going to give us any tools or matches. They really scared the hell out of everybody. But soon after we arrive in the wilds, Richard goes into the bushes and comes out holding a small film canister that he waves around—and it's full of matches. He says to everybody, 'I can make a fire…I've got matches!' Everybody kept asking him, 'Richard, where'd you get the matches?' And he finally admits, smiling that trademark smirk, that he'd smuggled them in *up his ass!*

"Now just to top that, here's a story I'm revealing for the first time ever—the scoop even Mike Walker never got. At the show's finale, one of our producers showed up with a truly astounding souvenir. We couldn't believe our eyes as he proudly showed us Richard's secret canister—the guy had actually saved it."

Eeeeewwww…thanks for sharing, Rob! And no early parole for you, Richard Hatch! And here's a tip for all you "Survivor" fans…watch for that canister on e-Bay.

*

To sum up, it's all about sex. Or, as Howard Stern insists, it's all about lesbians!

If network and cable Reality TV ever starts to bore you, there's always the hard-core of Stern's "On Demand" pay-per-view. Howard's art is to hone in on the offbeat sexual fantasies we all think about, but rarely mention in polite—or even impolite—conversation.

That's why America needs Howard: to interview lesbians and educate the general public about them; to let us watch real women surrendering to the robotic stroking of a Sybian machine; and demonstrate how a true master of reality can elicit even the "Most Shocking Secrets" from a reluctant subject—like the time he pried from co-host Robin Quivers the mind-boggling confession that she has enjoyed pleasuring herself with meats and vegetables (raw and uncooked, of course).

But, alas, reality programming is still in its infancy here on Earth, shaking to free itself from the surly bonds of earth and the censorship prudes of the FCC. That's why Howard Stern has been forced to figuratively leave the planet and broadcast from a satellite in outer space where—like a super-hero in self-imposed exile—he's free to continue his daring explorations into reality for the sake of all mankind.

* * *

Chapter *Twenty*

NEXT STOP: THE FUTURE!

Here is an experiment so dangerous I specifically warn Jennifer Aniston not to participate.

Stop reading NOW, Jen!

Everyone else...please sit back, relax, close your eyes—and try to imagine the phantasmagorical future of Reality TV. What riveting, sensational new shows will ratings-hungry Hollywood invent for our prurient delectation over the next decade? Remember, showbiz can never stand still. The audience ruthlessly demands ever-fresher chills, thrills and giggles! So the illusionists, whose lust for our money is insatiable, must keep topping themselves with new plots and fresh, way-out gimmicks designed to exploit our fears, tickle our funny-bones and feed our addiction to voyeurism.

To quote that endlessly-talented old perv Woody Allen, "The heart wants what the hearts wants"...whatever that is! But therein lies the question: How far will the escalation go? Where will it end? Remember the question posed at the beginning of this book:

Is "The Running Man" right around the corner?

Will we ever see a TV reality show based on a death-hunt game, with condemned convicts literally running for their lives to evade licensed-to-kill pursuers and win the grand prize of freedom on a faraway isle where they pose no further danger to civilized society? Make no mistake, dear reader, ideas like this are discussed in the creative community more often than you might think. It starts as a joke, usually, then someone says, "Well...why not?"

One Hollywood writer-producer told me he was approached by a woman who asserted that she had made the decision to end her life, which had become unbearable, by committing suicide with a pistol—so she wanted to propose a reality show that would climax with her self-inflicted death, on-camera!

Now *that's* showbiz! Talk about ending your 15 minutes with a bang.

Profits from her show, the woman said, would go to her surviving family members, thus ensuring their future security—and, at the same time, providing a noble, feel-good premise that would make everyone, both producers and viewers, feel less guilty about serving up that soupcon of *schadenfreude* so necessary to reality's recipe. It's a sordid premise, unquestionably; but totally fascinating! Even Jennifer Aniston might be tempted to tune in. And, trust me, there are network Suits who'd green-light that baby in an eye-blink—if lawyers and insurance companies would give them the thumbs-up.

Now, let's continue with our experiment....

...Eyes closed, please, and concentrate first on Reality TV as it exists today...relax...let the mind smile as happier images come swirling up...ah, look there....

...people singing on "American Idol"...dancing on "Dancing with the Stars"...getting goofy on "America's Got Talent"...frenetically flitting around the world on "The Amazing Race"...designing dreamy fashions on "Project Runway"...and a real heart-warmer, "Little People, Big World," that truly touching series about Matt and May Roloff, 4-foot-tall little people raising a large family on a 34-acre farm in Oregon, and teaching their kids—three of average height, one born a dwarf—that you must never let physical size get in the way of your dreams....

...Uh, oh!...hold tight now...the swirling images get progressively more frightening as....

...UGH!...look at "real people" just like you and me, eating bugs and pig rectums...jumping off cliffs...swapping spouses...seducing others into adultery... suffering painful plastic surgeries that go horribly wrong...exposing embarrassing personal secrets...back-stabbing their closest friends and family...betraying lovers...throwing orphans into the street...entrapping pedophiles....

Entrapping pedophiles…?

Oops, sorry, that show's actually not in the future—it's already here!

(AUTHOR'S NOTE: The next few pages are exactly as I wrote them in the first-draft manuscript of this book. Following that is an update written as we go to press. I'm keeping the original words intact because they proved to be so uncannily prophetic, and to convey that initial unease I felt so strongly when I saw alleged journalists (1) corrupting our craft to score ratings for a TV reality show, (2) carelessly setting the stage for a man's death, then (3) bragging that despite it all, they really "sleep well." To them I say: May this book be your worst nightmare!)

Astoundingly—or perhaps not so astoundingly, depending on your view of human nature—a whopping 10 million people per episode view a pedophile entrapment reality show staged by these so-called "newsmen" of "Dateline NBC" who have airily abandoned the journalistic ethics they once so dearly loved to brag about by paying cold cash to sources, and even law enforcement agents. The show is called "To Catch a Predator," and it works like this:

NBC News pays a watchdog website called Perverted Justice, whose members go online posing as underage girls, then try to lure male perverts into meeting them for sex in a house that's rigged with hidden cameras. Once the sucker perp walks in the door, of course, the blow-dried NBC correspondent Chris Hansen pounces, interviews and humiliates the rattled creeps—then gives the audience a blow-by-blow after he orders them out of the house and cops arrest them.

Admittedly, watching male perverts freak out and panic as they get busted for preying on children makes for great television. But as a journalist, this show made me more than a little uneasy. Throwing these child-perv scumbags in jail is admittedly a noble pursuit. But it's a job for law enforcement and the cops—NOT so-called "investigative" journalists. Newsmen report news, they don't conspire to invent it. Make no mistake, NBC News is not "investigating" one damned thing with their hit show, "To Catch a Predator." What they're doing is providing money, cameras and prime TV time to produce a whiz-bang perp-bust show that racks up monster ratings and big, big bucks—which is absolutely what Reality TV is all about, of course.

But here's the crucial point: shows like this should be produced by the network's entertainment division—not the news department.

In the first draft of this book, I wrote that it was unsettling to watch people who call themselves "journalists" corrupting our craft just to score ratings for a TV reality show. I sensed that there might be bad times ahead for "Dateline," as did other experts in our field. NBC News was carelessly setting the stage for disaster, and finally faced it when they launched an ill-considered witch-hunt that ended in a man's death. Even in the face of that sobering experience, "Dateline" frontman Chris Hansen told an interviewer that he "sleeps well" at night. To him I say, as one journalist to another, Reality TV is *entertainment*. Mixing it up with real-life journalism can conjure up nightmares! So take a nap, Chris, while I explain to my readers just how dangerous you and your kind are.

First, NBC's show-bizzy "Predator" extravaganza thumbs its nose at accepted journalistic standards. It clearly flouts the legal definition of entrapment, which says that a person is entrapped when "induced or persuaded by law enforcement officers or their agents to commit a crime that he had no previous intent to commit." Get that, folks? Journalists aside, even cops are not allowed to entrap by throwing out bait. For a cop, or a journalist, reporting that Britney Spears ingested cocaine in a nightclub is perfectly legitimate, if true. But sending a nickel bag of pure over to her table just to see if she'll take a snort is NOT.

Now don't get me wrong. My personal belief is that there should be life sentences without parole for sick monsters who prey on our children, because any expert will tell you that there's no recidivism—no chance of rehabilitation. You can't cure or control that creepy, kiddie-sex urge, even by castration. (Too bad the law won't allow adding that ratings-getter to NBC's show!) But here's my advice to Chris Hansen and all the other "wannabe" cops on "Dateline": If you want to make a career out of apprehending dirtbags, quit journalism and join the police force.

When "To Catch a Predator" first launched, it was attacked by many outraged journalists—and defended by few. When the Public Eye blog on CBSnews.com chided their competitor on NBC News, animatronic anchor Stone Phillips, he scoffed at the charge that he's engaging in entrapment—even though he admitted, in a monumental lapse of logical thought, that when a suspected perv makes Internet contact with the decoy "underage girls," it's often the "girl" who actually introduces the idea of sexual contact.

To illustrate Stone Phillips' point, here's an online exchange between "Dateline" decoy "Shia" and "Rob" (rkline05), in which the target clearly expresses concern about their age difference and whether a sexual encounter would be appropriate—but Shia calms him down, then flashes him a greenlight:

rkline05: but idk [I don't know] about everything we talked about

shyshia girl: why not

rkline 05: well you sure you wanna do all that

shyshiagirl: yeaa why not

skline05: idk I just wasn't sure you wanted to you are a virgin and all. you sure you want it to be me that takes that

shyshiagirl: yea why not. ur cool

skline05: I just…you really sure I feel weird about it. You being so much younger than me and all

shyshiagirl: ur not old. Don't feel weird

Thus reassured and lured by "shy" Shia, Rob hustled over to the "Dateline" house, got busted and later pleaded guilty to soliciting a minor.

So…it *is* entrapment, right? Here's what Great Talking Head Stone Phillips wrote on his blog:

"In many cases, the decoy is the first to bring up the subject of sex. However, the transcripts show that once the hook is baited, the fish jump and run with it like you wouldn't believe."

Say what? Then why not call the show, "Trolling for Pervs!" Is Phillips' bizarre justification for entrapment the fact that it works beautifully, so it must be okay?

The illogic of his reasoning apparently dawned on Stone Phillips in retrospect, because he "refined" his argument shortly thereafter and wrote: "Enticement? Yes. An entrapment? I don't think so. The closer I look at the online conversations (which are available on Perverted Justice website) the more obvious it becomes that these men are not first timers when it comes to engaging minors in graphic online chats. They tend to be remarkably matter of fact in their approach, as if it is part of an all too regular routine."

So…"Psychic" Stone Phillips peers into the past and *knows for certain* that each and every man who responds to *Dateline*'s siren call to sex has committed these crimes before? *Puh-leeze!* Internet junkies goof around and talk dirty in sex chat rooms for anonymous titillation and/or "just to fuck with people's heads," as one geek put it, all the time—with no intention of committing a crime. Disgusting, yes. A crime? Probably. Under most state statutes designed to combat online pedophilia, intent to solicit sexual acts from a minor is unlawful, even if the minor is willing to engage. But if that's true, why isn't disgraced ex-Congressman Mark Foley in the pokey? In May 2006, this hypocrite stood before Congress and railed against "online predators," urging tougher laws because "we must stop playing Russian Roulette with our children's lives!" Just months later, Foley was under FBI investigation for sending creepy, sexual e-mails to underage congressional pages. He admitted he was gay and resigned his House of Representatives seat, but he's still walking around free. How's that investigation coming along, FBI?

CBS Public Eye quickly responded to Stone Phillips' dim-bulb argument, saying, "He writes that because [he thinks] the man had engaged minors in graphic chats before, he can be enticed to the house by any means necessary. That's a Machiavellian argument, and not necessarily an incorrect one, depending on your perspective. But it is not an unassailable response to the charge of entrapment…one can, of course, argue that potential child molesters should be exposed to the public. Some law enforcement agencies do so. 'Dateline,' however, is not the law. Even if you think it is appropriate for these men to be exposed, is the decision to do so one that should be made by the media? I*s it too much to think that a little thing like 'ratings' might play a part as well?"*

BUSTED!

Shortly after this exchange, CBS canned Stone Phillips. Was it because he'd proven, in writing, that he lacks the intellect to practice journalism at a network level? One can only hope.

Let's cut right to the chase. The very, very smart people who run network TV know that their show, "To Catch a Predator"—which shamelessly puts cops and journalists in bed together—stays in business because it's like exterminating rats and cockroaches: nobody questions your methods much, as long as you get the job done.

The average viewer doesn't know much about journalistic ethics and could care less, probably, so they're not going to complain. And there are no bleeding hearts for kiddie-sex sickos. Despite the fact that even vile murderers like Scott Peterson get sympathy and love letters from pathetic, lonely women, nobody loves a child molester. So what's the big deal if a news organization—in the course of busting these monsters—hands out cash money to sources and law enforcement personnel? It's a huge journalistic no-no, even by NBC News standards, but…who cares, right? The targets are kiddie pervs? It's a feel-good show. And star-struck cops, who want their 15 minutes of fame just like the next guy, play along. And why not? What could go wrong? Molesters are rarely hard-case, violent criminals who might actually whip out a gun and start shooting when confronted by candid cameras. It's not like anyone's gonna get killed, right?

WRONG!!

In November 2006, NBC's "To Catch a Predator" and its hit squad of wannabe-cops/journalists descended on the town of Murphy, Texas, to conduct a sting operation.

"The only honest thing that followed was the gunshot," wrote Luke Dittrich in a riveting *Esquire* magazine piece, ominously headlined:

"Tonight on Dateline This Man Will Die."

NBC's team arrived and quickly went into action. A rented decoy house was wired for video and sound. A weird vigilante group of self-styled pedophile hunters called Perverted Justice, who are paid a consulting fee by "Dateline," fired up their computers and entered online chat rooms posing as underage teens living in the area. Whenever an adult male hit on one of the fake kids online, Perverted Justice saved transcript of their conversations, then informed "Dateline" producers. Targets were chosen for takedown and invited to show up for a sexual liaison at the wired decoy house—where Chris Hansen would suddenly pounce with a microphone and cameras, humiliate the perv, then send him outside for a wildly dramatic arrest by the "Showbiz Police," who'd run hollering at the suspect with guns drawn and throw him on the ground like he'd just assassinated the President.

Those who've observed *Dateline*'s weird symbiosis with local cops are shocked at how easily police officers let themselves be ordered around by TV producers who have no law enforcement authority whatsoever. "Those camera-loving cops would line up and high-kick like the Rockettes if the producers asked them to," one Reality TV producer told me.

Speaking about the tragic and horrifying incident that occurred during the taping of this episode, the district attorney of Kaufman County, Texas, labeled the cops involved as "the most incompetent bunch of buffoons you've ever seen."

It's important to note that Chris Hansen and NBC News vehemently deny that "Dateline" and law enforcement are working hand-in-glove to create an exciting TV show; on the contrary, they insist, they're simply conducting "parallel investigations" that never influence each other. But on this episode, notes Luke Dittrich in *Esquire*, "whatever wall may have once divided 'Dateline' and the police... essentially collapsed."

Here's how it went down: Perverted Justice reported to "Dateline" producers that a man using the screen name "inxs00" had engaged in sexual exchanges with a decoy pretending to be a 13-year-old boy. Under Texas law, it is a felony to communicate lewdly with someone under the age of 14, even if there is no sexual contact. Incredibly, the man was identified as Lewis Conrad Jr., 56, a veteran district attorney from the nearby town of Terrel, Texas. An upstanding conservative who'd been president of his high school class and voted Most Likely to Succeed, "Bill" Conrad had become the D.A. of his home county in his thirties. His peers—the judges and lawyers who'd worked with him for years—rated him as a very good prosecutor. An expert in Texas law, Conrad had apparently been breaking it for two weeks in sexually explicit online chats with a Perverted Justice decoy posing as a 13-year-old boy named "Luke." Conrad presented himself to Luke as a 19-year-old named "Wil." According to Dittrich's *Esquire* story, some of the things he wrote to Luke included:

"could I feel your cock"

"how thick are you"

"i want to feel your cock"

"maybe you can fuck me several times"

Finally, Luke invited Wil to visit him at the decoy house. Wil accepted, then didn't show. Luke repeated the invitation several times. Will kept saying he'd come, but never did.

And then the insanity began.

The local yokel police chief got a call from one of his men working with "Dateline," and was told: Chris Hansen wants the police to get an arrest warrant and a search warrant for Bill Conrad because he's no longer answering his computer or his telephone, and they don't think he's coming to the decoy house. Incredibly, the star-struck chief talked a judge into issuing a warrant, then sent a SWAT team to Conrad's house. When he didn't answer the doorbell, the cops eventually decided to make a forced entry—rather than, say, wait for him to show up at his office the next day and arrest him without incident. Although it can't be proven, there's little doubt that Bill Conrad saw the SWAT team and NBC cameras swarming on his lawn. When the cops busted his front door open with a prybar, he slowly stepped into view, said something like, "Guys, I'm not going to hurt anyone"—then fired a bullet from a .380 handgun into his brain.

A forensic analysis of Bill Conrad's laptop computer months later showed that he had indeed chatted online with "Luke," but his computer's hard drive "was otherwise devoid of anything illegal or indicative of sexual predation," according to Dittrich.

Of the 23 would-be pedophiles captured by "To Catch a Predator," the local prosecutor dropped charges against them all, citing flaws in the joint NBC/police investigation.

Conrad's sister, disputing the alleged transcripts notated by Perverted Justice, filed suit against NBC, seeking $105 million in damages.

And in another lawsuit, Marsha Bartel, 49, alleges that she was fired from her job as "sole producer" of "To Catch a Predator" when she insisted on "ethical and accurate reporting on the Predator series." Bartel charges NBC covered up the improper relationship between law enforcement officials and the show's producers, and further charges that cops acted wrongly when arresting suspected pedophiles, "goofing off by waving rubber chickens in the faces of Sting targets while forcing them to the ground and handcuffing them."

Bartel added the incredible charge that Perverted Justice, the shadowy vigilante group, does not provide "complete transcripts from its trolling operations," so NBC "cannot independently verify the accuracy" of the transcripts. In answer to her complaints about the group, she says, the show's executive producer, David Corvo, told her, "We all know they're nuts." NBC's answer to all this, in an official statement, is:

"NBC News is proud of its reporting and we believe this lawsuit is without merit."

Proud?

A man who may or may not be innocent was hounded to death by journalists who are supposedly dedicated fact-seekers, duty-bound to report news, not create it—and who want the truth, not TV ratings.

Proud?

So why, asks Brian Stelter in the *New York Times*, does NBC "seem to be scaling back its commitment to 'To Catch a Predator'? The network has filmed only one sting operation so far this year (2007), compared with seven in 2006. In several ways, the high ratings for 'Predator' have come at a high price for NBC. Some advertisers say they are wary of being associated with the show's content...."

Stay tuned.

As we try to predict Reality TV's future based on the above, let's imagine a hot new show called..."Home Invasion." Its premise is to lure criminals into robbing homes where police lie in wait. (NBC...call me!)

In the riveting pilot episode, a producer goes online posing as a little old lady. She says her bank was rude to her, so she's withdrawn her life savings of nearly $1 million and will keep it at home—in cash—until she finds a nicer bank. She asks people to recommend one in her area—and is "conned" into giving out her address. Pistol-wielding thugs break into the house. They're confronted by cops, but start shooting—and are quickly executed in a blaze of gunfire. Great TV, right?? But the "Home Invasion" show can't happen in our era, because even criminals have rights, right? (Damn. Sorry, NBC.)

Ah, but the laws, they are a-changin' in post-9/11 America. And with shows like "To Catch a Predator" pushing the envelope, can "The Running Man" be far behind?

Preposterous?

Perhaps. But ask yourself this question:

Will Reality TV escalate from the freak show it is today into a genre that's even more cartoon-ish? It's the TV equivalent of slowing down to get a better look at a car crash, so why not a show called "The World's Greatest Car Crash"…real people risking life and limb as they compete for a big-bucks prize by staging violent vehicle smashups?

Will we ever accept real-life bloodshed on TV? Will there be any limit to the bad taste already sucking in the "suckers" that, as showman P.T. Barnum put it, are born every minute?

You want bad taste? Here's bad taste:

When British Reality TV producers advertised for contestants for a new show called "Let's Make a Baby"—in which total strangers compete in a race to conceive a child—more than 200 people applied. They were told they would live in a "fertility house" with a group of other total strangers, and the least attractive couple would be voted out each week. When only two couples remained, they would race against each other to make a baby.

Shortly after "Let's Make a Baby" was announced, the producers were offered vast sums of money for rights to the show from TV channels all over the world. Famed British TV personalities offered to host it, including that notorious "Big Brother" on-camera sex star, hottie Makosi. But it wasn't until after the auditions were held that the so-called "producers" revealed the shocking truth:

"Let's Make a Baby" was a total hoax!

It had been conceived by a BBC current affairs series called "Mischief." The idea was to come up with the ultimate tasteless Reality TV show and see if people were either (a) willing to take part, or (b) willing to watch. It was first pitched to focus groups, who agreed that it was completely offensive, morally questionable—and (c) they could hardly wait to watch!

Professor David Wilson, an academic who walked out as a consultant on the U.K. "Big Brother" for ethical reasons, said he wasn't surprised that so many people applied to make a baby with a total stranger on TV.

"Those who take part are considered odd or bizarre for wanting to do so, but they are merely products of a society that now holds fame above anything else. All cultural reference points are now rooted in being a celebrity…not attached to having an intrinsic skill."

It takes two to tango, however. Everyone wants to be a star, but you can't be a star unless people are willing to watch you. Hard as it is to believe, the Reality TV phenomenon proves that showbiz stars like George Clooney or Scarlett Johansson don't have a lock on the fame game. Hollywood's just discovered something truly amazing:

Real people are people, too.

In the 1990 movie "The Truman Show," Jim Carrey starred as the only person in the world who didn't know that his whole life had been recorded since birth for the world's most popular TV show. His house, his office, every store and building in his town had been constructed for "The Truman Show"—and his wife, his mother, his friends and all the townspeople were actors in the carefully constructed plot that was his life. And the hint of things to come for all of us is summed up at the end of the movie by Ed Harris, who plays the TV show director, when he tells Truman:

"You were real. That's what made you so good to watch."

Okay, our experiment has worked nicely, so...wake up, everyone!

Take a deep breath...relax...and let's reconsider what the future holds for Reality TV, based on what we've just discussed. Let's go back to "The Running Man." If the idea that convicts might someday be hunted down and executed on a national TV show makes you snicker, will you agree that it sounds less far-fetched after hearing Stone Phillips pompously defend journalists who play perv-busting cops for fun and profit on "To Catch a Predator"?

Remember: entrapment is illegal. If you can get away with that, you might eventually get away with...murder!

Can't you just hear some network Suit arguing, "Well, it's not *really* murder because the people you'd be executing are criminals, right? And bad guys don't have rights, right? Are you sure the lawyers are okay with it? And the insurance guys? Well...what the heck! I say, let's green-light it, babe!"

Trust me, dear reader, the Stone Phillips argument is the same one that will be used someday by ratings-mongers posing as journalists to justify "The Running Man"—a show that will be reviled by TV critics, but will unquestionably be a monster success if it airs. To the future producers of that show, I hereby bequeath the promo line I wrote for "National Enquirer TV":

You *Know* You Want to Watch!

Here's one more harbinger of the future from Reality TV super-producer Mark Burnett: the controversial idea of pitting teams divided by race against each other on "Survivor: The Cook Islands."

When Burnett first confirmed in news reports that his show would feature whites *vs.* blacks *vs.* Asians *vs.* Latinos, it was like throwing a bomb right into the heartland of Politically Correct America! Posturing politicos, pandering race-baiters and bleeding-heart liberals exploded with predictable, over-heated rhetoric:

"What will be next? Nazis versus Jews? This is blatant racism of the worst kind designed to pump the ratings...blah, blah, blah."

Rush Limbaugh hit the racial-stereotyping equivalent of a home run right out of the park on his radio show, huffing gleefully that he hoped there were *"not going to be a lot of water events"* because blacks are not good swimmers. Huh? When challenged on that point, the ever-resourceful recovering drug addict referred to a survey that says *more blacks than whites drown in the U.S.* Rush identified Asians as *"the brainiacs out of the bunch."* He then opined that the Latino team would come on strong because they *"will do things other people won't do."* And how do you assess the white team's chances, Rush? Ah, they'll have problems, he predicted, because of their "guilt at oppressing all these people."

Mark Burnett scored a huge public relations coup by heading off to the races, so to speak, with this groundbreaking idea. But a quick, informal poll of sociologists and academic eggheads reveals no incipient fear that "Survivor: Rainbow" will trigger race riots. In the contrary, the consensus seems to be that healthy competition might even lead to valuable dialogue—and funny dialogue, certainly, on jolly old Rush Limbaugh's show.

Now here's a tidbit most people missed: the Reality TV giant who first came up with the idea of playing the race card to raise ratings was...Donald Trump! Unhappy with the sagging ratings of "The Apprentice," the billionaire admitted that he'd toyed with the idea—but then backed off. He told the *New York Post:* "Because of the enormous success of 'The Apprentice,' people are always calling and e-mailing us with ideas for the show. This idea was suggested by numerous people. But I personally don't like it, so it will never happen."

The *Post* turned for comment on that to a black contestant from the previous season of "The Apprentice," Tara Dowdell, who snapped, "This is a sick, desperate attempt to try and boost ratings for a show that's stooped to Jerry Springer level."

Even though The Donald passed on race-teaming, his Reality TV partner, Mike Burnett, quickly picked up on the colorful idea and ran with it. The show has aired, but—so far, at least—the streets are quiet. The calm before the storm, perhaps?

My favorite report on the debut of "Survivor: The Cook Islands" was penned by the hilariously thoughtful Joel Stein of the *Los Angeles Times,* a nice young Jewish humorist who wrote:

"I've never been interested in 'Survivor,' but the new, racist 'Survivor'—that, I was psyched about. If 'Battle of the Network Stars' made good TV, weekly competitions between poorly fed 'tribes' of African-Americans, whites, Asians and Latinos were going to be awesome. So...I got some brie and water crackers, put on a J. Crew sweater vest and settled down on the settee to root for whitey. None of my white friends wanted to watch with me because—although it was fine for the other races—they felt it was unbecoming for Caucasian-Americans to root for their own kind."

Stein reports that he immediately began "to turn on my own people" because they were "too preppy, too frat-boy, too happy with themselves. While other teams were fighting over hut building, the white folks were making toasts to each other over little bits of coconut milk...thrilled with their total super awesomeness." Stein found that the black people loved themselves almost as much as the white people did, and they indulged in too much "sexism, infighting and talk about representing and feeling each other's vibes."

He found that the Latinos were likable, hard-working and quiet, "but those Asians—they were terrific. In fact, better yet, they were like me. They were laid-back and self-effacing. There was a journalist, a lawyer, a management consultant—just like my friends."

Overall, Joel Stein liked the show mostly because it allowed him "to make these kinds of racist comments in public." Speaking of the race factor, he concluded, "...if we're going to survive, we really need to band together against the yellow people."

"Survivor: Cook Islands" opened big with 18 million viewers. The reaction at "Survivor" fan sites was mixed, with comments ranging from, "I wasn't offended at all," to "The race thing is way too divisive," to "I haven't watched 'Survivor' for several seasons and decided to check it out due to the twist...it was okay, but not enough to hook me back in as a regular viewer."

A *New York Daily News* reader got it exactly right when he wrote that the race issue isn't the reason for pitting ethnic groups against each other on a TV series: "The money is!"

So if I'm right, and decades in the future TV viewers will be watching "The Running Man," here's a tip if ratings begin to sag: get "race-y"—have white criminals running from black executioners, Latinos from Asians, Muslims from Christians, and just to get really kinky...men from women, and vice versa.

Wow! The future looks bright, don't you agree? Whatever form Reality TV takes—game show, soap opera, hidden-camera show or quasi-documentary—it will thrive and grow forever if producers don't forget this basic recipe:

Throw real people, preferably strangers, into claustrophobic spaces—physical or psychological. Add liquor, allow the mix to simmer, roll cameras and....

...wait for the dynamite!

* * *

Chapter *Twenty One*

Okay, here's The Big Finish!

Like my wife always says, "Every story ends up being about him." (No, that's not my Big Finish...it's just what my wife always says. Anyway....)

One day, a major Suit at MGM phones me, we do lunch, and a few days later I get a letter that says:

Dear Mike,

As we discussed over lunch, MGM-TV wants to produce an exciting reality show starring you as The Donald Trump of Gossip!

It's this simple: Hard-nosed, world-renowned editor cracks the whip over wannabe journalists competing for a job as a celebrity reporter working for your legendary column, the #1 feature in the *National Enquirer!*

The show is a perfect follow-up to the huge success of "The Apprentice." It's always fun for people to watch a pro—like you, or Donald Trump—mold talented people who are competing for a prize. This project is tailor-made for you, and will reinforce your image as a respected news-breaker.

Here's more good news: Andrew Glassman, the reality show genius who produced the hit series "Average Joe" and others, has expressed a strong interest in making this his next project. He knows your work—and as a former reporter himself, he's a fan.

Mike, MGM believes this is a great project with exciting opportunities. We hope you feel the same way.

Sincerely Yours,

Hank Cohen
Senior VP, Development

WOW, a major studio wants to make me a star.

But wait, this is Hollywood—it gets BETTER!

A couple of days later, I'm joking around with a pal about insane ideas for Reality TV shows. My pal, who knows a Suit or two around town, says that over at Fox—the masters of the genre—they insist that no matter what idea anybody brings them, they've already heard it. In other words, there's nothing new under the reality sun.

"Ridiculous," I say.

Joking around, I invent a way-out idea on the spot. The next day my pal phones and says, "I tossed your idea at a guy. He wants to see you."

The "guy" is a Fox development exec, and the next day I'm in his office. I say jokingly, "So, I hit you with an idea you've never heard, eh?"

"I've heard the idea before—but I like your take on it," says the Suit.

So I write a five-page treatment, they "love" it, things are looking good, but...they decide to take a pass. Okay, I'm a big boy. After a good cry, the Suit says, "Sorry, but we would like to do something with you. You have any other ideas?"

I pitch him an idea that clicks so fast, his head spins. Just two months later, my show is officially "green-lighted." It's a "go" project, signed contracts, option money…a real deal. A show-runner is hired, office space is committed for, we've got a production schedule….

And then, as you may have read in the papers, media giant Rupert Murdoch puts one of his sons, Lachlan, in charge of Twentieth-Century Fox. Lachlan comes in and, like these guys always do, hires new folks, fires old folks, suggests new projects, and kills some existing projects…including *mine!*

"But…but…I was green-lighted. I've got a contract," I sputter to my $600-an-hour entertainment lawyer.

"That's right, Mike," he says. "And you can sue Fox. You want to sue Fox, Mike?"

At $600 an hour?

"No," I whine. "But…."

"Mike, you know how it works. They feel bad, they're going to pay you the option money…and they'll always be open to your next idea. You know this town. Be a pro. Take the hit."

Okay, I took the hit. And I won't tell you that show idea because I know I'm going to sell it someday. (The folks at the Lifetime network heard about it, liked it, contacted me the day before this book was finished to schedule a meeting in two weeks. Wish me luck, gang.)

Because this book is about adventures in Reality TV—and you're a fan, or you wouldn't be reading it—I'll show you the brilliant treatment that "Average Joe" producer Andrew Glassman wrote after we kicked the MGM idea around. And I'll show you the treatment for my "way-out" reality show that never got produced. If you're somebody who wants to break into the reality biz, it might give you ideas on how to pitch your own projects to the Suits.

And who knows…maybe some Suit will green-light one or the other. First, here's the MGM project—which never got made after the studio got sold to Sony and disbanded its TV division. Andrew says he still wants to make this show with me "because you're loud, fast on your feet—and hilarious when somebody pisses you off, Mike."

See? Rob Cesternino was right. These producers are looking for train wrecks who can curse loudly and make great TV. And frankly, I want to do a reality show because of…SURPRISE!…all that free booze! (And just wait'll I take my top off.)

* * *

Chapter *Twenty Two*

The Walker Amendment
By Mike Walker, Andrew Glassman, Hank Cohen, and Rob Lee

"Congress shall make no law respecting an establishment of religion, or prohibiting the free exercise thereof; or abridging the freedom of speech, or of the press; or the right of the people peaceably to assemble, and to petition the Government for a redress of grievances."

—*The First Amendment of the U.S. Constitution*

"Get me the bleep-ing story. Write it so it grabs my attention. Don't waste my bleeping time."

—*The Walker Amendment*

REALITY COMPETITION: 10 ONE-HOUR EPISODES

THE FRONT PAGE:
is where you want to be. This is where the best writers with the best information tell the best stories.

IT IS:

nearly impossible to get there. You need talent. You need instinct. You need luck. And you need a mentor.

SOMEONE:

who has been there on the front lines. Someone who can tell it to you straight. Someone you respect and fear.

THE TOUGHEST BOSS:

in the business is about to take a new crop of recruits into his confidence. THEY WILL ENTER HIS SECRETIVE WORLD, of confidential sources, unorthodox tactics, and sheer will, in an attempt to be part of the world's most aggressive pursuit of the truth.

They will get the story—his way—or they will get out.

OUR AUDIENCE:

We are about to take everyone who reads *People, Us Weekly, Entertainment Weekly, In Touch, The National Enquirer, Star,* or *The Globe* every week DEEP INSIDE the reality of the world they are so fascinated with.

Fortunately for us, these are EXACTLY the same people who LOVE Reality Television.

OUR HOST:

And the most trusted name in that world also happens to be one of the most colorful, animated personalities on television and radio.

On THE WALKER AMENDMENT, Mike Walker welcomes a group of aspiring celebrity writers and columnists to Beverly Hills and puts them through his information gathering and writing boot camp.

CAN THEY SURVIVE ON THE STREET?

These young men and women will live and work immersed in the celebrity culture of Hollywood—BUT in Mike Walker's Hollywood—you learn how to get to the truth, and learn what's really going on.
The show will feature ongoing celebrity cameos, as stars volunteer to be covered by our reporters.

NO CELEBRITIES' privacy will EVER BE VIOLATED during this reality show, however, <u>the methods and tactics used by the contestants on celebrities who are cooperating with us will be real every step of the way.</u>

HERE'S HOW THE SHOW WORKS:

MIKE WALKER welcomes a class of recruits to his new BEVERLY HILLS NEWSROOM. He presides over the corner office and they work in the Bullpen.

These young men and women are here for their dream shot (*a job with Mike at a guaranteed salary of 50k/year—or a job at the* National Enquirer) and they all have a hunger in their eyes. Some are graduates of the finest journalism schools like *Northwestern* and *Columbia*. Others are fresh off the mean streets.

This group also lives together in a house or apartment complex in Hollywood.

WEEK ONE:
starts off with an assignment which figures to be easy enough. The reporters get sent to cover a movie premiere. Walker hands out credentials to each of them. Off they go to see some movie stars in person and they report to the red carpet area (complete with publicists/gate-keepers and agitated photographers to push them around).

Inevitably, most of them follow "the pack" and stand behind a barricade, gawking at stars, noting what they are wearing, shouting out a question or two.

AND THEN

there are the information-hungry wolves, who sneak in through the back entrance, pose as waiters, and get the inside story for themselves.

WHO doesn't have what it takes to survive on the streets. AND WHO has gone too far?

These field challenges will escalate in intensity. Other examples: (Note to network buyers: our challenges will make headlines!)

OVER THE COURSE OF THE SERIES

Mike will show us, and the recruits, how even a casual stop in Starbucks can be turned into a network of information which can lead to a celebrity scoop. We will see him tutor the contestants on how to cultivate sources, gain access to insiders, massage difficult celebrity interviews, and trust your own sense of reporting instincts.

We will watch hidden camera encounters with real-life sources as they dangle information in front of our hungry contestants and try to negotiate a higher price for the information.

All along the way, Mike will tell us about the reality of the inner workings of celebrity journalism. No one has better stories than Mike Walker. The same principles used by our cast members have been used in Mike's own experience.

GETTING THE STORY IS ONLY HALF THE ASSIGNMENT ON THE WALKER AMENDMENT. YOU MUST BE ABLE TO PRESENT THE STORY AND CAPTIVATE THE READER.

In addition to the pressure of the street, on THE WALKER AMENDMENT there is the constant pressure of the newsroom. Anyone who has ever worked in the news environment can tell you a bullpen of people in competition with each other, writing away under deadline pressure, produces its own infectious jealousy.

Our reporters will be looking over their shoulders at every turn. And they will have the toughest editor in the business breathing down their back.

Mike will set a deadline for each reporter to turn in a draft of his or her story. He will tear each story to pieces in front of the nervous writer.

News is full of tough characters. None are tougher on young writers than Mike. His criticisms will bring some to tears. But they will be leveled with the best of intentions. Our young reporters will be growing as writers. Mike will hone their craft.

In the end, their headlines will grab your attention. A viewer will see how even a relatively mundane piece of celebrity fluff can be worked into a headline-generating story.

You must be able to write with passion to excel on THE WALKER AMENDMENT.

OVERALL:

The reporters have hit the streets and performed their news gathering task (covering an event, or working a source).

They will have lived with each other and either formed alliances to work together (you can share a byline) or tried to undermine each other (get a "source" to peddle false information which is the basis of their article).

They will have faced the wrath of Mike, reading over their first draft of their story.

At 5 p.m., the deadline is reached, and the copy is submitted and we GO TO PRESS.

Mike studies all of the articles, which have been blown up on his wall as life-size color pages.

He paces around the newsroom, making the editor-in-chief's decision.

THAT EVENING:
they all meet and Mike walks out with the printed edition in hand.

There are 15 contestants, but the edition is 14 Pages long.

PAGE 1:
belongs to the top writer, who receives a cash bonus, or advantage in the game.

Mike continues announcing the subsequent pages, and congratulates those writers on making the paper.

UNTIL FINALLY we are down to the weakest performer.

Mike pronounces them "YESTERDAY'S NEWS," and they remove their credential and are shown the door.

At the conclusion of 10 Episodes, Mike is left with a sharp, talented, aggressive, yet likeable young reporter, who begins his career with a lucrative job in journalism. And a chance to continue learning from one of the legends in the business.

ENDS

Incredibly, just after Andrew finished writing that treatment, a British production company called Radar contacted me out of the blue with a similar idea— except that I take over a real newspaper in the U.K. and try to drive its circulation up. They actually had a newspaper willing to put itself in my hands. Talk about Reality TV fever. It's driving us all insane. Anyway, read on for that brilliant proposal as pitched to Brit TV networks.

* * *

radar

March 2006

Hold the Front Page

6x60'

"Over 14 million people read a regional newspaper but do not use the internet". *The Newspaper Society*

Can one of the world's greatest journalists apply his skill, expertise and experience to revive the fortunes of an ailing local newspaper?

We're inviting top American journalist and media mogul The National Enquirer's Mike Walker to come to the UK to breathe life back into our local newspapers.

Why Now?

Nearly 85% of all British adults - 40 million people - read a regional newspaper, compared with 69.6% who read a national newspaper. They are an integral part of their communities - championing local causes, spearheading campaigns and fighting on behalf of their readers.

There are 1,300 regional and local newspapers in the UK today. Read by the vast majority of adults every week they embody the identity of the villages, towns and cities they serve, and are considered to be the most trusted and responsible medium of all...

But the latest batch of audited circulation figures for regional press titles shows sales and circulation are in decline. Out of the top 20 regional evening papers in the UK, only one has increased its circulation year-on-year and that increase is by a mere 0.5%.

The other 19 lost up to 15% of their copy sales in one year. The truth is, circulation figures for regional newspapers have been quietly falling for many years. For example, in 1986 the Manchester Evening News sold 310,682 copies every day - today they are selling just 141,737.

There are three main reasons for this: A stale image due to lack of innovation, little editorial relevance and failure to attract young readers on a regular basis.

It's time for some new ideas – enter Mike.

Contact Simon London Creative Director 020.7729.9595

radar

For the two weeks he spends with them, Mike has carte blanche to do whatever he likes – this could be anything from redesigning the layout to firing the staff. Mike can do whatever he thinks it will take to turn this paper around – and he intends to...

Like Gordon Ramsay in **Kitchen Nightmares**, Mike will bring his no-nonsense approach to getting the job done - proving just why he has been at the top of his game for the last 30 years.

Contact Simon London Creative Director 020.7729.9595

Chapter *Twenty Three*

A nd now…(drum roll)…my BIG FINISH!

Here's the "way-out" treatment I wrote that intrigued fearless Fox—but they finally passed after a few serious meetings. Was my topic too taboo even for the guys who green-lighted "Who's Your Daddy"? Come on! My show is delightful, innocent fun. It's about…virginity!

How hot is that…right, Paris???

As usual, I was way ahead of my time. But this is an idea whose time, I think, finally *has* come, reality fans, because even now—and I'm not joking—MTV is auditioning MALE virgins for a new show.

I say that's sexual discrimination. I demand equal treatment for females—and here it is!

Rupert Murdoch, look no further. Here is your next "American Idol."

*

VIRGIN ISLAND

A Reality TV Series Synopsis….

by Mike Walker

Squaring off in a TV battle royal for mankind's Ultimate Prize, hot young studs compete for the right to deflower a beautiful virgin!

"Virgin Island!" kicks off with an exciting nationwide search for three virgin girls of legal age who aren't quite ready for marriage—but are definitely ready to Give It Up!

To widen the girls' horizons, our panel of experts—guided by Viewer Voting—hand-pick a dozen eligible young bachelors.

The games begin as the lucky guys compete head-to-head for the once-in-a-lifetime favors of an unsullied virgin—PLUS big bucks, including their show fee of $20,000!

The rules are simple: Each girl gets—in addition to her fee of $50,000 for doing our show—a "Virgin Dowry" of $200,000. The dowry is split between the girl and the guy who leads her into womanhood. If a girl decides not to surrender her chastity, she forfeits her dowry and it's split between the remaining virgins (or virgin).

THE VIRGIN SEARCH—Lovely young American girls-next-door show off their bods in "Virgin Island!" beauty contests, including tests for talent, congeniality, etc.

THE VIRGINITY CHECK—Nail-biting suspense as six finalists sign affidavits stating that they're virgins, undergo a lie detector test—then are examined by a doctor, who certifies that their whatchamacallits are truly intact. Only then are they awarded our panel's coveted certificate (suitable for framing), which reads….

CERTIFIED INTACT!

Guys don't get off scot-free. They undergo medical tests for STD's—and their certificate says....

GOOD BOY!

Next, guys and panel of experts vote and eliminate three girls. It's time to meet....

THE THREE VIRGINS!—Fast thumb-nail look at each girl in her home environment, with family snaps, intvus with pals, teachers, etc.

OH, BOY!—A look at our 12 guys—dubbed "Beaus"—is less in-depth because...hell, we all know what *they're* after. And it's off to....

VIRGIN PARADISE!—Contestants are flown to an exotic, isolated retreat—an island, perhaps. The Three Virgins live in a luxurious house staffed by a butler, housekeeper and chaperone/maid. They share one big bedroom. The boys are bunked in a more modest "frat house."

"Virgin Island!" is hosted by a guy and a girl. Besides usual duties—interviewing, conducting upcoming elimination rounds, etc.—they contribute their male vs. female viewpoints on the action.

Presiding over the series is our panel of experts—i.e., a psychologist, a dating service exec, women's mag editor, sex columnist, etc. They critique our mating dance with witty, no-holds-barred comments heard only by viewers—NOT the contestants. After contestants settle in, rules are explained (more on that later) and the fun events kick off with....

THE VIRGINS' DANCE—First contact between Virgins and Beaus is a formal dance—boys in tuxedos, girls in long gowns—in the main room of the girls' mansion, "Chastity House." It's an elegant soiree with live musical combo, buffet, wet bar, etc.

The evening begins with a formal receiving line. Nerves jangle as each Beau is announced by the male host as he enters the main room. He marches up to the Three Virgins, and is introduced by the female host.

Pressure's on! Cameras catch the sweat—and the sweetness—as boys and girls finally meet face-to-face, trying desperately to come off all cool.

The dance begins—a fascinating mating ritual. The Three Virgins are whirled around briefly by each boy. Cutting-in is cued by our hosts.

The dance gets looser. The Three Virgins are flushed and excited as they take the measure of the boys and hold court…sipping punch, chatting, dancing, flirting. Sparks fly…and we get our first hints of which boys make girlish hearts beat faster.

Later in the evening, the girls retire to the Powder Room. We hear ad-lib comments, how the boys measure up, etc. Our experts analyze this amazing mating dance—and start the handicapping on who might end up with whom, based on what they've seen so far.

Our male host circulates among the boys, soliciting comments on the girls. Our female host chats with The Three Virgins as they primp in the Powder Room. Then it's back to the dance until midnight, when the guys are thrown out—and warned that security systems are being triggered to KEEP them out!

POOL PARTY!—Next day, Virgins and Beaus check out each other's hot bods in bathing suits.

VOLLEYBALL GAME!—Virgins bounce and Beaus get physical as the sexes play rough together for the first time. Bodies sweat on the sun-drenched beach. Strict NO-GROPING rules.

THE DINNER PARTY!—It's a formal sit-down dinner, allowing girls to observe boys' social graces…table manners, talent for polite conversation, etc.

But what makes it VERY edgy for boys and girls alike is…the parents of the Three Virgins are flown in to attend. Grumpy Dads alone should make this sequence hilarious.

VIRGINS' HORROR!—It's "Ohmigod!" time for the girls as we interview their moms—and dads! It's must-see TV!

Host: "So, folks, what's it like knowing your daughter's on a timetable for giving up her virginity—and all America is watching?"

(To qualify for our show, virgins must get formal agreement that mom & dad—or at least one parent—will give us an interview after the dinner party!)

DAREDEVIL DAY!—Boys get to show off their bravery and sway female hearts! They bungee jump, dive off high places, lie down with snakes, plus other fear factor stuff. Cash prizes for Top Three Daredevils!

GAME NIGHT—Time to chill after these whirlwind events, so there's an informal evening get-together at Chastity House. Games like Trivial Pursuit, Scrabble, Charades, etc., are played. Cash prizes—or promotional gifts—for winners. It's a chance to check out each other's smarts.

FLIRT FIESTA—An outdoor barbecue/dance with a hot band. Girls are scored by our panel on how outrageously they flirt—batting eyes, flipping hair, showing cleavage, flashing legs, etc. A cash prize goes to the winner.

SADIE HAWKINS DAY—The Dating Round begins ….each Virgin gets to ask one guy for a date ALONE. Rules up to this point disallowed touching or kissing—and the girls were never left alone with a guy. Twist here is that a girl CANNOT tell the others which guy she picked. This will drive the girls nuts. We'll overhear them trying to wheedle hints from each other on who dated whom.

THE BITCH/GOSSIP ROUND—Each Virgin gets to spread a rumor about each other among the boys. They're harmless, untrue rumors supplied by our panel, i.e., Virgin A snores like a wart hog; Virgin B bites her toenails; Virgin C is hiding a gas problem. Each girl knows the others are spreading a rumor, but don't know what it is. We watch them try to get the boys to tell them—then fight back with their own rumor. MEOW!

BUH-BYE, BOYFRIEND!—The Elimination Rounds begin. Goal is to eliminate nine Beaus, ending up with one for each Virgin. Viewers can vote, but it's the Virgin's final decision, always. There are infinitely variable ways to set up the Elimination Rounds, but the goal is ending up with three lucky Beaus.

NIGHT OF DELIGHTS!—It's the moment of surrender. We interview each Virgin and Beau on how they feel on this special night. Each couple waves to the audience as the door to The Virgin's Chamber closes….

DAWN OF WOMANHOOD!—Our hosts explain that in medieval times, custom had it that the bed-sheets from the Night of Defloration were hung out the window the next morning for the whole village to witness the…er, evidence that the girl had indeed been a maiden. Tipping our hat to the old custom, each couple hangs their sheet on a flagpole, and we see—hopefully—male and female Smiley Faces pinned to it!

If there are Frown-y Faces, we get the gory details of A Night in Sex Hell!

(Strictly speaking, our doc should certify that the…er, veil has been pierced, but that may be too clinical even for today's Reality TV.)

SHOTGUN WEDDING!—If any of the three couples emerge from the Virgin Chambers to declare they're in love and want to get married, we double the dowry AND pay for the televised wedding!

Host: "Just one last question…did it hurt?"

*

THE FOLLOWING ARE VARIOUS EPISODE IDEAS, RANDOM NOTES, ETC.:

Our sex columnist interviews girls about what turns them on sexually.

Following that, we get a fly-on-wall listen to how they reacted to the lusty questioning.

Intvu each Virgin's mom—and dad!

Intvu Virgin's best girlfriend back home—who they think she'll pick…if anybody!

Elimination rounds. If girls give in, they're eliminated.

Before a girl makes her final pick, she can interview the last girlfriends of her two possibles.

"OH, BOY!" ROUND …boys are chosen. How about winnowing down to 24 by our judges and/or viewers?

VIRGINS' CHOICE…virgins get to pick the lucky dozen???

VIRGIN'S DANCE…the first time Virgins meet the boys who'll compete for their prize.

POOL PARTY…Virgins and boys check each other out in bathing suits.

VOLLEYBALL GAME…Virgins and boys get physical for first time. Strict NO-GROPING rules.

VIRGINS' DINNER PARTY…formal sit-down dinner so girls can observe boys' social graces, talent for polite conversation, etc. Catch is that the Three Virgins' parents/family members attend. Could be hilarious.

GAME NIGHT…informal evening get-together at The Virgins' mansion. Games like Trivial Pursuit, Scrabble, Charades are played. Virgins get to judge guys' mental acuity.

RULES:

If two V's pick same guy, he gets bonus. If all three pick same guy, he gets HUGE bonus!

We state that if V ends up marrying Her First Time guy, we pay for wedding.

Our doctor confirms officially that it's a done deal. We fly the happy flag—two smiley faces??

Suggested Titles:

It's My First Time, Be Gentle!

Give It Up!

Virgin Sacrifice!

The Virgin Chronicles!

Virgin Search!

*

ALSO NOTE: Join my fun contest, "Name Mike's Virgin Show!" by e-mailing me at mikegossip@nationalenquirer.com.

I'll pick the winner—judged solely by me—and pay a $100 prize, plus mention your name in my column. Entries must be received by December 31, 2008.

*

Good luck and let me leave you with one last thought…. It's tough to crack showbiz, but you must *never* give up. Remember, for one brief shining moment, I had THREE Reality TV shows cooking….

…and then I had NONE!

But…as we go to press, that meeting with Lifetime is just around the corner. Hope, as they say, springs eternal.

And that's Reality, folks!

* * *